SIMMERING SUPPERS

Classic & Creative One-Pot Meals
From Harrowsmith Kitchens

Edited by Rux Martin & JoAnne B. Cats-Baril

COMPILED FROM THE PERSONAL RECIPE COLLECTIONS OF THE
EDITORS, READERS, CONTRIBUTORS AND STAFF OF HARROWSMITH,
THE MAGAZINE OF COUNTRY LIFE

CAMDEN HOUSE

Published simultaneously in Canada by
Camden House Publishing, a division of Telemedia Publishing Inc.

Library of Congress Cataloging-in-Publication Data

Martin, Rux, 1950-
  Simmering suppers.

  "Compiled from the personal recipe collections of the editors,
readers, contributors, and staff of Harrowsmith, the magazine of country life."
  Includes index.
  1. Stews.   2. Casserole cookery.   3. Soups.
I. Cats-Baril, JoAnne B., 1949-   II. Harrowsmith.
III. Title.
TX693.M28   1988   641.8'21   88-28491
ISBN 0-920656-81-1
ISBN 0-920656-69-2 (pbk.)

Trade distribution by
        Firefly Books
        3520 Pharmacy Avenue, Unit 1-C
        Scarborough, Ontario M1W 2T8

Printed in U.S.A. by
Boyd Printing Inc., Albany, New York, for:
Camden House Publishing Inc.
The Creamery
Charlotte, Vermont 05445

Cover illustration by Roger Hill
Back cover photograph by Ernie Sparks

To our readers: The editors have made every effort to ensure that the recipes in this cookbook are clear and accurate. Readers who discover errors or other problems are encouraged to draw them to our attention so that they can be corrected in future printings. Please write:
Rux Martin
Harrowsmith
The Creamery
Charlotte, Vermont 05445

SIMMERING SUPPERS

Classic & Creative One-Pot Meals From Harrowsmith Kitchens

Editors
Rux Martin, JoAnne B. Cats-Baril

Contributing Editors
James M. Lawrence, Pamela Cross, Sarah Fritschner

Test-Kitchen Coordinator
Meredith Gabriel

Testers
Mary Ann Avolizi, Janet Ballantyne, Ina Fitzhenry-Coor,
R. Kent Cummings, Nancy Davis, Liz Foster, Sarah Fritschner, Carolyn S. Gregson, Pamela Lord,
Melissa McClelland, Lynne E. Smith, Elisabeth Weltin, Janet Wilson, Gregg Wilson

Graphic Designer
Susan McClellan

Graphic Artist
Eugenie Seidenberg

Photography
Ernie Sparks

Art Director / Photography
Linda J. Menyes

Food Design
Mariella Morrin

Illustration
Alexandra Schulz

Production Manager
Alice Z. Lawrence

Copy Editor / Typesetting
Wendy S. Ruopp

Associate Copy Editors
Wistar Rawls, Suzanne Seibel, Ina Fitzhenry-Coor, Pat Paquin, Euan Bear, Barbara Panter Harris

Office Administrator
Diane Lamphere

Special Thanks for Assistance

Elizabeth Alexander
Jean Alexander
Glen E. Anglin
Diane Berry
The Fish House, Kingston, Ontario
Mitchell Kelsey
Kitchen Cargo, Kingston, Ontario
Sarah Mason-Ward
McCallum's China and Gifts Ltd., Kingston, Ontario
J. Shirley Menyes
Mike Mundell's Surf and Turf Stores, Kingston, Ontario
N.J. Pollitt
Jackie Sparks
Wilton Pottery, Wilton, Ontario
Pamela Wimbush

Photographic Properties Courtesy of:

Page 65
Wicker basket: Cellar Door Antiques, Kingston, Ontario
Page 66
Bowl, cups and platter: Wilton Pottery, Wilton, Ontario
Page 68
Quilt: Sydenham Street United Church women, Kingston, Ontario
Page 70
Marble: Spada Tile Inc., Kingston, Ontario
Page 72
Plate: McCallum's China and Gifts Ltd., Kingston, Ontario
Page 73
Marble: Spada Tile Inc., Kingston, Ontario
Page 74
Tureen and bowl: Kitchen Cargo, Kingston, Ontario
Page 76
Bowl: Wilton Pottery, Wilton, Ontario
Page 77
China: McCallum's China and Gifts Ltd., Kingston, Ontario
Velvet: Whitney Wal-Flair, Kingston, Ontario
Page 78
Chopper: Cellar Door Antiques, Kingston, Ontario
Page 80
Chafing dish, cream and sugar dishes: Cellar Door Antiques, Kingston, Ontario

CONTENTS

FOREWORD

*"Nonetheless, if you have the time
and the fuel, make a stew for your soul's sake."*
M.F.K. Fisher

At the age of six, I was already working alongside my father in the kitchen, in training as his assistant, vegetable peeler, dishwasher and general go-fer. Though my apron reached all the way to my ankles and I had to stand precariously on a stool to work at the counter, I must have been of some use or my father, who took his cooking very seriously, would undoubtedly have banished me from the kitchen. Garlic and onion were in every dish he prepared, and being Lebanese, he believed in the medicinal as well as the provocative culinary powers of these indispensable aromatic alliums. His sauces and stews were authentic peasant fare, but he was as strict as any French chef about the routines we followed: "You've got to cut them up real fine, then brown them real good, almost black, to give the dish a good taste." After the pot had bubbled for hours under a cloud of steam, he would urge me back into the kitchen and up onto the stool. Doubling over a slice of crusty bread, he would dip it into the rich sauce and allow me to taste.

As the recipes in this sixth HARROWSMITH cookbook suggest, a simmering pot throwing off mouth-watering aromas from favorite stew and soup recipes occupies a vital place in the family traditions of many of our contributors. "I vividly remember a huge gray enamel stockpot simmering on the back of the old black cookstove, warming our bones on a winter night," wrote Sharon Kostka of Frazee, Minnesota, expressing a sentiment common to the many hundreds of readers, editors, staff members and friends who opened their private recipe boxes to make this cookbook possible.

Many of the recipes that follow—Greek *stifado*, Hungarian goulash, Tuscan minestrone, Rumanian *ghivetch*, Indian *biryani*—were carried directly from their country of origin to North America and subtly adapted to local ingredients, often under the watchful eyes of an exacting parent. "In a tradition passed on by word of mouth and measured in the palm of the hand," wrote Viola Gay of Westport, Massachusetts, "this recipe for a complete pot-roasted dinner made its way from the tiny Portuguese island of San Miguel in the mid-Atlantic Azorian archipelago to a small fishing and farming community in southern New England, carried by my husband's homesick maternal grandmother, who immigrated here in the early 1900s. The dish has found a home in the North, relying on homegrown beef, potatoes, carrots, onions and a particularly sweet white turnip developed by the local farmers." Still other recipes in this cookbook—Loughborough Chowder, Chicken Letter Soup, Kentucky Burgoo, Texas Chili and Jambalaya—represent other diverse but equally flavorful traditions of North America.

Like all one-pot dinners, the stews, soups and casseroles included here are appealingly simple meals for everyday eating, and when company is planned, they can be wonderful alternatives to the fussy four-course productions that keep the cook shuttling from kitchen to table.

To be sure, simple does not necessarily mean fast, and most of these recipes require extended cooking times—taking anywhere from two to six hours to reach full flavor. Nevertheless, once in the pot, they can simmer on their own virtually unattended, perhaps punctuated by an occasional stir.

Even though they are eminently suited to frugal shopping lists and a minimum of preparation effort, these one-pot suppers reward one's patience with rich, complex flavors. Not the least of their appeal is that they can—indeed should—be made well in advance, as their flavor appreciates greatly with a day or two of aging.

From the standpoint of health, these one-pot suppers also have much to recommend them, since many rely on vegetables and grain rather than upon meat. In "Substitutions," beginning on page 16, nutritionist Sarah Fritschner offers sensible advice on how to decrease the amount of fat and increase fiber in one-pot dishes without sacrificing good taste.

Since one-pot dinners are traditionally made from what is on hand, whether in the garden, the freezer or the pantry, this cookbook is organized by ingredient. Within the individual chapters, similar dishes are grouped near one another, with stews at the beginning of the chapter and soups near the end. For convenience, the vegetable chapter is organized seasonally, beginning with stews and soups made with spring and summer produce. We have also included a chapter on casseroles, which, although they do not simmer, are squarely within the one-pot tradition. The concluding section, "Finishing Touches," provides accompaniments to one-pot dishes—winter salads, dumplings and quick breads that can be made in less than an hour to round out the meal. To assist in meal planning, we have included total preparation time necessary to complete each dish.

The process of recipe selection was, of course, not only the most rewarding part of the project, but also the most difficult, thanks to the generous participation of our readers. Of the thousands of submissions we received from all parts of Canada and the United States, we excluded from consideration recipes containing canned cream soups (canned bouillon was, however, acceptable) and other highly processed ingredients. Recipes taken directly from a newspaper or cookbook, and those that were inexact, were also rejected. In addition, those recipes that did not fit our admittedly arbitrary definition of "simmering suppers"— stir-fries, pizzas, lasagnas and the like—and soups that were too light to serve as a complete meal, were set aside in anticipation of future HARROWSMITH cookbooks.

The remaining recipes, together with an evaluation form, were given to 11 testers from a variety of backgrounds: some are gourmet world travelers, others are trained in the Cordon Bleu tradition, others have extensive experience in restaurant cooking, while others are simply good home cooks with daily experience in satisfying the critical palates of their own families. The recipes that are included here are those that found unequivocal and enthusiastic endorsement from the testers and those who sampled the dishes. In many cases, our testers also added successful submissions from their own recipe files.

In the test kitchen of HARROWSMITH, Meredith Gabriel daily turns out a variety of vegetarian soups and lofty biscuits for our staff. She quickly adopted a number of submissions into her file of Favorite Recipes to Serve Guests, including a garlicky Chilled Buttermilk Soup and a spectacular Mexican Chicken studded with prunes.

As in previous HARROWSMITH cookbooks, the striking photographs beginning on page 65 are the work of Ernie Sparks, with food presentation and arrangement by cooking instructor Mariella Morrin. Many other collaborators also worked to make this cookbook come to life, from kitchenware suppliers who generously provided properties for the photo sessions, to highly critical proofreaders whose mandate was to clarify each and every confusing or vague instruction.

The recipes that follow, patiently simmered and carefully evaluated, offer ample proof, we believe, that too many cooks do not spoil the broth.

—*JoAnne B. Cats-Baril & Rux Martin*

TECHNIQUES & EQUIPMENT

"The greatest dishes are the simplest dishes."

Escoffier

"Faites simple"—'Make it simple'— counseled the great Escoffier, who created over 7,000 legendary recipes in an era when, he said, " . . . a thousand worries of industry and business occupy the mind of man, and he can devote only a limited place to eating well." If Escoffier's description of his age sounds uncannily similar to our own, then his advice on cooking simply but eating well is as appropriate today as it was in nineteenth-century France.

Stews and soups are among the least complicated forms of cooking, traditionally using but a single pot and a single source of heat. Although many one-pot dishes have evolved considerably since their rudimentary beginnings, a grand kitchen filled with gourmet appliances and utensils is hardly a prerequisite. Contributor Carolyn Gregson's recipe for Olivier's Moroccan Chicken, for example, was conceived in the cramped quarters of a Paris apartment, "in the smallest room known to man, with only a double-burner hot plate as our kitchen."

While precision is not necessary and can even hamper the making of a good stew, a sense of proportion, timing and a knowledge of technique are essential. "Stews, above all, were responsible for the brilliance of old French cookery, yet it is stews which bring disgrace on contemporary cuisine," complained Alexandre Dumas back in the nineteenth century. Made without a guiding recipe or well-honed instincts, a stew can easily become a mushy amalgam of ill-combined ingredients, greasy, harshly seasoned or insipid.

Despite minor differences in individual recipes, the process of making a stew is reassuringly similar. Meat should be blotted dry and dusted with flour; vegetables should be washed and those with similar cooking times should be cut into uniform sizes.

Before they are added to the pot, both meat and vegetables are often browned to intensify their flavors. The pan and the oil should be thoroughly hot and the individual pieces of meat must never be crowded, lest they steam rather than sear. Salt should not be added until after the meat has been browned.

The choice of liquid in which to braise will vary according to the nationality of the dish, though in practice, it is most often dictated by convenience. Adding stock rather than water will produce a richer, more full-bodied broth. In the case of vegetable one-pots, however, many cooks prefer to use water so as to show off the flavors of the vegetables to their best advantage. Tomato juice, canned tomatoes, wine, or a combination, will also add to the body and flavor and will tenderize the meat, as in the French dish Coq au Vin, in which a tough old rooster was originally the featured ingredient. While a fine wine is unnecessary, a vinegary vintage will ruin the stew: if it isn't fit to drink, it isn't fit for the stewpot. In general, the less liquid used, the more concentrated the flavor.

Although cooking times are notoriously vague in soup and stew recipes, proper timing can be important, especially when vegetables are concerned. "Flavoring" vegetables like leeks, onions and carrots are added early in the cooking, along with dried herbs, while "garnish" vegetables—additional onions, carrots, potatoes and so on—are added later and cooked until fork-tender, but not so long that they lose their individual flavors and textures. Vegetables like green peppers and broccoli that are high in vitamin C, which is destroyed by long cooking, should be added near the end. When garlic is added near the beginning of cooking, it ripens to a mellow softness; added near the end, it can be assertive and pungent.

Meat, in particular, benefits from very slow simmering. One of our favorite stew recipes, Beef with Carrots, is cooked in the oven on low heat (250 degrees F) for 6 hours, at which temperature it can cook, without danger of scorching, until it becomes silkily tender. Fish and shellfish, on the other hand, have little connective tissue and fat, and are added in the final stages of cooking and cooked only briefly so they do not toughen or disintegrate.

During the cooking process, fat contributes flavor and keeps meat moist, but it is crucial to remove as much of it as possible before serving the stew, both for reasons of health and taste, since fat will mask the flavors of the dish. The fat can be removed when the dish is still hot by collecting it with a ladle or spoon or by blotting it up with several thicknesses of paper toweling. Even better, the dish can be cooled in the re-frigerator, causing the fat to congeal at the surface, where it can easily be skimmed away.

Thickening can be accomplished by one of several methods. The liquid may be reduced by boiling, resulting in intense flavor and velvety texture. Or flour can be added to an equal portion of butter and cooked, then added to the stew and cooked until the floury taste is gone. Either cornstarch or arrowroot can be used instead of flour to achieve a glossier, more transparent finish.

The only essential piece of equipment needed to make a good stew—beyond a sharp knife—is a good, heavy pot with a lid. In fact, the pot is so indispensable to the stew that many stews are named for the pots in which they are cooked: casseroles, hotpots and daubes being but a few examples. The most efficient stewing vessels are enamel-covered iron Dutch ovens, or heatproof casserole dishes, in which the ingredients can be browned as well as simmered, eliminating extra pots. The only disadvantage of enameled pots is that they will chip. Some cooks swear by their heavy, old-fashioned black iron cookware, and a well-seasoned skillet fitted with a lid is an excellent choice for making fricassees and other stews because its surface gives the best crust when browning.

Unglazed earthenware cookers, also called clay cookers, make respectable stews, if browning is first done in another pot, since they cannot be placed directly on the flame. They must be soaked before heating. Because they are porous, it's a good idea to check during the cooking to make sure that the juices have not been soaked up. Slow to warm, clay cookers hold the heat well and can be brought to the table to become a practical centerpiece with a pleasingly rustic appearance.

That old-fashioned time-saver, the pressure cooker, can greatly speed the making of a stew, reducing preparation time to less than one hour. Invented in the nineteenth century by an Englishman, and called the "digester," it was originally created to cook the tough Argentinian beef that was imported to Britain. It did the job well, but it also had a lethal side, being capable of exploding without warning. Recently streamlined and made fail-safe by new technology, the current generation of pressure cookers, such as Tefal, are free of the alarming jiggling and hissing of their precursors of the 1950s, and are as simple and worry-free to use as any other pot.

The process of cooking the stew in a pressure cooker is fundamentally the same as in the traditional method: the meat is first sautéed in the cooker with the lid removed, and after the flavoring vegetables, herbs and liquids have been added, the cooker is brought up to pressure. After about 20 minutes of cooking, the pressure is released, and the garnish vegetables and thickening agent are added. Again the pot is brought up to pressure, and the stew is cooked for a short time longer. We found the flavor of pressure-cooked stews perfectly acceptable, but in side-by-side tastings, they were noticeably less rich than the long-simmered versions. Better results can be obtained by refrigerating the stew overnight and slowly reheating it with the lid removed.

A stew that has bucked at a rolling boil for a couple of hours will not give as flavorful a result as one that has been kept at a guarded simmer, suggesting, once again, that the critical ingredient in great soups and stews is simply time, for which there is no substitute.

MAKING STOCK

"A big man can carry a heavy load; a good soup can carry a dinner."

Country Proverb

Since lunch means soup here at the lake," writes contributor Mary Loucks of Godfrey, Ontario, "there is a large red soup pot that lives permanently on the back burner and gently simmers each day—a collection of leftovers, discards, worn-outs and useless bits and pieces. Once a week, it is strained and skimmed and the meat goes to the dogs, who think they've died and gone to heaven, while the stock itself becomes the basis of all my soups."

Despite its disreputable appearance while being prepared, homemade stock is essential for the best soups and stews—it is not for nothing that the French call stocks the *"fond de cuisine"*—the foundation of cooking. While commercial substitutes are available, nothing approaches the rich, rounded fullness of a soup or stew made with a homemade stock.

Though many cooks imagine that making a stock is a complex process, nothing could be simpler, except perhaps boiling water. There is little or no measuring involved and only simple, everyday utensils are needed. Essentially, a homemade stock consists of a few meaty bones, or simply vegetables, covered with water and with a few aromatics added, such as pepper, parsley, thyme and a bay leaf.

Stock does take time to make, for the pot must simmer for about 6 hours or as long as 12 hours, if possible, to extract the flavor and desirable gelatin from the bones. The pot can be left to percolate untended for all but the first half hour; stirring will actually muddy the result. Stocks are models of frugality, since bones can usually be had for pennies.

The age-old rule is that the older the animal supplying the bones, the stronger the flavor of the meat and the richer the stock will be. Chicken stock can be made with a leftover carcass or from a whole hen; young frying chickens, however, are not good for stock, because they lack the desired mature flavor. In the case of beef, veal shin and knuckle bones are prized, because they are laden with desirable gelatin. Marrowbones are also excellent. Liver and giblets should never be added to the stockpot, because they become bitter.

For fish stock, lean, nonoily fish like cod, whiting, hake, pike or bass are best. Look for whole fish, gutted and scaled. The squeamish may be less than pleased to learn that a fish head is wonderful for making stock because of its ample reserves of gelatin. If none can be had, make do with carcasses and skin.

The first step in making stock is to wash the bones and trim them of excess fat. Cover with cold water and bring to a boil. If you want, skim the layer of foam that rises to the surface; it is simply albumin, the protein released by the bones. If it is not removed, the broth will be somewhat cloudy, but the taste will not be adversely affected. Because a clear broth is not essential for the soups and stews in this cookbook, skimming is purely optional.

Vegetables added to the pot should be left whole: carrots with their skins on, celery with its leaves. All members of the cabbage family, including broccoli and cauliflower, should be shunned, because they develop a strong, sulfurous flavor. Fresh herbs like parsley may be added whole, and similarly, peppercorns are always left whole or the flavor will be too harsh. Oregano and dill become bitter, and are best left out.

Whether to add salt is a matter of some debate. Purists say that it is not necessary, since the soups and stews themselves usually contain salt. Others contend that salt helps draw the gelatin out of the bones. If you do choose to use salt, the kosher brands offer "softer" taste and freedom from impurities, but common table salt will do.

As the stock cooks, the fat rising to the surface may be skimmed, or it may be removed when the stock is finished cooking. The liquid is then strained through a colander. Ideally, cheesecloth should be stretched over the colander to strain out impurities, but cooks who never seem to have cheesecloth in the house at the right moment will quickly find that one can make perfectly good stock without it.

After it is ready, the stock should be chilled immediately, and preferably frozen if it will not be used within three days. The rich, gelatinized liquid makes an ideal breeding ground for bacteria, which is why it is the medium of choice for scientists growing certain strains of bacteria in laboratories. If refrigerated, stock must be boiled every two to three days to prevent spoilage. To make longer-term use of a batch of stock, freeze in small quantities in plastic food-storage bags suspended in straight-sided containers, leaving a little space for expansion. Then, once hard, the bags of frozen stock can be removed from the container and sealed. If space is limited, the stock can be reduced by boiling. Pour into ice cube trays, freeze, and empty cubes into freezer bags.

The basic stock recipes that follow offer fundamental guidelines; liberties may, of course, be taken, for stock-making is marvelously adaptable to whatever ingredients happen to be on hand. For the most sophisticated gourmet chef and the unassuming country cook alike, there is great satisfaction in distilling the essences of meats and vegetables into a stock that will provide the foundation for many a dish to come.

Beef Stock

Caramelized vegetables and meaty bones give rich flavor and color to this robust stock, which is essential for bold soups and stews.

Note: The use of a whole, unpeeled bulb of garlic rather than a single clove in chicken and beef stocks gives them a softly mellow dimension.

Yield: 2½-3 quarts
Preparation time: 6-8 hours

♦

3 lbs.	assorted beef bones (shin, shank, short ribs or marrowbones)
4 lbs.	veal bones
2	large onions, studded with 3 whole cloves each
5	carrots
2 Tbsp.	cooking oil
1 large bulb	garlic, unpeeled
2 stalks	celery
1	leek, green and white parts
	bouquet garni: bay leaf, parsley, lovage and thyme
1 tsp.	salt, preferably kosher

Place bones, onions and carrots in a flat roasting pan, drizzle with oil, and bake in a preheated, 375-degree F oven for 40 minutes, or until golden brown. Remove bones and vegetables to a stockpot, and cover with 5 qts. cold water. Slowly bring to a boil, and skim surface foam. Add remaining ingredients, lower heat to a low simmer, and cook for 5 hours. Strain the finished stock and degrease for immediate use, or refrigerate overnight and lift off the surface fat once it has congealed. To store up to six months, freeze in 1-pt. containers.

Chicken Stock

A simple and flavorful chicken stock that is a versatile foundation for a variety of dishes.

Yield: 2 quarts
Preparation time: 3 hours

♦

7-8 lb.	stewing hen (if smaller, use wings to bring to weight)
1	large onion, studded with 3 whole cloves
2	carrots
1 bulb	garlic, unpeeled
	bouquet garni: bay leaf, parsley, lovage and thyme
1 tsp.	salt, preferably kosher

Put chicken in stockpot and add 4 quarts cold water. Slowly bring to a boil and skim off surface scum. Add remaining ingredients, lower heat to maintain a low simmer, and cook for 3 hours. Strain the stock and degrease for immediate use, or refrigerate overnight and remove the surface fat once it has congealed. For storage of up to six months, freeze in 1-pt. containers.

Vegetable Stock

This quickly made, light stock is widely used in vegetarian dishes.

Yield: 4 quarts
Preparation time: ¾ hour

◆

3 Tbsp.	vegetable oil or sweet butter
2	medium onions, chopped
2	leeks, chopped
4	carrots, chopped
2 stalks	celery, with leaves
6-8	mushrooms, sliced
1	tomato, quartered
5 sprigs	parsley
3 sprigs	thyme
	bouquet garni: bay leaf, lovage and marjoram
1 tsp.	salt, preferably kosher

Place oil or butter in stockpot, add onions, leeks, carrots and celery, and cover. Sweat over medium heat for 10 to 15 minutes, until vegetables are limp and very lightly colored. Add 4 qts. cold water and the rest of the ingredients. Bring to a boil, skim sediment as it rises to the surface, and continue to boil for 30 minutes. Strain the stock and either use immediately, or refrigerate. For storage of up to six months, freeze in 1-pt. containers.

Fish Stock

A clear, aromatic essence of fish, for seafood chowders, bisques and stews.

Yield: 3½ quarts
Preparation time: ¾ hour

◆

4 lbs.	fish heads, skin and bones, gills removed
3 Tbsp.	sweet butter
2	large onions, chopped
2 stalks	celery, chopped
2	leeks, chopped
¼	lemon, with rind
1 tsp.	salt, preferably kosher
6 sprigs	parsley
3 sprigs	thyme
1	bay leaf
1 clove	garlic, unpeeled but slightly crushed

Rinse fish in cold water. Melt butter in pot, add fish and vegetables. Cover the pot and sweat the mixture for 10 minutes over medium heat. Add 4 quarts cold water, lemon and seasonings. Simmer for 40 minutes. Strain through a fine sieve and use immediately, or freeze for up to six months in 1-pt. containers.

SUBSTITUTIONS

"Congealed fat is pretty much the same, irrespective of the delicacy around which it is congealed."

Sigmund Freud

For the cook who wilts at the thought of making several different dishes for a balanced meal at the end of the day, soups, stews and casseroles are a study in nutritional convenience, incorporating the four basic food groups into one dish. Minestrone, the classic example, contains pasta, beans, a little meat, lots of vegetables and a topping of cheese, all in the same bowl.

Soups and stews stretch meat or poultry for four into dinner for eight, provide a ready use for bits of leftover meat and vegetables, and appear hearty and filling while placating our appetite without heavy foods. In fact, studies show that we tend to consume fewer calories when we eat soup because the liquid fills us up with nutrients without adding fat to our diet.

Even when they are fattening and stodgy — and many traditional recipes date from the nutritionally unenlightened past — one-pot suppers can be easily adapted to become healthier — higher in fiber and lower in fat — without substantially altering their taste. When a piece of broiled, lean top round is substituted for a well-marbled strip steak on the dinner plate, the change is immediately noticeable, since fat makes meat more palatable. In stew, however, lean meat is more flavorful and just as tender as the fatty cuts.

For those of us trying to make healthy adjustments to the ways we cook, changes are perhaps best made subtly and gradually, so that suspicious family members will accept them: uneaten food, after all, has no nutritional benefits. Fiber-rich foods can be introduced in tandem with old favorites. One friend floats two or three pieces of frankfurter on top of a lentil-rich dish and bills it as Hot Dog Soup to entice her six-year-old, who normally regards beans as art supplies.

Other "invisible" or apparently modest changes may be made as well. Skim milk can be substituted for whole milk, or 2 percent for half-and-half in cream soups. Ham in pea soup can be reduced by one third; there is plenty of protein in the dried peas and you'll be eliminating fat and salt besides. An extra cup of kidney beans slipped into soup or chili, or some fresh spinach tucked into a casserole, may be noticed but is unlikely to cause a commotion. In fact, making a dish more nutritious usually creates a one-dish meal where none existed before. A meat-filled chili needs a salad, but when bulgur and carrots are substituted for half the meat, the meal becomes nutritionally complete.

To increase the healthfulness of soups and stews, scrutinize each recipe for overreliance on meat, the main source of fat in the North American diet. According to health professionals, Americans now consume about 40 percent of their calories as fat, rather than the 30 percent or less that is recommended to lower the risk of heart disease, stroke and cancer.

Any discussion of fat reduction often makes meat sound evil. It isn't, of course. Meat is nutrient-rich, a good source of protein and essential minerals, such as iron and zinc. Some cuts, however, are better choices for one-pot meals than others. Beef graded "select" is lower in fat than prime or choice meat, and any cut from the round will be lower in fat than chuck or loin portions. Flank steak, eye of round, arm and rump are all lean. 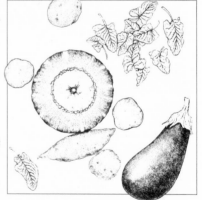 Hamburger, browned and drained on absorbent paper, will be reasonably low in fat. Before browning the meat, remember to trim all visible fat. Removing the skin and fat from chicken will cut its calories in half.

Whenever possible, replace red meat with turkey or chicken. Many cooks combine hamburger with ground turkey in chili to reduce saturated fat content. Turkey breast is also an admirable substitute for veal.

Often the fat used in the browning process can be reduced by at least a tablespoon. Each tablespoon eliminates about 120 calories. Consider a substitute for butter in the first step of a recipe, because much of its fat is saturated and its flavor is lost in most one-dish meals. Save it for when you can taste it: on bread. Substitute olive oil, which has been shown to lower total blood cholesterol without affecting the reserves of "good" blood cholesterol that protect against heart disease. Although you can omit the browning step entirely and simmer the onion and garlic in broth instead, we opt for a little fat in return for a lot of flavor. After browning, drain all fat in the pan before adding the rest of the ingredients. When the dish is finished cooking, it can be refrigerated for 30 minutes so that the fat that rises to the top can be spooned off.

After meat, dairy products are the second highest sources of fat in the North American diet, and unfortunately, casseroles often lean heavily upon them. Use hard cheeses judiciously. Most of them—Cheddar, for instance—get 70 to 80 percent of their calories from fat. Reduce cheese by leaving it out of the casserole proper and sprinkling a small amount on top instead.

Another hidden source of fat and sodium is the "binder" sauce, an almost universal ingredient in casseroles, often made with cream cheese, mayonnaise or canned cream soups, which receive almost all of their calories from fat. A low-fat béchamel (recipe below) may be made by thickening skim or low-fat milk with flour or cornstarch. Cottage cheese or ricotta cheese blended with plain, low-fat yogurt also makes a good binder and adds other nutrients.

Although adding kidney beans to chili may be anathema to Texans, it makes healthy sense: high fiber foods help reduce the risk of heart attack by lowering blood cholesterol. Lentils and split peas, high in both fiber and protein, cook more quickly than other beans. Whole grains like bulgur (cracked wheat berries), barley and brown rice should be used liberally, too, with meat used merely as a flavoring ingredient.

The blender is a boon to healthful cooking, because it adds "hidden" nutrients and fiber to one-pots while thickening them. Creamy, rich-tasting soups without fat can be produced simply by blending cooked vegetables with broth. Potatoes, sweet potatoes, winter squash, carrots and cooked dried beans are all effective thickeners, and add a delicate, creamy or nutty

taste. While a blender does reduce some of the benefits of fiber—some findings suggest that larger pieces of fiber are better for our health—it doesn't detract from the nutritional reserves like beta-carotene, a vegetable form of vitamin A.

Although many people think that making a more nutritious meal will take more time, there are convenience foods that make the job easier. Canned beans, for example, add plenty of fiber but require no soaking and simmering. Canned tomatoes or tomato-juice cocktail can act as the base of a broth or help bind a casserole, adding flavor and nutrients with few calories and little fat.

For a nutritious final flourish, top the one-dish meal with a touch of yogurt, chopped green, red or yellow bell pepper, a sprinkling of cheese, or croutons sautéed in garlic-flavored olive oil. The '60s notion that healthy food must be drab, tasteless and require a martyr's palate is long obsolete, and the creative cook need not doubt that good health and good taste can be married in the same pot.

—Sarah Fritschner

Sarah Fritschner is a nutritionist and food editor of The Louisville Courier Journal in Louisville, Kentucky. She is the co-author, with Michael Jacobson, of The Fast Food Guide (Workman Publishing, 1986).

LOW-FAT BÉCHAMEL SAUCE

In this cholesterol-free, nonfatty binder, which can be used to thicken cream soups or casseroles, skim milk or buttermilk takes the place of cream or half-and-half, and olive oil replaces the traditional butter.

2 Tbsp. olive oil	pinch cayenne pepper
¼ cup flour	1 qt. skim milk, or butter-
½ tsp. salt	milk, or part skim milk,
pinch black pepper	part chicken stock

Heat olive oil in medium saucepan. Add flour and stir well. Add seasonings and stir to blend over medium heat for about 1 minute. Remove pan from heat and whisk in a little milk. Add a little more milk, working it into flour paste. Keep working in milk until the flour paste no longer seizes into a tight mass and can be stirred easily. Beat in the remaining milk and bring to a boil, stirring frequently, over fairly high heat.

BEEF & VEAL

"Beef is the soul of cooking."

Antonin Carême, *Le Cuisinier Parisien* (1828)

An occupational hazard in the preparation of this cookbook was the all-too-frequent temptation to abandon work and slip into the kitchen to test a particularly tantalizing recipe. So we understand how one of our contributors, John Thorne, the author of the "Simple Cooking" newsletter, felt when he encountered a casual reference to a beef stew in his reading.

"For reasons I'm still not sure I understand," he wrote, "the simple name of one of the dishes, '*Boeuf aux Carottes*' or simply, 'Beef with Carrots,' resonated so deeply in my appetite that when I had closed the book it was the single culinary image that lingered. . . . Those three words were enough to summon up not only the dish but all its individual components, assembling together in bursts of flavor that obediently clustered around two central players: a gentle braise of chunks of beef and carrot, slowly simmering in no more liquid than they cared themselves to exude, fragrant with braised onion, parsley, garlic and thyme." Midway through Thorne's description of the stew he was inspired to create, we yielded to temptation and set out to discover for ourselves whether the dish was all its author promised.

There is something about beef stew that, at least for those of us who eat meat, tugs powerfully at the senses. Beef's complexity makes it a protean resource for the stewpot. Root vegetables like carrots and onions are apt complements, as are a variety of sweet, spicy or sour flavors. Savory herbs, such as rosemary, thyme, bay leaves and garlic, enhance it, and so do cinnamon and cloves in the Greek stew *stifado*.

Unless you are acquainted with the cow's anatomy, selecting a cut for the stewpot can be an uncertain proposition. In general, the well-exercised parts closer to the forequarters and the hoof are the most suitable for stewing, since they are tougher but also highly flavorful. Sirloin and tenderloin portions, which are composed mostly of muscle fibers, shrink and become mealy under long, slow cooking, while the tough cuts become silkily tender, as their collagen is coaxed into gelatin, thickening the broth and giving it sheen and depth.

Our first choices for stewing are shin and shank, which come from just above the hoof, and are lean and juicy. Although scorned for steak because it is tough and veined with irregular streaks of fat, the chuck, from the forequarter, is also a good choice for stew. Short ribs, from underneath the shoulder, are fatty and flavorful, and are commonly available boneless. The brisket, a striated, tough cut from the forequarter, also responds well to long simmering and is favored for corned beef and sauerbraten. Oxtails, the joints of the tail of the steer, have a succulent sweetness and are worth watching for in the market.

Rump and round portions have the advantage of being low in fat, but because they shrink and become dry, we prefer to reserve them for daubes, in which the meat is first marinated so that it is tenderized.

For stewing, locally raised "red" veal, from calves that are allowed to roam and eat solid food, is preferable to the more expensive milk-fed veal, from calves that are confined—not only because of its fuller flavor, but for humane reasons.

All of the fattier cuts can be made acceptable from the standpoint of health by carefully trimming the fat before cooking, and making the stew in advance—preferably the day before—so that the congealed grease may be skimmed off.

Most stews should be cooked long and slowly for two to four hours, at a gentle simmer or on low heat in the oven. They can be warmed the next day and refreshed with a jolt of garlic; a paste of garlic, basil, tomato paste and Parmesan cheese; or, following John Thorne's lead, a bracing touch of lemon.

Jane's Sweet Basil Stew

Fragrant with sweet basil, this tomato-red stew is an easy dish for company.

◆

Yield: 6-8 servings
Preparation time: 2½ hours

◆

3 Tbsp.	olive oil
4 cloves	garlic, crushed
1	medium onion, sliced
3 lbs.	stewing beef
6½ cups	crushed tomatoes in tomato puree
5 Tbsp.	sweet basil
1 cup	dry sherry
2 Tbsp.	sugar
3	onions, quartered
4	carrots, quartered
6	potatoes, quartered
1 tsp.	salt, or to taste

Put oil in a large Dutch oven. Add garlic and onion and cook until golden brown. Blot beef dry and add it to the pot, brown thoroughly. Add tomatoes, basil, sherry, sugar and 1 cup water. Cover and simmer for 1 hour.

Remove cover and simmer for ½ hour longer. Add the remaining vegetables and salt to taste, simmer for 40 minutes longer or until potatoes and carrots are fork-tender.

Jane Easton Brashares ◆ *Chevy Chase, Maryland*

Quilters' Ragout

See photo page 68.

"A lovely looking ragout with which to end a day of quilting." For a particularly striking effect, serve it in a "bowl" made from a hollowed-out loaf of bread, garnished with oranges and broccoli. Rice or broad egg noodles are a good accompaniment.

◆

Yield: 6 servings
Preparation time: 2½ hours

◆

1 package (about ½ oz.)	dried wild mushrooms
2 Tbsp.	vegetable oil
2 lbs.	stewing beef, in 1½" cubes
3 Tbsp.	flour

2 cloves	garlic, minced
2	large onions, finely chopped
1 cup	beef stock
1 Tbsp.	tomato paste
½ tsp.	dried thyme, crumbled
½ tsp.	dried rosemary, crumbled
2 Tbsp.	red wine vinegar
¼ tsp.	freshly ground black pepper
2 Tbsp.	butter
1 lb.	fresh mushrooms, halved if large
2 cups	small white onions, peeled

Serving Suggestion: While the ragout is cooking, prepare bread shell. Hollow out bread, leaving a sturdy shell about an inch thick. Fit a bowl into the hollowed loaf or line it with foil.

Soak dried mushrooms in 1 cup warm water for 30 minutes, or until soft. Strain soaking liquid through several layers of cheesecloth and set aside. Rinse mushrooms well to remove any grit, chop finely and set aside.

Heat vegetable oil in a large heavy pot or Dutch oven. Toss meat with 1 Tbsp. of the flour, and brown in batches in the hot oil. Remove and set aside. Pour off and discard all but 2 Tbsp. fat.

Add garlic and onions and cook until tender. Stir in the remaining 2 Tbsp. flour and cook for a few minutes until onions are browned. Whisk in mushroom-soaking liquid, beef stock, tomato paste, thyme, rosemary, vinegar, pepper and chopped wild mushrooms, and stir well. Add beef and bring to the boil. Reduce heat and simmer, covered, for 1½ hours.

In a small frying pan, heat butter and cook fresh mushrooms until all liquid has been absorbed. Add mushrooms and onions to the meat mixture. Cover and simmer about 30 minutes longer, or until meat and onions are tender. Adjust seasonings.

GARNISH

1 small bunch	broccoli
10" loaf	crusty bread such as sourdough Italian or rye
2-3	oranges, sliced
¼ cup	chopped fresh parsley
sprig	fresh rosemary

Just before serving, cut broccoli into florets and blanch lightly in boiling water. Place bread on a large serving plate, surround with broccoli and orange slices. Spoon ragout into hollowed-out bread loaf. Sprinkle with parsley and a few slivers of orange rind, and add a sprig of fresh rosemary.

Irene Louden ◆ Port Coquitlam, British Columbia

Spanish Cocido

Variation: Hot Italian sausage may be substituted for chorizo.

"This spicy stew is the result of a 70-year love affair with the language, people and countries of the Spanish-speaking world and our own southwestern United States. Present it with squares of hot Mexican Corn Bread [page 228] and a lightly dressed green salad, garnished with orange slices, thin rings of red onion, stuffed green olives, sliced avocado and a sprinkling of pine nuts."

◆

Yield: 6-8 servings
Preparation time: 2½ hours

◆

2 lbs.	top-round of beef, cut into 1"x ½" squares
3 Tbsp.	olive oil
½ lb.	chorizo (Mexican sausage), cut into ¼" slices
1	medium onion, finely chopped
2 large cloves	garlic, minced
1	small bay leaf
¼ tsp.	marjoram
⅛ tsp.	thyme
8-oz. can	tomatoes, chopped
2 cups	beef stock
2 1-lb. cans	chick-peas
	salt & pepper to taste
¼ cup	dry sherry

Sauté beef in oil in heavy pot until lightly browned. Add sausage, onion, garlic, bay leaf, marjoram and thyme. When onion is limp and golden, add tomatoes and stock. Puree 1 can chick-peas in a blender, and add.

Cover and simmer 1½ to 2 hours or until very tender. Drain second can of chick-peas and add to stew. Season with salt and pepper and add sherry just before serving.

Corenne Smith ◆ *Aptos, California*

Down-Under Beef Bourguignon

"A fine stew to help February along, this beef stew, made with Burgundy, is worth coming home for and tastes even better the next day. Crusty bread is a must to sop up the gravy."

◆

Yield: 8 servings
Preparation time: 6½ hours

◆

2	small onions, chopped coarsely
2 Tbsp.	chopped fresh parsley
1 tsp.	dried leaf thyme, crushed
2	bay leaves
2 Tbsp.	coarsely ground black pepper
2 Tbsp.	pickled green peppercorns, crushed
2 Tbsp.	olive oil
3 cups	Burgundy wine
3 lbs.	beef, bottom round (or lean shin beef), cut into 1" pieces
2 Tbsp.	vegetable oil
¼ cup	brandy
1¼ cups	beef stock
2 Tbsp.	butter
3 cups	small white onions, peeled
1 large clove	garlic, crushed

Pickled green peppercorns have a piquant taste that is halfway between capers and black peppercorns. They are available in specialty food shops and in some super-markets.

Combine onions, parsley, thyme, bay leaves, pepper, green peppercorns, oil and wine in a large glass or pottery bowl. Stir to blend. Add cubed beef, stir well and let stand 2 to 3 hours at room temperature, stirring occasionally.

In a large heavy saucepan or Dutch oven, heat oil. Drain beef cubes, saving the marinade. Remove the bay leaves and discard. Blot the beef dry and add to the saucepan; cook until browned, stirring as needed. Add the brandy and ignite with a match, averting face.

Add reserved marinade and stock. Bring to a boil. Reduce heat, cover and simmer 2 to 3 hours, or until the beef is tender.

Melt butter in a heavy frying pan, add white onions and garlic, cook and stir until the onions are a golden brown.

Stir onions into stew and simmer another 30 minutes. Adjust salt and seasonings as needed.

Irene Louden ◆ *Port Coquitlam, British Columbia*

Best-Ever Hungarian Goulash

Paprika, a favorite seasoning in many Hungarian recipes, adds color and flavor and is believed to stimulate the appetite. It contains more carotene than a carrot, and vitamins C, B_1 and B_2 besides.

"A staple of Hungarian cooking, goulash, or 'gulyas,' can be traced back to the ninth century. Serve this on a cold winter evening with well-cooked cabbage seasoned with brown sugar and a pinch of caraway seeds. Accompany it with hard bread and pickled beets."

◆

Yield: 6-8 servings
Preparation time: 2½ hours

◆

	vegetable oil
4 slices	bacon
¼ cup	flour
1 Tbsp.	paprika
1½ tsp.	salt (optional)
½ tsp.	coarsely ground pepper
dash	cayenne pepper
2 lbs.	boneless beef chuck, cut into 1½" cubes
1 cup	sliced onions
14½-oz. can	stewed tomatoes
4	medium potatoes (2 cups), peeled and sliced in wedges
6-oz. can	tomato paste
2-3 cups	beer, or strong chicken stock

Thinly coat Dutch oven with oil. Brown bacon until fat melts but bacon is not yet crisp. Remove from pan. Put flour, paprika, salt, pepper and cayenne into a large bag. Place beef in bag and shake until coated. Brown beef in bacon fat. Add onions, tomatoes, potatoes, tomato paste and beer or chicken stock. Lay bacon strips on top. Cover, bake in 325-degree F oven for 1½ to 2 hours, or until tender. After 1 hour, stir and add more water if necessary.

Sandra Helmacy Chenevey ◆ *New Wilmington, Pennsylvania*

Oxtail Ragout

"This is a treasure from a Bohemian neighbor 25 years ago." The juices of oranges and lemons complement the sweetness of raisins and red pepper.

◆

Yield: 4-6 servings
Preparation time: 3¾ hours

◆

3-4 lbs.	oxtails
	flour
2 Tbsp.	oil
2 tsp.	chili powder
2 tsp.	dry mustard
2 tsp.	cornstarch
2 tsp.	salt
1½ cups	orange juice, preferably freshly squeezed
2 Tbsp.	fresh lemon juice
¼ tsp.	Worcestershire sauce
½ cup	sultana raisins
1	sweet red pepper, thinly sliced
3 stalks	celery, chopped
1 cup	chopped black olives

Dredge oxtails lightly in flour. Heat oil in a Dutch oven or heavy skillet and brown oxtails on all sides.

In a separate bowl, combine chili powder, mustard, cornstarch and salt, and stir in orange juice, lemon juice and Worcestershire sauce to make a smooth paste. Add to meat along with raisins and simmer, covered, for about 2½ hours, or until the meat is tender.

Stir in red pepper, celery and olives. Simmer 25 to 30 minutes longer. Cool, skim fat and reheat.

Monte Thompson ◆ Omaha, Nebraska

Oxtails are proof that the nearer the bone, the sweeter the meat. Because most butchers don't cut their own meat from hanging carcasses, oxtails can be hard to find. Stock up when you do find them.

Belgian Beef Braised in Beer

This oven stew is simplicity itself. Beer is the secret ingredient, providing amber color and subtle complexity.

◆

Yield: 6 servings
Preparation time: 3 hours

◆

2 Tbsp.	vegetable oil
3 lbs.	boneless beef chuck, fat trimmed, cut into bite-sized pieces
2 Tbsp.	flour
1½ tsp.	salt
¾ tsp.	pepper
2 sprigs	fresh rosemary, or 1 tsp. dried, crumbled
5	medium onions, thinly sliced
2 cloves	garlic, crushed
1	small bay leaf
2 cups	dark beer

Preparation Hint: Use a clay cooker or crockpot for best results.

Place oil in ovenproof pot and heat. Coat beef cubes with mixture of flour, salt and pepper. Brown beef in hot oil. Add all of the remaining ingredients and stir well. Cover the pot and place in a preheated 325-degree F oven; bake for 2½ to 3 hours, stirring occasionally. If mixture seems dry after 2 hours of baking, add ½ cup water. Finish baking and serve.

JoAnne B. Cats-Baril ◆ *Charlotte, Vermont*

Beef Stew with Leeks & Mushrooms

For this voluptuously rich French stew, we like to use shin, a highly flavorful cut, which becomes tender and gelatinous when slowly simmered in the oven.

◆

Yield: 6 servings
Preparation time: 3½ hours

◆

2½ lbs.	beef shin with marrowbones
6 Tbsp.	vegetable oil
2	medium onions, chopped
3 cloves	garlic, minced
3	leeks, well washed and cut into 1" lengths
3 Tbsp.	flour

1½ cups	beef stock made from shin marrowbones
1½ cups	dry red wine
½ cup	cognac
2 Tbsp.	tomato paste
1	bay leaf
½ tsp.	rosemary
½ tsp.	thyme
¼ tsp.	nutmeg
¼ tsp.	allspice
1 tsp.	salt
1 tsp.	pepper
3	carrots, sliced into 1" rounds
8	small red potatoes, washed, with skins on, cut into 1½" chunks
6	onions, quartered
½ lb.	mushrooms, halved
½ cup	chopped fresh parsley

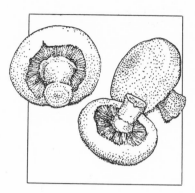

Cut meat from marrowbones, trim excess fat and cut meat into 1½-inch pieces; set aside. To make stock, brown marrowbones in heavy pot, then add 2½ cups cold water. Simmer 30 minutes. In a Dutch oven, brown meat on both sides in 2 Tbsp. hot oil and set aside. Add 2 Tbsp. oil, or as necessary, and sauté chopped onions, garlic and leeks until soft. Stir in flour and cook for a few minutes until it colors slightly.

Strain broth and add 1 cup to the pot, along with wine, cognac, tomato paste, meat and seasonings. Simmer, covered, in a 300-degree F oven for 1½ hours. Add carrots, potatoes, quartered onions and ½ cup stock. Simmer for 1 hour longer, or until vegetables are tender. During the last 30 minutes, sauté mushrooms in 2 Tbsp. oil and add to pot. Skim fat. Stir in parsley just before serving.

Rux Martin ◆ *Underhill Center, Vermont*

Sheena Stew

Suggested Accompaniment:
Oatmeal Biscuits (page 225).

"Our grandfather brought this stew home from Scotland after the Second World War, and it has provided us with many enjoyable evenings in the company of friends ever since." Chutney, red currant jelly and mustard combine in a tangy gravy.

◆

Yield: 4-6 servings
Preparation time: 3¼ hours

◆

8-12	small, whole onions
1½-2 lbs.	top-round beef or stewing beef, cut into 2" cubes
¼ cup	flour
	salt & pepper
2 Tbsp.	drippings or oil
14 oz.	stewed tomatoes
1-2 Tbsp.	prepared mustard
1-2 Tbsp.	red currant jelly
1 Tbsp.	chutney
2 cloves	garlic, crushed
1½ cups	small, whole mushrooms

Peel onions. Trim excess fat off meat. Toss meat in flour seasoned with salt and pepper. Heat drippings in heavy casserole pan and brown meat. Add tomatoes with juice and mustard, blending well. Add remaining ingredients. Stir well. Cover and simmer for 2¼ to 2½ hours until meat is tender.

The Drennans ◆ Stouffville, Ontario

Double Beef & Barley Stew

Pearl barley has been milled to remove the tough hull and some of the bran. Though that process removes a few nutrients, it greatly shortens the cooking time. Pearl barley is found in the grain section of most supermarkets.

Doubly delicious, too! The beefy, flavorful gravy becomes thick and luxurious when the pearl barley is added.

◆

Yield: 6 servings
Preparation time: 2½ hours

◆

1½ lbs.	chuck steak, or other lean meat
	flour
2 Tbsp.	oil
1	onion, chopped
1 clove	garlic, crushed
1 lb.	ground chuck (beef)
1 Tbsp.	soy sauce

½ tsp.	seasoned salt
½ tsp.	sesame seeds
2 cups	beef stock
¼ cup	pearl barley
2 cups	sliced carrots
½ cup	chopped celery
	pepper to taste

Additional salt is not needed since the soy sauce provides plenty of sodium.

Trim fat and bones from meat and cut into bite-sized cubes. Dust beef with flour. Using a heavy pot, brown the beef in hot oil, browning all sides. Remove meat and set aside. Add onion and garlic to drippings and cook until onion is transparent. Remove from heat.

Form ground meat, soy sauce, seasoned salt and sesame seeds into small balls. Push onion and garlic aside and brown meatballs. Return steak cubes to pan. Add broth and barley. Cover and simmer for 45 minutes. Add carrots and celery and simmer until meat is tender, about 40 minutes. Add ½ to 1 cup water as needed and season with pepper as desired.

Donna Jubb ◆ *Fenelon Falls, Ontario*

Hot Beef with Sugar

(La Viande Chaude)

"This is my own creation, and so far I have been rewarded by many compliments. Sweet, spicy and easy to prepare, it has a Cajun flair. The consistency is just right for serving over rice."

◆

Yield: 4-6 servings
Preparation time: 70 minutes

◆

2 cups	beef, cut into 1" cubes or thin strips
2 large or 3 small cloves	garlic, finely chopped
¼ cup	granulated sugar
¼ tsp.	salt
1 tsp.	cayenne
1 Tbsp.	soy sauce
15-oz. can	tomato sauce
½ cup	onion, chopped
2 cups	sliced carrots
2 cups	sliced or cubed potatoes

Place beef, garlic, sugar, salt and cayenne in a large bowl and toss together thoroughly, making sure the beef is well coated. Place in a skillet and set over medium heat. Sauté beef mixture for 5 minutes, keeping mixture moving while cooking. Add soy sauce and tomato sauce and stir until completely mixed. Turn down heat to medium-low and continue cooking and stirring for an additional 10 to 15 minutes, until all is thoroughly cooked. Taste and adjust seasonings, if necessary. Add vegetables and 1 cup water and cook until vegetables are tender.

Ann Davey ◆ *Seattle, Washington*

Redmond's Beef or Venison Stew

Venison, which is exceptionally low in fat, can sometimes be bought from local game wardens.

"This family recipe has been served at family get-togethers for generations. It can be halved for smaller families. The large quantity of onions is no mistake; they make for a very sweet stew."

◆

Yield: 8-12 servings
Preparation time: 3 hours

◆

1 cup	flour, or as needed to dredge meat
4 lbs.	beef or venison, cut into 1½" cubes
¼ cup	oil
5 lbs.	onions, peeled and cut into 1" slices
6 large cloves	garlic, crushed
1 cup	brown sugar
3	bay leaves
1 tsp.	thyme
1 Tbsp.	seasoned salt or to taste
¼ tsp.	ground pepper
¼ cup	wine vinegar
3 cups	beer
¼ cup	dry red wine
4-8	peeled, sliced carrots (about 1 per person)
4-8	small potatoes, peeled and quartered
¼ cup	flour, dissolved in ½ cup cold water

Put flour into paper bag, add half the meat and shake to coat; set aside. Repeat with the remaining meat.

Heat oil to medium-high heat in Dutch oven. Brown half the meat, do not crowd. Brown the remaining meat. Set aside. In the same pot, sauté onions and garlic until golden brown.

In a bowl, mix brown sugar, bay leaves, thyme, seasoned salt, pepper and vinegar. Add to onions in Dutch oven. Pour in beer and wine. Return meat to pot, stir and bake, covered, for 2 hours at 350 degrees F.

During the last hour, add carrots and potatoes. Half an hour before the stew is done, whisk in flour-water mixture.

Sally Lord ◆ *Shelburne, Vermont*

Daube of Beef

In this intensely flavored, savory stew of French origin, the beef is marinated with vegetables in white wine for several hours and braised in the marinade, without being browned.

◆

Yield: 6-8 servings
Preparation time: 7 hours .

◆

3 lbs.	beef, cut into 2" squares

MARINADE

1½ cups	dry white wine
¼ cup	brandy
3 Tbsp.	olive oil
3 sprigs	fresh thyme, or 1 tsp. dried
1	bay leaf
3 cloves	garlic, crushed
4	onions, sliced (about 2 cups)
6-8	carrots, sliced (about 2 cups)
½ tsp.	pepper
2 tsp.	salt

½ lb.	bacon, cut into 2½" pieces
½ lb.	mushrooms, sliced (about 2 cups)
	flour for dusting meat
2 cups	crushed tomato puree
1-1½ cups	beef or veal stock (enough to cover contents of casserole once all else has been added)

Variation: For fresher flavor, fresh tomatoes mixed with 4 Tbsp. puree may be substituted for crushed tomato puree.

Place beef in a bowl and add marinade ingredients: white wine, brandy, olive oil, thyme, bay leaf, garlic, onions, carrots, pepper and salt. Cover and marinate for at least 3 hours. If refrigerated, marinate at least 6 hours.

Blanch bacon in boiling water, and preheat oven to 325 degrees F. Remove beef from marinade and separate out vegetables. Roll beef in flour. Alternate layers in casserole dish starting with the bacon. Next add the marinated vegetables, mushrooms, tomatoes and finally the floured beef. Finish with a few pieces of bacon. Pour marinade and stock over top, cover, and bake for 3 to 4 hours, until beef is tender.

JoAnne B. Cats-Baril ◆ *Charlotte, Vermont*

Minty Beef & Noodle Stew

Tarragon and mint add an unusual twist to this otherwise traditional stew. Simmer it slowly with the lid off to make the thick, flavorful gravy.

◆

Yield: 4-6 servings
Preparation time: 2½ hours

◆

¼ cup	butter
2	large onions, chopped
1½ lbs.	beef, cut into ½" cubes
2	large tomatoes, cored and chopped
¼ cup	finely chopped fresh mint
2 cloves	garlic, crushed
1 tsp.	salt
1 tsp.	pepper
½ tsp.	tarragon
¼ lb.	wide noodles

In a large saucepan, melt butter, then add onions and sauté until they are golden. Blot beef dry, add to pan and brown. Add remaining ingredients—except noodles—and 4 cups water. Simmer for 2 hours, uncovered, or until meat is very tender and sauce is thickened. Stir in noodles, cover pot and simmer 10 minutes longer.

Irene McKay ◆ Wahnapitae, Ontario

Middle Eastern Beef & Green Bean Stew

Potatoes may also be added to this zesty, spicy stew, which reminded our tester of dishes she had enjoyed while living in Syria.

◆

Yield: 3-4 servings
Preparation time: 2 hours 20 minutes

◆

1 lb.	lean beef, cubed
2 Tbsp.	oil
1	large onion, peeled and chopped
2	tomatoes, peeled and diced, or 8 oz. canned
2 cups	tomato juice
2 Tbsp.	lime or lemon juice
¼ tsp.	turmeric
¼ tsp.	cinnamon

2 Tbsp.	chopped fresh mint, or 2 tsp. dried
	salt & pepper
1 clove	garlic, minced
1 lb.	fresh green beans, tipped and sliced

Brown beef in hot oil in a Dutch oven. Add remaining ingredients, except green beans, cover and simmer for 2 hours.

Steam green beans for 15 minutes or until almost tender, then add them to the stew. Cover and cook 10 minutes more. Serve.

Bertha F. Small ◆ *Ste. Anne de Bellevue, Quebec*

Mediter-ranean Beef Stew

Green and black olives and cherry tomatoes are the distinguishing flavors in this dish.

◆

Yield: 6-8 servings
Preparation time: 2½ hours

◆

2 Tbsp.	olive oil
3 lbs.	top-round steak, cut into cubes
1	large onion, chopped
3 cloves	garlic, minced
3	carrots, sliced
3 stalks	celery, sliced
1 tsp.	thyme
½ tsp.	marjoram
1 cup	tomato puree
2 cups	beef stock
12	pitted black olives
12	pitted green olives
18	cherry tomatoes

Heat olive oil in a heavy pot. Brown beef cubes a few at a time, removing pieces as they brown. Set aside. Sauté onion, garlic, carrots and celery in the pot for 5 minutes. Add beef, seasonings, tomato puree and stock and simmer for approximately 2 hours, covered, until the beef is tender. Just before serving, add olives and tomatoes and heat through.

Laurie Bradley ◆ *Surrey, British Columbia*

Serving Suggestion: "Serve over rice or with a thirsty loaf of French bread."

Cider Stew with Herb Dumplings

The day we cooked this stew, the sweet aroma of apples and beef lured our staff into the kitchen all morning to ask what was cooking. Cider imparts a sweet-tart depth to the beef.

◆

Yield: 6 servings
Preparation time: 2 hours

◆

3 Tbsp.	flour
¼ tsp.	thyme
1 tsp.	salt
¼ tsp.	pepper
2 lbs.	stewing beef
3 Tbsp.	cooking oil
2 cups	apple juice or cider
2 Tbsp.	cider vinegar
4	carrots, chopped
3	potatoes, peeled and quartered
1	onion, chopped
1 stalk	celery, chopped
1	apple, peeled and chopped
1 cup	whole mushrooms

Combine flour, thyme, salt and pepper. Dredge meat in flour mixture to coat. In a large saucepan or Dutch oven, brown meat in hot oil. Stir in apple juice or cider, ½ cup water and vinegar. Cook and stir to boiling. Reduce temperature and add carrots, potatoes, onion, celery and apple. Cook slowly until meat is tender, 1½ to 2 hours. Add mushrooms in last 15 minutes of cooking. If necessary, thicken with a little flour dissolved in cold water, and top with dumplings.

DUMPLINGS

2 cups	flour
4 tsp.	baking powder
½ tsp.	salt
½ tsp.	parsley
¼ cup	Parmesan cheese
2 Tbsp.	shortening
1 cup	milk

Mix dry ingredients, parsley and cheese. Work in shortening with pastry blender. Add milk gradually and, with a knife, mix to a soft dough. Drop by spoonfuls onto stew mixture, allowing space for the dumplings to rise. Cover pot closely and do not peek for 12 to 14 minutes. Lift dumplings out carefully onto a platter and serve with stew.

Emily-Jane Orford ◆ Kingston, Ontario

Beef with Carrots

Although no liquid, save for the juice of half a lemon, is added to this stew, the long, slow oven-cooking sweats out copious juices to produce a rich gravy. The carrots are moist and sweet without being mushy and melt on the tongue.

◆

Yield: 4-6 servings
Preparation time: 4½ hours

◆

1 lb.	carrots
2-3	medium onions
	flour for dredging meat
	salt & freshly ground pepper to taste
½ tsp.	thyme
¼ cup	olive oil
2 lbs.	boneless beef short ribs
1 Tbsp.	parsley
2 cloves	garlic, minced
1 tsp.	minced lemon peel
	juice of ½ lemon

Preheat oven to 225 degrees F. Scrub and peel the carrots, trimming away the tops. Cut them into bite-sized chunks. Put them into a lightly oiled cast-iron 3-qt. casserole dish. Peel onions and coarsely cut them into bite-sized chunks. Set aside.

Season a cup or so of flour with a generous pinch each of salt, pepper and dried thyme. Heat olive oil in large sauté pan until it starts to smoke. Dredge strips of short rib (or any inexpensive, rich-textured stewing beef) in seasoned flour, shaking away any excess. Put meat in hot oil and sear on all sides, transferring each, as finished, into the casserole dish.

When all the meat has been seared, put onion in the pan, adding more oil if necessary to keep it from burning. Cook until the pieces are translucent and edged with brown, turning them often with a spatula while at the same time scraping up any burnt bits of meat and flour. Scrape all this into the casserole dish onto the meat and carrots.

Mince parsley, garlic and lemon peel. Add these to the casserole dish, pour over lemon juice, generously season with salt and pepper, and toss well to mix the seasonings throughout. Cover the casserole dish, place in the preheated oven, and cook for 4 hours, checking occasionally to make sure that the contents remain at bare simmer. Taste for seasoning.

John Thorne ◆ *"Simple Cooking," Castine, Maine*

"Simple Cooking" is a quarterly newsletter about food, full of essays, recipes and reviews. It is available for $12/year from: P.O. Box 622, Castine, Maine 04421.

Viennese Beef Goulash

"Please don't be taken aback by the quantity of onions; they stew away until they become part of the gravy."

•

Yield: 8-10 servings
Preparation time: 4 hours

•

½ cup	chicken fat
2-3 lbs.	cooking onions, sliced or coarsely chopped
2 Tbsp.	Hungarian sweet paprika
1 Tbsp.	dried marjoram
2 tsp.	salt
1 tsp.	caraway seeds
1 Tbsp.	lemon juice
3 lbs.	stewing beef, in 1½" cubes
1 Tbsp.	flour, dissolved in 1 Tbsp. cold water (optional)

Preparation Hint: "If you can, make this a day ahead; the fat is more easily removed and the goulash tastes better."

In a heavy stewpot set over medium flame, heat the fat. When sizzling hot, stir in onions and cook until soft. Stir in 1 Tbsp. paprika, marjoram, salt, caraway seed and lemon juice. Add meat and ½ cup cold water. (Don't bother to brown the meat first.) Cover and simmer for 2 or 3 hours, until the meat is tender.

If time allows, chill and skim off the fat. Reheat and blend in the remaining paprika, and the flour and water if the gravy isn't thick enough. Simmer for 15 additional minutes.

Lynne Roe ◆ *Orangeville, Ontario*

Chili Parmesan

This thick, stick-to-your-ribs chili is quicker to make than most.

•

Yield: 6-8 servings
Preparation time: 1¼ hours

•

2 lbs.	ground chuck
1	large green pepper, diced
2 cloves	garlic, crushed
2	large onions, chopped
2 stalks	celery, diced
28-oz can	whole, peeled tomatoes, quartered

1 tsp.	black pepper
2 scant tsp.	salt
2 Tbsp.	chili powder
29-oz. can	tomato puree
1 Tbsp.	Worcestershire sauce
4 Tbsp.	Parmesan cheese

Brown ground chuck, green pepper, garlic, onions and celery in Dutch oven. Drain off fat. Add tomatoes with liquid, pepper, salt, chili powder, tomato puree and Worcestershire sauce; stir well. Heat until it boils; reduce heat and simmer 45 minutes. Stir in Parmesan cheese; cook 5 minutes longer. Sprinkle with more Parmesan cheese; serve with garlic bread.

Sue Gifford ◆ *Lansing, Illinois*

Texas Chili

" '**R**eal chili con carne is a haunting, mystic thing,' writes Frank X. Tolbert in *A Bowl of Red*. This chili is mysteriously delicate rather than searingly hot. It is wonderful served immediately, at room temperature or even cold, but seems to lose its flavor edge on reheating."

◆

Yield: 4 servings
Preparation time: 3¾ hours

◆

Masa harina, a finely ground white cornmeal, is available in the Mexican section of many supermarkets, but coarse cornmeal, ground in a blender or food processor for several minutes, can be substituted.

	olive oil
3 lbs.	chuck roast, cut into bite-sized pieces, all fat trimmed
2-3	onions, minced
5 fat cloves	garlic, minced
¼ cup	chili powder
1 tsp.	oregano
2 tsp.	cumin
½-1 tsp.	salt
1-2 Tbsp.	masa harina
1-2	jalapeño peppers, minced (fresh preferred, but pickled peppers can be rinsed and used)

When preparing the meat, remove as much fat as possible, as it seems to dull the delicate flavors of this chili. Heat olive oil to smoking in a heavy kettle and add meat. Cook until meat is light-colored. Add onions and garlic. Add 2-3 cups water to cover, and mix. Bring to the boil, then cover and simmer for 1 hour.

Add chili powder, oregano, cumin and salt; cook slowly for 1 hour more, stirring occasionally. You may want to adjust the seasoning after a half hour. Stir masa harina into ¼ cup cold water. Add to chili. Add jalapeño peppers. Continue to cook until the chili thickens, about 10 to 15 minutes, stirring frequently to avoid sticking.

Stephen Cummings ◆ *London, Ontario*

Mucho Gusto Chili

Preparation Hint: "Leave out the salt until the end of cooking or it will toughen the beans."

The addition of water makes this more a Mexican soup than a true chili. A bit of cornmeal mixed with water will thicken it without detracting from the flavor. "Serve with grated cheese and finely chopped onion and either corn or flour tortillas, heated, buttered and rolled up tight to serve as a scoop."

◆

Yield: 12 servings
Preparation time: 4-5 hours

◆

1 lb.	coarsely ground beef
1 lb.	ground pork (lean shoulder)
1 lb.	red beans, washed
1	large onion, diced
1 cup	celery, sliced into ¼" pieces
3 Tbsp.	hot chili powder
1 Tbsp.	cumin seeds
1 qt.	tomatoes
1½ cups	V8 juice
1½ cups	beer
3	bay leaves
3 large cloves	garlic
3-oz. can	green chilies, diced
1	bell pepper, diced
1 Tbsp.	oregano
½ tsp.	black pepper
	salt to taste
2 Tbsp.	cornmeal mixed with 3 Tbsp. warm water (optional)

Brown meat slightly. Add to beans in soup pot. Add water to half full. Add onion, celery, chili powder, cumin, tomatoes, V8, beer, bay leaves, garlic, green chilies, bell pepper, oregano and pepper. Bring to a simmer and cover. Cook for 3 to 4 hours or until tender, adding water if necessary so beans do not stick and stirring frequently. Add salt. If too runny, stir in cornmeal mixture.

Pat Dunkel ◆ *San Diego, California*

Corned Beef Stew with Gruyère

"This hearty stew provides the cook with a different way to serve corned beef."

•

Yield: 4 servings
Preparation time: 2¾ hours plus soaking time

•

2 lbs.	corned brisket of beef, trimmed of fat
2 cloves	garlic, finely chopped
3 Tbsp.	Dijon mustard
2 Tbsp.	vegetable oil
2 lbs.	leeks, trimmed and washed, chopped into ½" pieces
2 Tbsp.	Worcestershire sauce
1 cup	beef stock or consomme, diluted with ½ cup water
2 cups	grated Gruyère cheese

Serving Suggestion:
Accompany with boiled new potatoes and a salad.

Soak corned beef in fresh water at least six hours, changing the water several times to remove the salt.

Chop beef into 1-inch cubes and place in a large mixing bowl. Preheat the oven to 350 degrees F. Mix garlic and mustard and stir them together with the beef.

Using a large flameproof casserole dish, heat oil over moderate heat. Add meat cubes and fry, stirring constantly, for about 7 minutes until meat is browned. Add leeks and Worcestershire sauce. Pour beef stock over meat and bring contents of casserole dish to a boil. Taste for saltiness, and if the beef seems too salty, add ½ cup more water.

Remove casserole dish from stove and place in oven. Cook, covered, for about 1½ hours, then uncover and cook for another ½ hour, stirring occasionally. The meat should be very tender, almost crumbly.

Remove casserole dish from oven and sprinkle the meat with grated cheese. Return it, uncovered, to the oven and cook for 10 to 15 minutes until the cheese is bubbling and golden brown. Remove from oven and serve immediately.

Ina Fitzhenry-Coor ◆ Burlington, Vermont

Lucifer's Short Ribs

Despite its incendiary name, our tester assures us that this dish contains the proper amount of warmth for tame palates.

•

Yield: 4-6 servings
Preparation time: 3½ hours

•

3 cups	soaked pinto beans
1	bay leaf
3 lbs.	lean, boneless short ribs
1 Tbsp.	oil
1	medium onion, chopped
3 cloves	garlic, minced
1	green pepper, cut into strips
2 cups	chicken stock
6 oz.	tomato sauce
1½ cups	beer
½ tsp.	cumin
½ tsp.	oregano
1 tsp.	chili pepper

Cook pinto beans with bay leaf in enough water to cover beans, until they are tender. Meanwhile, trim excess fat from ribs. Heat oil in heavy pot and brown meat. Discard all but 1 Tbsp. fat. Add onion, garlic and green pepper, and sauté until limp. Pour liquids over meat and add spices. Cover pot, simmer for 2 hours. Serve beans topped with ribs and sauce.

Laurie Bradley ◆ *Surrey, British Columbia*

Greek-Style Beef Pot Roast

"**F**or those who are tired of the usual New England-style pot roast."

◆

Yield: 4-6 servings
Preparation time: 2½ hours

◆

4-5 lbs.	beef pot roast, chuck or round
	salt & pepper
¼ lb.	butter
2	onions, quartered
3 cloves	garlic, crushed
2 stalks	celery, cut into chunks
⅛ tsp.	cinnamon
¼ tsp.	cloves
1 tsp.	allspice
3	bay leaves
1	cinnamon stick, broken in half
28-oz. can	whole tomatoes
8-oz. can	tomato sauce
1 cup	dry red wine

Sprinkle roast with salt and pepper and brown in 2 Tbsp. butter in a heavy pot. Set meat aside and drain fat. In the remaining butter, sauté onions, garlic, celery, cinnamon, cloves, allspice, bay leaves and cinnamon stick. Return meat to pot. Add tomatoes, tomato sauce, red wine and 1 cup water. Cover and simmer for 2 hours, or until meat is tender, adding more water if necessary.

Mary-Eileen McClear ◆ *Baden, Ontario*

Corned Beef Dinner

Low-salt corned beef is excellent in this traditional dinner, according to our tester.

◆

Yield: 5 servings
Preparation time: 4¾ hours

◆

2½-3 lbs.	corned beef brisket
1	medium onion, sliced
1	bay leaf
¼ tsp.	black pepper
1 clove	garlic, crushed
1 tsp.	celery seed
6	medium onions, whole
6	medium carrots, halved
6	medium potatoes
1	small turnip, cut in sixths
1	small cabbage, cut in sixths

Simmer brisket, onion and seasonings in 6 cups hot water, for 3 to 4 hours. Add vegetables, except cabbage, and simmer for 30 minutes more. Add cabbage and simmer 10 more minutes.

Remove meat and vegetables from the broth. Slice meat and arrange with vegetables on a serving platter. Spoon a little broth over top.

Kathryn Jane Christie ◆ *Singhampton, Ontario*

Mongolian Hot Pot

A brass hot pot is a worthwhile investment for this meal. It comes in two parts: a large, round basin to hold the broth and a base in which coals are burned. Hot pots are available for about $45 in Chinese specialty shops. A meat fondue pot is an acceptable substitute. All the ingredients may be obtained from a Chinese specialty store or the Chinese section of the supermarket.

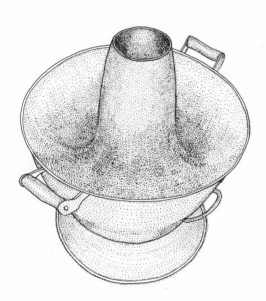

"Introduced into China by the Mongols in the thirteenth century, this fondue-like meal has become a ceremonial event at our house, reserved for company and special family occasions. It's ideal for entertaining on a busy schedule because the ingredients can be assembled in less than an hour, and the guests do all the cooking. The sight of the platters piled high with raw, thinly sliced beef, vegetables and shrimp and the exotic pot enthroned in the center of the table fills everyone with expectation. First, the food is dipped into the boiling broth and cooked using chopsticks or fondue forks and dipped into various sauces around the table. Then when it is gone, Chinese noodles are added, and the meal concludes with a soup."

◆

Yield: 6 servings
Preparation time: 1 hour

◆

DIPPING INGREDIENTS

2-3 lbs.	boneless top round
3	boneless chicken breasts, cut into thin strips
30	large raw shrimp, peeled and deveined
3 qts.	homemade chicken broth, heated to boiling
½ head	celery cabbage, trimmed to bite-sized pieces
½ lb.	fresh spinach, cleaned
1 lb.	tofu, cut into bite-sized cubes
1 lb.	fresh mushrooms
1 package	Chinese plain noodles

MASTER SAUCE

½ cup	sesame oil
½ cup	red wine vinegar
¼ cup	hot oil
½ cup	fish sauce
½ cup	red bean curd sauce
½ cup	sesame paste
¾ cup	brewed tea
scant ½ cup	sugar
¼ cup	light soy sauce
	salt

Place beef in freezer until it is partially frozen, slice into paper-thin slices. Arrange dipping ingredients, beef, chicken, shrimp and vegetables attractively on a platter.

Place hot pot on a fireproof surface. (We use two firebricks.) Place hot coals in base of hot pot. (Coals from the wood stove are ideal, but lighted charcoal briquettes may be used.) Place basin on top and add boiling chicken broth, or place broth in a fondue pot.

To make the master sauce: combine all ingredients and divide it into small dipping bowls for each person. Place additions to the sauce in small bowls around the table.

Using chopsticks or a fondue fork, guests lift up pieces of meat or vegetables and dip them into the boiling liquid and then into sauce. The master sauce may be individually embellished by adding scallions, soy sauce or hot chili sauce to taste.

After the guests have eaten as much as they want, the noodles are added to the pot and cooked. Then the liquid is spooned into individual soup bowls. If they wish, guests may add some of the dipping liquid to the soup.

Rux Martin ◆ *Underhill Center, Vermont*

Additions to Sauce:

- finely chopped garlic in Chinese cooking wine
- finely chopped scallions, green part included
- finely chopped fresh coriander
- light soy sauce
- hot oil
- chili paste with garlic
- minced ginger in Chinese cooking wine

Beefy Borscht Stew

"It is difficult to decide whether this is a soup or a stew. Just a small bowl can fill you up. I make a whole batch and freeze it in small portions." Chunky and satisfying, it has good zip.

◆

Yield: 4-6 servings
Preparation time: 1½ hours

◆

2 lbs.	stewing beef, cut in 1" cubes
8 cups	beef stock
5	beets, 3 grated, 2 julienned
1 small head	white cabbage, chopped
3	carrots, julienned
2 stalks	celery, chopped
1	onion, finely chopped
4	tomatoes, chopped
1 Tbsp.	red wine vinegar
1 Tbsp.	sugar
1	bay leaf
1½ tsp.	salt
½ tsp.	pepper
1 Tbsp.	lemon juice
1 Tbsp.	dill
1 Tbsp.	parsley
1 cup	sour cream

Simmer meat in stock for 45 minutes. Remove scum as needed. Add all vegetables, except tomatoes, and simmer 20 to 25 minutes. Add remaining ingredients, except sour cream, and simmer 15 minutes more. Add sour cream. Heat through but do not boil. Serve with extra sour cream.

Wendy MacQueen ◆ *Petawawa, Ontario*

Veal Shanks with Buttermilk, Lemon & Capers

Health Tip: The use of buttermilk makes this stew relatively low in fat. Buttermilk is made from skim milk or low-fat pasteurized milk. A cup of skim buttermilk contains just 2 percent fat compared to the 20 percent in a cup of light cream.

"Originally put together from ingredients on hand, this quickly became a favorite." It makes a festive savory-tart supper from an inexpensive cut of veal. Serve over fettuccine.

◆

Yield: 6 servings
Preparation time: 2½ hours

◆

1½ cups	buttermilk
3 cloves	garlic, minced
1 Tbsp.	coarsely ground black pepper
¼ cup	fresh lemon juice
3 lbs.	veal shanks, cut 1" thick
2 Tbsp.	olive oil
2 Tbsp.	butter
4	leeks, cut in ¼" strips lengthwise
2 cups	dry white wine
1 Tbsp.	capers
	salt & pepper

GARNISH

3 cloves	garlic, chopped
1 cup	finely chopped fresh parsley
	grated rind of 1 lemon

Mix buttermilk, garlic, pepper and lemon juice together in a bowl or pan large enough to marinate veal shanks. Add veal and marinate for 1 to 2 hours at room temperature, or refrigerate overnight.

Pat shanks dry and reserve marinade. In a heavy stockpot or Dutch oven, heat oil and butter and brown shanks on both sides. Remove and set aside. Add more oil and butter if needed and sauté leeks until browned lightly. Add wine and buttermilk mixture and bring to a gentle boil, return shanks to pot and simmer, covered, for 1 hour. Add capers and simmer, uncovered, for 30 minutes more. Season with salt and pepper, and garnish with a mixture of garlic, parsley and lemon rind.

R. Kent Cummings ◆ North Ferrisburg, Vermont

Blanquette de Veau

"This traditional French veal blanquette combines veal, pearl onions and mushrooms in a lemony cream sauce."

◆

Yield: 6 servings
Preparation time: 2 hours

◆

3 lbs.	stewing veal, cut in 1" cubes
2 cups	chicken stock
1	onion, stuck with cloves
1	carrot, peeled and quartered
½ tsp.	thyme
1	bay leaf
2 sprigs	parsley
½ lb.	mushrooms, quartered
4 Tbsp.	butter
20	pearl onions, peeled
3 Tbsp.	flour
	juice of ½ lemon
½ cup	cream
	salt & pepper to taste

Health Tip: Because they contain lots of cream, most blanquettes are high in fat. This one gets by with less and is healthier than its rich taste would lead one to believe.

Place veal in a heavy pot and cover with 2 inches of water. Boil for 3 minutes, skimming foam as necessary. Drain. Bring veal, chicken stock, 1 cup water, onion, carrot, thyme, bay leaf and parsley to a boil, skimming foam as necessary, for about 5 minutes. Lower heat, cover and simmer for 1 hour.

While the veal is simmering, sauté mushrooms in 1 Tbsp. butter, and boil onions in water until tender. When veal is tender, drain, reserving the liquid. Remove onion, carrot, parsley and bay leaf.

In the casserole dish, make a roux with 3 Tbsp. butter and flour. Add the reserved cooking broth. Bring to a boil, whisking constantly and boil for 5 minutes. Lower heat, add lemon juice, cream, salt and pepper to taste. Return veal to casserole dish, add mushrooms and onions and simmer for about 10 minutes. Serve with rice or steamed potatoes.

Carolyn Gregson ◆ *Underhill Center, Vermont*

Veal Stew with Winter Vegetables

Fresh dill, which is feathery and delicate, gives best results, but 1 tsp. dried may be substituted.

"Red" veal, which has been fed a diet of grain and allowed to roam, is a fine choice for this delicately seasoned, aromatic stew.

♦

Yield: 6 servings
Preparation time: 2 hours

♦

4 Tbsp.	butter
3 Tbsp.	olive oil
3 lbs.	boneless veal chuck roast, trimmed, cut in 1½" cubes
	freshly ground pepper
¼ cup	brandy or cognac
2	leeks, cut into 1" rounds
4	carrots, cut into 1" rounds
2	medium onions, quartered
1 tsp.	dried thyme
1 cup	dry white wine
4 cups	chicken stock
4" strip	orange peel
1	butternut squash, peeled and cut into 1" cubes
4	potatoes, peeled and quartered
1½ tsp.	Dijon mustard
1 cup	light cream
1 Tbsp. plus 1 tsp.	fresh dill
½ cup	chopped fresh parsley
	salt to taste

Preheat oven to 350 degrees F. In a large, flameproof Dutch oven, melt 2 Tbsp. butter and 1 Tbsp. oil over moderately high heat. Lightly brown veal in batches, on both sides, seasoning with pepper; don't crowd the pan. Set aside.

Add brandy to Dutch oven and, averting face, ignite with a match. When the flames subside, add remaining butter and oil. Add leeks, carrots, onions and thyme. Simmer, stirring, until vegetables are softened, about 15 minutes. Add wine, stock and orange peel and scrape up any browned bits. Return veal to pot, and add squash and potatoes. Heat just to boiling; bake in the oven for 1 hour, or until meat and vegetables are tender.

Skim fat. Remove vegetables and meat to serving dish; discard orange peel. Boil broth and reduce by half. Whisk in mustard, cream and herbs, heat briefly, adjust seasonings and pour over vegetables and meat.

Rux Martin ♦ Underhill Center, Vermont

Veal, Mushroom & Cider Stew

Carrots and hard cider lend a mellow sweetness to the sauce. Mushrooms, sautéed and put in at the last moment, add earthy undertones.

◆

Yield: 4 servings
Preparation time: 2 hours

◆

4 Tbsp.	sweet butter
1	large onion, chopped
2 lbs.	veal, cut in bite-sized cubes
2 Tbsp.	flour
1 tsp.	salt
½ tsp.	pepper
4	carrots, peeled and sliced
1 cup	chicken stock
2 cups	hard cider
½ cup	chopped parsley
1 tsp.	dried thyme, or 3 fresh sprigs
2 cloves	garlic, crushed
1 lb.	fresh mushrooms, sliced

Melt 3 Tbsp. butter in an ovenproof pot. Add onions and sauté until golden brown. Meanwhile, blot veal with paper towels to dry, dust with flour, salt and pepper. Add meat to the pot and sauté until brown and crisp. Add sliced carrots, stir until coated with pan juices. Add remaining ingredients except the remaining 1 Tbsp. butter and the mushrooms. Cover pot and place in preheated 325-degree F oven and bake for 1½ hours or until veal is tender. Stir occasionally.

During the last ½ hour of the cooking time, slice mushrooms and heat butter, until sizzling, in a skillet. Add mushrooms and sauté until nicely browned. Remove stew from the oven and add mushrooms. Stir.

JoAnne B. Cats-Baril ◆ *Charlotte, Vermont*

Hard cider or *cidre*, available in the wine stores, varies widely in price and alcoholic content, depending on whether it is made in Canada, France or Britain.

Blanquette of Veal with Apples & Two-Potato Crust

"I created this recipe for a fall menu featuring Ontario products at a cooking school where I was an instructor." Delicately flavored with apple, covered with pipings of sweet potato and white potato puree, this veal stew is time-consuming to make but well worth the effort.

◆

Yield: 6-8 servings
Preparation time: 3¾ hours

◆

3 lbs.	veal, cut into 1" cubes
1	medium carrot, split
1 stalk	celery
1	onion
1	small leek, split and well-washed
1	bouquet garni: 2-3 sprigs thyme, 1 bay leaf, 2 cloves, white peppercorns, 2-3 parsley stalks, all tied up in a cheesecloth bag
⅔ cup	diced carrot
⅔ cup	diced turnip
⅔ cup	diced parsnip
20	pearl onions
6 Tbsp.	unsalted butter
5 Tbsp.	flour
1 cup	dry white wine
½ cup	dried mushrooms, soaked, or 1 cup fresh button mushrooms
4 oz. piece	bacon, cut into strips, rind removed
2 Tbsp.	fresh chives or thyme
½ cup	whipping cream
2	McIntosh apples, peeled and sliced into thin wedges

To make the stew: Place veal in a large pot and cover with 7 cups of water. Set on medium heat and bring to a boil. Skim foam. Add whole vegetables: carrot, celery, onion, leek and bouquet garni. Reduce heat, cover and simmer approximately 45 minutes, or until veal is just tender.

Using a slotted spoon, lift out veal and set aside in bowl. Remove bouquet garni and whole vegetables and discard them. Add diced vegetables and pearl onions to the stock and simmer 7 to 8 minutes, or until tender. Using a colander, strain stock into a bowl and add the vegetables to the veal.

In a separate pot, melt 5 Tbsp. butter and stir in flour gradually until combined. Cook over low heat 3 to 4 minutes, do not brown. Slowly whisk in stock, and cook until smooth, about 5 to 6 minutes. Reduce wine to ½ cup by boiling, and add to stock. Add mushrooms, if dried are used.

Cut bacon into small pieces, drop into boiling water for 1 minute and drain well. Fry until crisp and add to veal. Drain fat, reserving 1 Tbsp. If fresh mushrooms are used, sauté 2 minutes in fat and add to veal. Add veal, vegetables, bacon, mushrooms, fresh herbs and cream to sauce and simmer 10 minutes. Place in an ovenproof dish. Sauté apples briefly in remaining 1 Tbsp. butter and arrange on top of blanquette.

POTATO PUREE

2 lbs.	potatoes, peeled and diced into ½" pieces
2	egg yolks
⅓-½ cup	whipping cream
	freshly grated Parmesan or Gruyère
	salt
	white pepper
	freshly grated nutmeg

Easy Variations:
- Tuck the stew under a pastry crust (page 201) and bake as a potpie.
- Cut veal and vegetables smaller and serve over pasta.
- Use canned yams in place of baked sweet potatoes.

Boil potatoes in salted water until tender. Drain and let stand 5 minutes in colander to dry. Push through sieve or a food mill into a bowl. Beat in egg yolks. Beat in cream. Mix in cheese and seasonings. Keep warm.

SWEET POTATO PUREE

2 lbs.	sweet potatoes or yams
2	egg yolks
⅓ cup	whipping cream
	salt
	white pepper
	freshly grated nutmeg

Bake sweet potatoes at 350 degrees F for 1¼ to 1½ hours, or until tender. Allow to cool slightly. Peel and put through a sieve or food mill. Beat in egg yolks. Beat in cream and add seasonings. Keep warm.

To decorate: Using a pastry bag, decorate the top of the blanquette with the purees, making stripes across the top, alternating sweet potato with potato. Or, mix the two purees and pipe over the top, using the pastry bag. Bake at 425 degrees F approximately 15 minutes, or until crust is lightly browned.

T.C. Seed ◆ *Toronto, Ontario*

LAMB & PORK

"Some hae meat and canna eat, And some wad eat that want it;
But we hae meat, and we can eat, And sae the Lord be thankit."

Robert Burns, *The Selkirk Grace*

It was the day of the Kentucky Derby when one of our testers, Janet Wilson, set out to make J. William Klapper's Kentucky Burgoo. The equivalent of Louisiana's gumbo and a close relative of Brunswick stew, burgoo is a hodge-podge of pork, lamb, beef, veal and vegetables, made in bathtub-sized quantities and served up at political functions, auctions, family gatherings and church socials. These days in the South, however, it takes pride of place on Derby Day.

Our tester, who grew up in Yankee country, breezed past the gargantuan portions of meat, corn, lima beans and okra, and was brought up short by the two cups of A-1 Sauce and two cups of Worcestershire sauce, "or to taste." Could the recipe mean two tablespoons?

With the measurements confirmed by telephone, and lingering skepticism in her heart, Wilson put her 16-quart canning kettle on the simmer. Ten hours later, long after the horses had crossed the finish line, the prodigious burgoo was ready. It was a thick, intriguingly spicy conglomeration of meats, no one distinct from any other, thickened by the natural unctuousness of the okra.

Both lamb and pork have the gumption to stand up to spicy Southern burgoos, powerful curries and tart borschts. The culinary link between the two meats is hinged on a mutual subtle sweetness and a chameleonlike capacity for responding to and agreeing with other flavors. While higher in fat and cholesterol than beef, lamb and pork are also more robust in flavor. A little goes a long way: a cured pork hock or a lamb neckbone will flavor a whole casserole of beans.

The flavor of lamb varies according to its age and diet. New Zealand and Australian lamb are older than American lamb and have a stronger flavor. In its turn, Western lamb, which grazes on the range, is more assertively flavored and less tender than most New England lamb, which reaches the market sooner because it is fed grain. Young lamb is the best choice for delicate dishes like Blanquette of Lamb or Lamb Stew in Avgolemono Sauce, and with vegetables like asparagus, artichoke hearts, peas or string beans; while older lamb or home-grown mutton has the character to hold its own in Lamb Chili with Black Beans, and with spices like curry, cumin, cinnamon and ginger.

Lamb shoulder is flavorful and well suited for stewing. Lamb shanks and breast may also be used. One cook who is famous for her lamb curries, however, prefers the more expensive, leaner meat from the leg, because it yields more symmetrical and tender chunks. Much of the fat in lamb is concentrated on the surface and should be trimmed before cooking. Browning the meat will melt most of the remaining fat away, which should then be drained from the pan. Because it is younger than beef, lamb does not require as much cooking. Curries, in particular, do not benefit from overcooking— their spices become bitter and muddy-tasting.

The mild flavor of pork makes it agreeable in stews where lamb would be out of place; for instance, with sweet potatoes and maple syrup, or green chilies and tomatoes, or a variety of Chinese seasonings, including soy, star anise and ginger.

Without question, the best pork cut for stewing is the ingloriously named butt, from the shoulder. It is meaty, fairly lean and reasonably priced. Smoked butt, used in place of ham, contributes honest flavor at a fraction of the price. Overcooking used to be practically mandatory, both to tenderize the meat and to kill the parasite, trichina, which is sometimes found within. New research shows that the parasite is killed when the meat is heated to 137 degrees F—still medium-rare. Too much cooking is not only unnecessary but will make the meat tough and stringy.

Like Kentucky Burgoo, many of the pork and lamb dishes in this chapter take well to freezing. In what may be the beginning of a Yankee tradition, tester Janet Wilson plans to trot the rest of the burgoo out of her freezer later this year for a garage sale/block party.

Maple Pork Stew

This sweet, savory stew of white beans, pork and sweet potatoes uses low-grade, dark maple syrup, which is more potent than Fancy or Grade A.

◆

Yield: 6 servings
Preparation time: 2½ hours, plus overnight

◆

¾ cup	white beans, soaked overnight and drained
4½ lb.	pork loin roast, trimmed, cut into 1" cubes
½ cup	flour
¼ cup	vegetable oil
1 Tbsp.	cognac or brandy
½ cup	dry red wine
1½ tsp.	salt
½ cup	dark maple syrup
6	sweet potatoes, peeled and cut into 1" cubes
1 tsp.	thyme
½ tsp.	sage
	black pepper
½ cup	chopped fresh parsley

Cook beans in 8 cups water for 10 minutes. Cover, turn off heat and allow to cool. Dredge pork in flour, and brown in hot oil in a Dutch oven. Drain in a colander. To the Dutch oven, add cognac, red wine, salt, maple syrup and 2½ to 3 cups water to cover meat. Stir, scraping up browned bits. Add sweet potatoes, pork, drained beans and seasonings. Cook, covered, for 2 hours in a 300-degree F oven, adding liquid as needed. Skim fat and adjust seasonings.

Meredith Gabriel ◆ *Ferrisburg, Vermont*

Pork Vindaloo

"Vindaloo, a traditional dish of Goa, located in the southwestern corner of India, is characteristically made by marinating meat in a vinegar mixture, so that it is exquisitely tender with a hot and pungent flavor. This one, made with pork, is rather mild, but of course can be made hotter by adding more chili powder. The contrast between tender pork and crunchy little mustard seeds is out of this world."

◆

Yield: 4 generous servings
Preparation time: 2½ hours plus marinating time

◆

2 Tbsp.	coriander seed
1 Tbsp.	cumin seed
2	green cardamom pods
1	cinnamon stick, 1" long
6	whole cloves
6	black peppercorns
2 tsp.	turmeric powder
1 piece	ginger, about 2" long
½-2 tsp.	chili powder
1 tsp.	salt
1 tsp. plus 2 Tbsp. plus ½ cup	white vinegar
2 lbs.	lean pork, chopped into stewing cubes
4	small bay leaves, crumbled
8 Tbsp.	vegetable oil
6 cloves	garlic, peeled and finely chopped
2 tsp.	mustard seed
	rice

Toasting the curry spices makes them more robust. A pinch of cardamom powder may be substituted for the pods, although the flavor is not as fresh.

Roast coriander and cumin seeds by cooking over medium heat in a small skillet. Take care not to burn them; they should be a darkish brown when properly roasted.

Mix coriander and cumin with cardamom, cinnamon, cloves, peppercorns, turmeric, ginger, chili powder and salt, and place in a food processor, processing until the spices form a paste, adding 1 tsp. vinegar, a few drops at a time.

Combine 2 Tbsp. vinegar and 2 Tbsp. water, and pour over pork. Add spice paste and mix with pork cubes. Prick meat so that it is well saturated with spices and vinegar. Sprinkle with bay leaves and cover with remaining ½ cup vinegar. Marinate overnight.

The following day, heat vegetable oil in a large, heavy skillet. Fry garlic. Add mustard seeds and fry until they "jump." Then add the pork and its marinating liquid and bring to a boil. Reduce the heat and simmer until the meat is tender, about 1 hour. No water should be added, as the dish is rather "dry" and thick. Serve hot with boiled rice, preferably the Indian basmatic type.

Ina Fitzhenry-Coor ◆ Burlington, Vermont

Curried Pork & Butternut Squash

Fresh coriander has a smoky, unusual flavor. When it is not available, flat-leaved parsley mixed with ½ tsp. coriander powder can be substituted.

"**K**nowing my passion for spicy foods, my brother gave this recipe to me."

◆

Yield: 6-8 servings
Preparation time: 3 hours

◆

3 lbs.	lean pork, cut in 1½" cubes
6 Tbsp.	butter or margarine
2	large yellow onions, chopped
2-3 cloves	garlic, crushed
1 Tbsp.	curry powder
	salt & pepper to taste
2 Tbsp.	tomato paste
⅛ tsp.	ground cloves
1 Tbsp.	crushed red pepper
¼ tsp.	ground coriander
¼ tsp.	ground cinnamon
2 cups	chicken stock
1	butternut squash, about 2 lbs., peeled, seeded and cut into 1" cubes
2 Tbsp.	brown sugar
1 Tbsp.	cornstarch mixed with 2 Tbsp. chicken stock
½ cup	chopped fresh coriander leaves

Brown pork in 4 Tbsp. butter. As the pork browns, transfer it to a heat-proof casserole dish and set aside. When the pork is done, add onion and garlic to the skillet and cook till soft (about 3 minutes). Then add the curry powder, salt and pepper, tomato paste, cloves, red pepper, coriander and cinnamon. Stir and gradually add the chicken stock. Combine the onion-spice-stock mixture with the pork and bake at 350 degrees F until the pork is fork-tender (about 2 hours).

Fifteen minutes before the pork is done, steam squash for 3 minutes. Melt 2 Tbsp. butter in a skillet, add brown sugar, and stir to melt. Add squash and toss to coat. Add squash to the pork and cook until the squash is tender but not mushy. Do not overcook.

Remove the pork and squash to a dish. Bring casserole juices to a boil. Whisk in the cornstarch mixture, taste and correct the seasonings. Add pork and squash and heat through. Sprinkle with chopped fresh coriander and serve.

Colleen Bruning-Fann ◆ *Clare, Michigan*

Curried Pork Stew

Crunchy peanuts, raisins and apples lift this simple pork stew out of the realm of the ordinary. Serve it with a fruit salad and rice.

◆

Yield: 4 servings
Preparation time: 1½ hours

◆

1 lb.	boneless pork, cut in cubes
2 Tbsp.	vegetable oil
½ cup	chopped onions
2 tsp.	curry powder
1 clove	garlic, minced
16-oz. can	tomatoes, cut up
2	medium carrots, in bite-sized pieces
2	medium potatoes, in bite-sized pieces
1 Tbsp.	quick-cooking tapioca
2 Tbsp.	raisins
1	large apple, peeled, cored, chopped
¼ cup	peanuts
2 Tbsp.	parsley flakes

In a Dutch oven, brown pork in batches in oil. Remove from pan and set aside. Drain all but 2 Tbsp. of drippings and sauté onions until soft. Return pork to pan. Add curry, garlic and vegetables. Simmer 1 hour. Add tapioca, raisins and apple in last 15 minutes of cooking. Sprinkle with chopped peanuts and parsley flakes.

Pamela England ◆ Central Butte, Saskatchewan

Oriental Pork Stew with Snow Peas

Transported to a potluck supper, this pork stew was the subject of "oohs and aahs" for the short time it lasted. Serve over rice.

◆

Yield: 6 servings
Preparation time: 2 hours

◆

3 Tbsp.	oil
2 lbs.	pork, cut in pieces
6	green onions, cut in 1" pieces
1	medium onion, chopped
½ cup	soy sauce
1 can	chicken stock
1 Tbsp.	sugar
2 cups	sliced carrots
1 can	sliced water chestnuts, drained
2 Tbsp.	cornstarch dissolved in ¼ cup cold water
10-oz. pkg.	frozen snow peas, or fresh if available

Heat oil in Dutch oven over high heat. Brown meat, ½ lb. at a time, and remove to bowl when browned. Put green onions and chopped onion in pan and sauté, stirring constantly, for 2 minutes. Return meat to pan and add soy sauce, chicken stock and sugar. Cover and simmer 40 minutes.

Add carrots and water chestnuts. Simmer 10 minutes. If desired, thicken with cornstarch and water mixture. Add snow peas and simmer about 3 minutes more.

Terry Braatz ◆ Mooresville, North Carolina

Chinese Pot Roast

Suggested Accompaniment:
Chinese Nappa Salad, page 221.

Star anise adds an exotic fragrance to this long-simmered Chinese-style pot roast. It is available in Chinese specialty stores. I like to serve this dish as part of a large buffet for company.

◆

Yield: 4 servings
Preparation time: 2¼ hours

◆

2 Tbsp.	oil
2 large cloves	garlic, peeled and crushed
2 quarter-sized slices	peeled ginger
2 lbs.	pork loin
3 Tbsp.	light soy sauce
3 Tbsp.	dry sherry
1 Tbsp.	sugar
½ tsp.	salt
1	star anise, whole
1 tsp.	Szechwan peppers
4	parsnips, cut in 2" lengths
4	carrots, cut in 2" lengths
4	onions, quartered

Heat oil in large heavy pot until hot. Reduce heat, add garlic, ginger and pork and brown on all sides. Add soy and sherry, turning meat to coat. Add 1 cup boiling water, sugar, salt, anise and Szechwan peppers. Add vegetables. Simmer for 2 hours, stirring occasionally.

Rux Martin ◆ *Underhill Center, Vermont*

Scalloped Sweet Potatoes & Apples with Pork Chops

T hough this dish cooks for a long time, it's child's play to assemble. At the end of cooking, the pork chops will be nicely brown and crusty, and the sauce light and fruity with the right amount of sweetness.

◆

Yield: 4 servings
Preparation time: 2¼ hours

◆

1 Tbsp.	oil
4	pork chops
2	large sweet potatoes, peeled and sliced
2	large apples, peeled and sliced
2	large onions, sliced
¼ cup	melted butter
1 Tbsp.	brown sugar
¼ cup	flour
1 tsp.	salt
¼ tsp.	nutmeg
¼ tsp.	freshly ground pepper
12 oz.	beer

Preparation Hint: Make this dish in advance up to the final ½ hour of cooking. It will keep in the refrigerator up to 3 days.

Heat oil and brown pork chops evenly on both sides. Layer sweet potatoes, apples and onions alternately in a greased, shallow casserole dish. Sprinkle them with half the butter and the brown sugar. Lay pork chops on top, in a single layer if possible. Mix flour, salt, nutmeg and pepper into remaining butter in a saucepan. Stir in beer and heat to boiling. Pour over pork chops. Cover and cook in 350-degree F oven for 1½ hours. Uncover and bake for 30 minutes longer.

F. Goodwin-Rogne ◆ *Sherwood Park, Alberta*

Pork & Apple Stew with Rosemary

Suggested Accompaniment:
Fluffy Biscuits, page 225.

J ust the sound of this combination — pork, apples, rutabagas and rosemary — is enough to make our mouths water. Apple juice, used to deglaze the pan, unites the flavors.

◆

Yield: 6-8 servings
Preparation time: 2½ hours

◆

¼ cup	vegetable oil
1 cup	chopped onions
5 cloves	garlic, minced
⅓ cup	all-purpose flour
1¼ tsp.	salt
¼ tsp.	freshly ground pepper
3 lbs.	lean pork, cut in 1" cubes
2 cups	apple juice
2 tsp.	crumbled dried rosemary
1 Tbsp.	Dijon mustard
1 Tbsp.	cider vinegar
3 cups	thickly sliced apples, peeled (preferably Northern Spy)
2 cups	chopped rutabaga, cut in ½" cubes

In large Dutch oven or flameproof casserole dish, heat 1 Tbsp. of the oil; add onions and garlic. Fry over low heat for about 5 minutes or until onions are tender. Remove with slotted spoon and set aside.

In sturdy bag, mix together flour, salt and pepper; add pork, in batches, and shake to coat. Add 1 Tbsp. of the oil to pan; cook pork, one layer at a time, over medium-high heat until browned, adding remaining oil as necessary. Remove with slotted spoon and set aside.

Pour apple juice into pan; increase heat to high and scrape up bits from bottom of pan. Return meat and onions to pan, along with rosemary, mustard, vinegar, apples and rutabaga; mix well. Cover and bring to boil.

Transfer Dutch oven to 350-degree F oven; bake, stirring occasionally, until meat is fork-tender, about 1½ hours. Taste and adjust seasoning.

Lucia Cyre ◆ *Logan Lake, British Columbia*

To reheat, bake at 325 degrees F for 30 to 40 minutes; or warm over low heat, stirring occasionally, until heated through.

The sheer simplicity of this dish, in which all the ingredients are tossed into the pot, appealed to our tester. Pork, veal and sausage harmonize without losing their individuality, with cabbage and sauerkraut striking assertive notes in a slightly sweet sauce.

Bigos with Prunes

(Polish Pork Stew with Prunes)

◆

Yield: 8-12 servings
Preparation time: 3 hours

◆

1	onion, chopped
1 clove	garlic, minced
2 Tbsp.	butter or lard
1 lb.	cabbage, shredded
1 qt.	sauerkraut, rinsed and drained
¼ lb.	mushrooms, sliced
1 lb.	boneless pork butt, cut in 1" cubes
1 lb.	boneless veal, cut in 1" cubes
½ lb.	Polish sausage, sliced ½" thick
1 cup	beef stock
1 cup	peeled and chopped ripe tomatoes
2	tart apples, peeled and diced
½ cup	pitted prunes
1	bay leaf
1 tsp.	salt
½ tsp.	freshly ground pepper
1 cup	red wine

Top-of-the-Stove Method

In a Dutch oven, sauté onion and garlic in butter until onion is transparent. Add remaining ingredients, cover and simmer for 2 hours.

Slow-Cooker Method

Combine all the ingredients, using only ½ cup each of stock and wine. Cook on low, covered, 8 to 10 hours.

Pressure-Cooker Method

In a pressure cooker, sauté onion and garlic in butter until onion is transparent. Combine the remaining ingredients, adding 1½ cups water, and cover and bring to full pressure. When steam appears, reduce heat and cook on low for 30 minutes. Reduce pressure completely and let stand 10 to 15 minutes to blend flavors.

Lucia Cyre ◆ *Logan Lake, British Columbia*

Kentucky Burgoo

Note: The voluminous
amount of A-1 and
Worcestershire sauces is no
mistake; our doubting tester,
who says she is ordinarily
not fond of spicy foods,
recommends no less.

"This traditional stew, served principally at
Derby time in Kentucky, was used for many years in our restaurant
and catering business and was originally given to me by a well-
known cook and caterer to some of the first families here. It yields a
cross between a soup and a stew that can be kept in the freezer for
several months."

◆

Yield: 3 gallons
Preparation time: 10-12 hours

◆

2 lbs.	pork shank or lean stewing meat
2 lbs.	beef shank or lean stewing meat
4 lb.	stewing hen
2 lbs.	veal shank or lean stewing meat
2 lbs.	breast of lamb
1½ lbs.	white potatoes, peeled and diced
2	green peppers, cored, seeded and diced
2 pods	hot red pepper, seeded and minced
2 cups	diced okra, fresh or frozen
1 cup	diced celery
1 bunch	carrots, peeled and diced
2 cups	chopped cabbage
2 cups	whole-kernel corn, fresh, frozen or canned
2 cups	lima beans, fresh or frozen
1 qt.	tomato puree
2 cups	A-1 Sauce
2 cups	Worcestershire sauce
	salt
	cayenne pepper
	Tabasco sauce
	chopped fresh parsley

Suggested Accompaniments:
Bran Corn Bread (page 227)
and green salad. Kentucky
Burgoo is often served in
mugs rather than bowls.

Put all the meat into 8 quarts cold water and bring to boil. Simmer until
tender enough to fall from bones, about 3½ to 4 hours. Remove meat
from stock, cool; bone and chop.

Return meat to stock and add vegetables, tomato puree, A-1 and Worcestershire sauces. Simmer until all vegetables are done and stew is thick but
still soupy. Stir frequently with a long-handled spoon, and adjust seasonings. Cooking will require 6 to 8 hours at a simmer. Garnish with parsley.

J. William Klapper ◆ *Louisville, Kentucky*

Kielbasa in Beer

(Bigos)

"**B**igos, now commonly served as a substantial dinner course, was originally a breakfast dish prepared in the forest for Polish aristocratic hunting parties. The sky is the limit as far as ingredients are concerned: sausages, cooked ham, a piece of boiled pork, roast duck, rabbit, venison and a glass or two of red wine thrown in." This version, enthusiastically recommended by our tester, confines itself to smoked kielbasa. Serve with coarsely sliced rye bread.

◆

Yield: 8 servings
Preparation time: 3¼ hours

◆

2 12-oz. cans	beer, at room temperature
4 Tbsp.	cornstarch
3 Tbsp.	Worcestershire sauce
1 tsp.	allspice
1	small cabbage, finely shredded
1	medium green pepper, coarsely sliced
8 oz.	fresh or canned mush-rooms, sliced
2 stalks	celery, chopped
1	medium carrot, finely chopped
2	medium onions, finely chopped
1	medium apple, cored and coarsely chopped
1 cup	chicken stock
2 lbs.	smoked kielbasa, cut into chunks
	salt & pepper to taste
2 cups	grated Swiss cheese

Variation: For a milder flavor, use pork in place of the smoked kielbasa.

Preheat oven to 350 degrees F. In heavy 4-to-5-quart casserole, stir in beer, cornstarch, Worcestershire sauce and allspice. Stir in vegetables and apple. Pour in chicken stock, add sausage, and season with salt and pepper. Cover the casserole and bake for 1½ hours; uncover and bake for 30 minutes longer or until the meat and vegetables are tender. Cover with cheese during last 10 minutes.

Ludwig F. Debski ◆ East Hanover, New Jersey

Kielbasa, New Red Potatoes & Sauerkraut

This classic Eastern European skillet supper has been updated with red potatoes, but ordinary potatoes may be used instead.

◆

Yield: 4-6 servings
Preparation time: 1 hour

◆

3-4 Tbsp.	butter
1	large onion, thinly sliced
1 lb.	sauerkraut, drained and rinsed
½ cup	dry white wine
1 cup	chicken stock
2 Tbsp.	wine vinegar
2 Tbsp.	brown sugar
1	bay leaf
	salt & pepper to taste
1 lb.	new red potatoes, cubed
1 lb.	kielbasa, sliced
2-3 Tbsp.	Dijon mustard

Melt butter and sauté onion until golden brown. Add sauerkraut, wine, stock, vinegar, brown sugar, bay leaf, salt and pepper. Bring to a boil and then simmer about 20 minutes. Add potatoes and kielbasa. Stir in mustard, and simmer until potatoes are tender.

R. Kent Cummings ◆ *North Ferrisburg, Vermont*

Kielbasa Simmer

"My grandmother used to make this dish. Serve on a platter, surrounded by halved orange slices. One orange is sufficient for the garnish."

◆

Yield: 4 servings
Preparation time: 40 minutes

◆

1 lb.	kielbasa or German sausage
1 Tbsp.	olive oil
1	large onion, diced
1	medium-firm head cabbage, finely sliced
1 cup	chicken or beef stock
1	apple, cubed, unpeeled
1	large potato, cubed

1 tsp.	crushed garlic
	salt & pepper to taste
4	medium-to-large carrots, sliced diagonally
1	orange for garnish (optional)

Slice sausage diagonally. Heat olive oil in a large skillet, add sausage and cook on low heat 15 minutes, covered. Add onion, cabbage and stock. Cover and cook 10 minutes, then add apple, potato, garlic, salt and pepper. Add carrots, cover and simmer, stirring occasionally, until carrots are cooked but still a little crunchy. Cabbage should be tender. If dry, add a bit more water. Pour out on a large platter and garnish with orange slices, or serve straight from the skillet with hard rolls.

Shirley Engle ◆ *Lynnwood, Washington*

Italian Sausage Stew

"This recipe was passed down for generations in my husband's family. It's good plain, served with bread to dunk or over noodles."

◆

Yield: 4-6 servings
Preparation time: 2½ hours

◆

¼ lb.	bacon
2 Tbsp.	olive oil
2½ lbs.	beef chuck, cut into cubes
2	onions, sliced
4 cloves	garlic, minced
1 cup	red wine
2 Tbsp.	flour
	salt & pepper
1 tsp.	oregano
1 tsp.	thyme
1-1½ lbs.	Italian sausage, hot or sweet

In a large frying pan, cook bacon until crisp. Remove, crumble and set aside. Drain fat, add olive oil. Brown beef cubes in batches over medium-to-high heat and place them in a large heavy kettle.

Add onions to skillet and cook over low heat about 3 minutes. Add garlic and cook another 1 or 2 minutes. Stir in wine, flour and 1 cup water. Bring to a boil, then add to meat in kettle. Add seasonings, cover pot, and cook slowly about 1 to 1½ hours, until meat is tender. Fry sausage until cooked through and add to stew along with bacon.

Carol LePree ◆ *Union, New Jersey*

Italian Tomato Soupstew

See photo page 65.

Aptly named, according to our tester, who used a combination of spinach and plain tortellini to make this Mediterranean meal-in-a-bowl even more colorful. Dill pickles are a surprise ingredient, adding a hint of sour to the sweet tomato-y richness.

◆

Yield: 10 servings
Preparation time: 2 hours

◆

4	fresh tomatoes, chopped
1 lb.	Italian sausage, cut into bite-sized pieces
14-oz. can	Italian tomato sauce
7 cups	beef stock
1 cup	chopped onion
1 clove	garlic, minced
1 cup	sliced carrots
1 tsp.	basil
1 tsp.	oregano
2 cups	sliced zucchini
1 cup	fresh mushrooms
1	green pepper, diced, seeds removed
¼ cup	chopped fresh parsley
1½ cups	sliced dill pickles
2 cups	frozen tortellini or small ravioli

Combine tomatoes, sausage, tomato sauce, stock, onion, garlic, carrots, basil and oregano in a large pot and simmer 30 minutes. Add remaining ingredients and simmer an additional hour, adding more water as necessary to cook tortellini.

Gabriele Quinn ◆ *Mountain, Ontario*

Italian Tomato Soupstew, page 64

North American Bouillabaisse, page 147

Quilters' Ragout, page 20

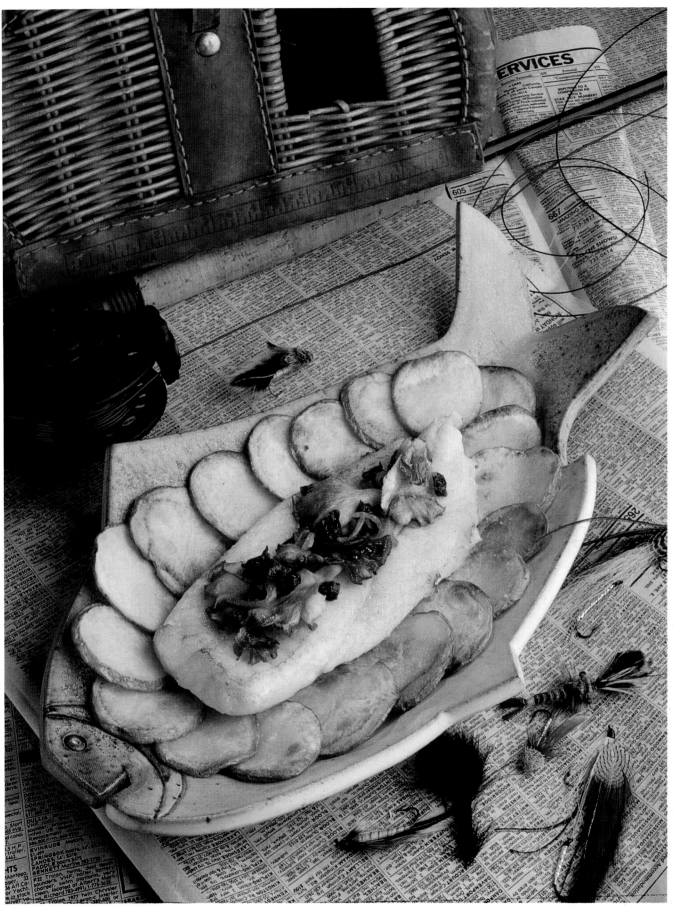

One-Dish Fish with Sun-Dried Tomatoes, page 146

Fast Russian Borscht, page 176

Chicken with Vegetables & Elephant Garlic, page 106

Vermont Cheddar-Crusted Scallop Pie, page 202

Creole Jambalaya, page 137

74

Meal in a Bowl Chinese Soup, page 82

Savory Pumpkin Soup, page 172

Torta Milanese, page 203

Chicken Marengo, page 102

Turkey Chili with Bitter Chocolate, page 112

Chinese Hot & Sour Soup

"**A**lthough this dish is extremely easy to prepare and is cooked in minutes, it offers a taste-punch. It goes well with steamed rice, hot tea and a cold day."

◆

Yield: 6-8 servings
Preparation time: 40 minutes

◆

Serving Suggestion: "The vinegar and pepper may be left out and passed at the table so diners may suit themselves."

5 cups	chicken stock
¼ lb.	lean pork or chicken, sliced into bite-sized pieces
1 tsp.	soy sauce
1 Tbsp.	sherry
¼ cup	sliced mushrooms, or 2-3 soaked and shredded Chinese dried mushrooms
¼ cup each	snow peas, cut in half
	carrots, thinly sliced or diced
	celery, thinly sliced
	Chinese cabbage stalk, thinly sliced
	spinach leaves, torn into bite-sized pieces
½ lb.	tofu, cut into bite-sized strips
¼ cup	coarsely shredded bamboo shoots
2 Tbsp.	cornstarch dissolved in ¼ cup cold water
1	egg, thoroughly beaten
2 Tbsp.	rice vinegar, or to taste
⅛ tsp.	ground black or red pepper, or to taste
	sesame oil
	sliced green onions

Heat stock to full simmer, add meat, soy and sherry. Simmer, covered, for about 3 minutes if using pork, less for chicken. Add mushrooms and any tough raw vegetables used, such as carrots or celery; simmer for an additional minute or two. Add tofu, bamboo shoots and any other tender vegetables, such as peas or spinach, and simmer to heat thoroughly, about 1 minute. Add cornstarch-water mixture and cook until clear. The soup should be slightly thickened; add additional water or broth if too thick.

Remove soup from heat and, stirring gently so as not to break up the tofu, slowly drizzle in beaten egg. Add vinegar and pepper to taste. Before serving, add a few drops of sesame oil and garnish with finely sliced green onions, including the green tops.

Mike Cheak ◆ Carbondale, Illinois

Meal in a Bowl Chinese Soup

See photo page 74.

The wontons may be made in quantity and frozen.

Filling yet light, this soup lives up to its name. Our tester pronounced it well worth the two extra steps of preparing barbecued pork and wontons. Wonton wrappers are found in most supermarkets.

♦

Yield: 8 servings
Preparation time: 2½ hours plus marinating time

2 lbs.	chicken backs and necks
2 lbs.	bony-cut pork, such as side ribs
1 tsp.	salt
1" chunk	ginger root, peeled
1	medium cooking onion, peeled
1-2 cloves	garlic
½ lb.	boneless chicken breast, sliced
½ lb.	raw shrimp, peeled and deveined
4-5 stalks	bok choi, sliced into 1½" lengths
¼ lb.	snow peas, ends and strings removed, cut in half, or regular peas
½ cup	sliced mushrooms, preferably oyster
4-5	water chestnuts, thinly sliced
12-16	wontons (*recipe follows*)
	Chinese barbecued pork, cut into slices (*recipe follows*)
	chopped scallions
	fried Chinese noodles
	steamed rice
	soy sauce
	Chinese vinegar (malt, cider or white wine vinegar may be substituted)

Put 3 to 4 quarts water in a heavy pot and add chicken backs, pork ribs, salt, ginger, onion and garlic, and boil for 5 minutes. Skim foam. Simmer 1½ hours. Cool, remove chicken and pork bones, and skim fat.

Add chicken breast, shrimp, bok choi, snow peas, mushrooms, water chestnuts, wontons and barbecued pork to stock. Bring stock to boil, reduce heat, and simmer for an additional 15 to 20 minutes, or until meats and vegetables are cooked. Serve, and pass the scallions, Chinese noodles, steamed rice, soy sauce and vinegar.

WONTONS

¼-½ lb.	ground pork
1 Tbsp.	finely chopped onion
½ tsp.	salt
¼ tsp.	sugar
2 tsp.	soy sauce
12-16	wonton wrappers

Combine filling ingredients. Place a tsp. of filling in the center of each wrapper. Fold bottom over filling, fold in sides and seal with water. Finish rolling up and seal again.

CHINESE BARBECUED PORK

2 lbs.	boneless pork, preferably tenderloin

MARINADE

1 Tbsp.	sugar
½ tsp.	salt
1 clove	garlic, minced
½ tsp.	freshly grated ginger
2 Tbsp.	catsup
2 Tbsp.	soy sauce
1 Tbsp.	sherry
½ tsp.	Five Spices Powder

BASTING SAUCE

1 Tbsp.	Hoisin sauce
¼ cup	honey

Barbecued pork may be tightly wrapped and frozen.

Place pork in marinade for 2 to 4 hours or overnight. Preheat oven to 375 degrees F. Place marinated pork on a rack over a pan of hot water. Bake for 20 minutes. Turn and bake for another 20 minutes. Switch oven to broil and baste pork with marinade and basting sauce and broil for 3 to 5 minutes each side, no closer than 2 inches from the broiling element. Cool before slicing. May be tightly wrapped and frozen.

Lynne Roe ◆ Orangeville, Ontario

"This popular Eastern European soup has survived many generations in our Ukrainian family. When it was made in the 'old country,' the kraut was brined in wooden barrels in the family cellar. Today, we achieve equally satisfying results using the store-bought variety. The tangy flavor of this soup is reminiscent of Oriental hot and sour dishes."

Kapusnyak

(Sauerkraut Soup)

◆

Yield: 6-8 servings
Preparation time: 2 hours

◆

1	ham bone, or ½ lb. spare ribs
1	onion, chopped
1	potato, diced
1	carrot, sliced
3 cups	sauerkraut
1 Tbsp.	butter or margarine
2 Tbsp.	flour
1 Tbsp.	sour cream
	salt & pepper

Cover bone or meat with 2 qts. water and simmer for 1 hour. Add onion, potato and carrot, and simmer until vegetables are done. Add sauerkraut. (If the kraut is too sour, rinse it in cold water before adding it to the soup.) Continue simmering for about 20 more minutes.

Make a roux from butter and flour, pour some soup liquid into it, stir until smooth, and return it to the soup. Add sour cream, season to taste with salt and pepper, and bring to a boil. Boil for a few minutes.

Irene Leush ◆ Underhill Center, Vermont

Sauerkraut Soup with Knockwurst

The apple and sauerkraut make this soup a wonderful mix of sweet and sour, and, with the knockwurst, a hearty meal.

◆

Yield: 8-10 servings
Preparation time: 1½ hours

◆

1-lb. jar	sauerkraut, drained and coarsely chopped
7 cups	beef stock
⅓ cup	diced bacon
1	large onion, coarsely chopped
1	large boiling potato, peeled and finely grated
1	large apple, peeled, cored and finely grated
1 tsp.	Hungarian sweet paprika
2	medium tomatoes, peeled, seeded and pureed
½ cup	dry white wine
1 tsp.	caraway seed
1	knockwurst (about ¼ lb.), thinly sliced
	parsley

Simmer sauerkraut in 4 cups beef stock in a saucepan over medium heat to mellow it.

Meanwhile, fry bacon in a Dutch oven over medium heat just until brown. Add onion and stir until golden, about 8 minutes. Reduce heat to low, add potato, apple and paprika, and stir 6 minutes. Gradually stir in remaining 3 cups stock. Blend in pureed tomatoes, wine and sauerkraut-stock mixture. Add caraway seed. Cover and cook 45 minutes.

Stir in knockwurst and heat through. Ladle soup into bowls. Sprinkle with chopped parsley and serve immediately.

Donna Sacuta ◆ *Prince George, British Columbia*

Blanquette of Lamb

"**L**amb and mushrooms are simmered together in a light lemon cream sauce. When asparagus is in season, I like to add it, too, during the final cooking minutes."

◆

Yield: 6 servings
Preparation time: 2 hours

◆

Suggested Accompaniment:
"For a great spring feast, serve this with new potatoes."

3 lbs.	lamb shoulder, cut in 1" cubes
2 cups	chicken stock
1	onion, stuck with cloves
1	carrot, cut in 4 pieces
1 stalk	celery, cut in 4 pieces
1	bay leaf
½ tsp.	thyme
2 sprigs	parsley
3 Tbsp.	butter
3 Tbsp.	flour
	juice of ½ lemon
½ cup	cream
½ lb.	mushrooms, quartered
	salt & pepper
	asparagus, cut in 2" pieces (optional)

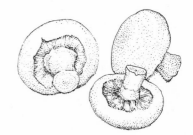

In a casserole dish, bring lamb, chicken stock, 1 cup water, onion, carrot, celery, bay leaf, thyme and parsley to a slow boil. Skim foam as necessary. Boil for 10 minutes. Cover, lower heat and simmer for 1 to 1¼ hours, until lamb is almost tender. Strain the mixture, reserving lamb and liquid, and discarding onion, carrot, celery, bay leaf and parsley.

In the casserole dish, make a roux with butter and flour. Add the reserved broth, bring to a boil, whisking constantly, and boil for 5 minutes. Add lamb and lower heat. Add lemon juice, cream, mushrooms and salt and pepper to taste. Cover and simmer for 15 minutes. If adding the asparagus, do so during the last 5 to 10 minutes of cooking. Serve with rice or new potatoes.

Carolyn Gregson ◆ *Underhill Center, Vermont*

Polly's Moroccan Lamb Stew

"We raise sheep and need to find recipes for all the cuts. This stew makes an elegant dish from the less tender portions." The ingredients may sound exotic, but this is an aromatic stew, with no harsh bite. If you like spicy food, add more red pepper.

◆

Yield: 4 servings
Preparation time: 3¾ hours

◆

2 lbs.	lean lamb, cut in cubes
¼ cup	olive oil
1 cup	chopped onion
1 clove	garlic, minced
¼ cup	dry sherry
¼ cup	raisins
1 tsp.	salt
½ tsp.	turmeric
1 tsp.	dried oregano
¼ tsp.	crushed red pepper or hot pepper sauce
1 lb.	tomatoes, peeled and diced (fresh or canned)
2 Tbsp.	toasted almonds, chopped rice

In Dutch oven, over high heat, sauté meat in batches in hot oil until lightly browned. Remove meat and set aside. Sauté onions and garlic until lightly browned. Add ½ cup water, sherry, raisins and seasonings. Stir in meat and cover pot. Simmer stew about 2½ to 3 hours.

Stir in tomatoes and cook 30 minutes longer. Stir in 1 Tbsp. almonds, spoon onto serving plate and garnish with remaining almonds. Serve with rice.

Polly Connell ◆ *Underhill Center, Vermont*

Lamb Stew in Avgolemono Sauce

"This Greek dish is elegant enough for a special dinner party. I constructed it with the aid of an obscure set of recipe notes from a newspaper and the expertise of my Greek sister-in-law."

♦

Yield: 6-8 servings
Preparation time: 2¼ hours

♦

4 lb.	leg of lamb, cut into 1"-square cubes
8 Tbsp.	olive oil
8 cups	chicken stock
3 tsp.	salt
½ tsp.	white pepper
⅓ cup	rice, washed and drained
2 packages	frozen artichoke hearts, thawed and coated with lemon juice
½ cup	finely minced fresh parsley
1-2 tsp.	minced fresh dill
3	egg yolks, or 2 whole eggs, at room temperature
	juice of 1 large, or 2 small, lemons
	minced parsley and dill

Suggested Accompaniments:
"Serve in a bowl, with slices of crusty country bread and a Greek salad of Romaine lettuce, cucumbers, tomatoes and feta cheese."

Dry lamb carefully so that it will not splatter when fried. Heat olive oil in a large, heavy skillet. Add lamb a few cubes at a time and fry until it is seared on all sides. Add chicken stock and season with salt and white pepper. Simmer until lamb is tender, about 1½ hours. Add rice during the last ½ hour of cooking. Add artichoke hearts, parsley and dill to the mixture and cook for about 10 minutes, until the artichokes are tender but still intact.

In a separate small bowl, beat egg yolks or whole eggs, and add the lemon juice, beating constantly. Add a ladleful of the broth to the egg mixture and beat well. Add another ladleful until the egg mixture has absorbed the broth. Then add the egg-broth mixture to the pan slowly, still beating constantly. Keep the heat very low and cook the mixture gently, stirring constantly. Do not allow it to boil or it will curdle. It will eventually thicken.

Taste and adjust seasoning, adding a little more lemon juice if necessary. Garnish with additional parsley and dill and serve immediately.

Ina Fitzhenry-Coor ♦ Burlington, Vermont

New Zealand Lamb Curry

"In New Zealand, I lived with a family who bought a hagget (a big lamb or young sheep) for the freezer. Of the many ways they used it, this curry was my favorite."

♦

Yield: 4 servings
Preparation time: 1½ hours

♦

2 lbs.	lamb, trimmed and cubed
¼ cup	flour
	salt & pepper
2 Tbsp.	oil
1 Tbsp.	curry powder
1 clove	garlic, crushed
4 stalks	celery, sliced
¼ tsp.	ginger
1 cup	tomatoes, peeled and chopped
2 or 3	onions, sliced
¼ cup	raisins
6-8	carrots, sliced

Coat lamb with flour, salt and pepper. Heat oil in a Dutch oven, and brown meat. Drain excess fat. Add remaining ingredients and cover with water. Simmer 1 hour.

Patricia Forrest ♦ Whitfield, Ontario

Lamb Curry with Cucumber Sauce

Cucumber sauce adds refreshing zing to this carefree oven-simmered lamb curry.

♦

Yield: 4 servings
Preparation time: 2 hours

♦

5 Tbsp.	butter
2 cups	thinly sliced onions
1 tsp.	minced garlic
2 cups	cubed cooked lamb
4 Tbsp.	lemon juice
1 tsp.	salt
2-3 Tbsp.	curry powder (to taste), mixed with 1 Tbsp. flour
1 Tbsp.	peanut oil
1 cup	chicken or beef stock

In heavy Dutch oven, melt 2 Tbsp. butter over moderate heat. Add onions and garlic and sauté, stirring, for 10 minutes. Transfer to small bowl.

Dip lamb in lemon juice, sprinkle with salt and coat heavily with the curry-flour mixture. In Dutch oven, heat remaining 3 Tbsp. butter and peanut oil over moderate heat. Sauté lamb until golden brown. Return onion-garlic mixture to the Dutch oven, add the stock and bring to a boil. Cover, bake in a 325-degree F oven for 1 hour or until dish has thickened to the consistency of a stew.

Marney Allen ◆ Edmonton, Alberta

Cucumber Sauce
1 cup chopped cucumber
2 Tbsp. minced fresh dill, or 1 tsp. dried
1 tsp. salt
¼ tsp. cayenne
2 cups plain yogurt
2 tsp. white wine vinegar

Mix all ingredients together and serve with curry.

Lamb Curry with Lemon & Walnuts

"A caterer I worked for many years ago in Washington, D.C., always received rave reviews from her clients when she served this curry. It is easy to prepare and great for those who are put off by the large number of spices in many curry recipes."

◆

Yield: 6 servings
Preparation time: 1½-2 hours

◆

3 lbs.	lamb shoulder, cut in 1" cubes
	flour
2 Tbsp.	oil
2 Tbsp.	butter
2	onions, chopped
1 clove	garlic, minced
2-3 Tbsp.	curry powder
1	apple, peeled and chopped
½-1 cup	walnuts, chopped
	rind and juice of 1 lemon
3 Tbsp.	yellow raisins
3 Tbsp.	shredded coconut
1½ Tbsp.	brown sugar
	salt & pepper to taste
	rice

Toss lamb in flour and sauté in skillet in batches in 1 Tbsp. oil and 1 Tbsp. butter. Remove to a casserole dish when browned. Add remaining butter and oil to skillet if needed, and sauté onions and garlic until transparent. Add curry powder and cook for another minute. Add curry mixture, 2 cups water, and remaining ingredients, except salt, pepper and rice, to casserole dish; bring to a boil, cover, lower heat and simmer for 1 to 1½ hours, until lamb is tender. Add salt and pepper. Serve with rice.

Carolyn Gregson ◆ Underhill Center, Vermont

Indian Lamb Stew with Spinach

Preparation Hint: "If you wish, the stew may be pre-assembled and simmered for about 40 minutes, set aside and warmed for 20 minutes just prior to serving. Take care not to overcook it."

"This traditional North Indian dish relies upon fresh ingredients and care in blending and cooking them. Overcooking will result in a loss of the individual characteristics of the various ingredients. The curry has a rich and unusual taste and is not too 'hot' despite the peppers."

◆

Yield: 6 servings
Preparation time: 3 hours

◆

4 10-oz. packages	frozen whole spinach leaves
2	large onions, chopped
2"-long piece	fresh ginger, peeled and coarsely chopped
6 cloves	garlic, peeled and chopped
1	fresh hot green chili, chopped, or 2 canned, peeled green chilies, chopped
8-9 Tbsp.	vegetable oil
3 lbs.	boneless lamb (shoulder or leg), chopped into stewing cubes and blotted dry with paper towels
3"-long	cinnamon stick
7	whole cardamom pods
1 tsp.	ground cloves
2	bay leaves
2 Tbsp.	ground coriander
1 Tbsp.	ground cumin
1 tsp.	ground turmeric
2	medium fresh tomatoes, chopped
2 Tbsp.	plain yogurt
1½ tsp.	salt

Briefly cook frozen spinach according to directions on the package, until it can be broken apart with a spoon. Remove it from the heat and drain it in a colander. Chop and set aside.

In a food processor, make a paste of onion, ginger, garlic and chili. Add 5 Tbsp. water gradually as ingredients are being processed. Heat 8 Tbsp. vegetable oil in a large, heavy skillet over medium-high heat. Drop lamb a few pieces at a time into the oil, being careful to avoid splattering. Brown lamb in batches. Set aside on paper towels to drain. Add a Tbsp. more of oil if needed.

Add cinnamon stick, cardamom pods, cloves and bay leaves to the hot oil. Cook until they darken, then add the paste from the food processor, taking care to avoid splattering. Stir, frying the mixture for about 10 minutes on medium heat until it becomes a light brown. Continue frying the mixture, adding coriander, cumin and turmeric, and cook for about 2 minutes. Add chopped tomato and cook for about 5 minutes, then add the yogurt. While the mixture is well blended but not overcooked, add lamb, then spinach. Add salt, bring the mixture to a boil, then cover it and simmer for about 1 hour.

Ina Fitzhenry-Coor ◆ *Burlington, Vermont*

Honeyed Lamb Stew

Variation: Cornstarch may be used in place of rice noodles to thicken the stew.

"**A**n excellent way to introduce lamb to a skeptical family."

◆

Yield: 8 servings
Preparation time: 1½ hours

◆

1 Tbsp.	oil
2 cloves	garlic, crushed
1	onion, chopped
2 lbs.	lamb, cubed
¾" piece	fresh ginger
4-6	young carrots
1-2 Tbsp.	honey
2 cups	chicken stock
½ cup	sherry
1 Tbsp.	soy sauce
1 Tbsp.	rice wine
3-4	tomatoes, chopped
2 squares	Chinese rice noodles (4x4")
	salt & pepper

Heat oil in large casserole dish. Brown garlic, onion and lamb. Peel and slice ginger and carrots. Add to casserole dish with honey, chicken stock, sherry, soy sauce and rice wine. Cover and simmer gently until meat is tender. Add tomatoes and rice noodles and cook another 10 minutes. Season with salt and pepper.

Janette Haase ◆ *Lyndhurst, Ontario*

Lamb Chili with Black Beans

Preparation Hint: Save soaking and cooking time by pressure cooking the beans. Rinse beans and place in cooker. Add 6 cups water. Cover, bring to a boil. When steaming, lower heat and pressure cook for 20 to 25 minutes.

"The use of lamb, black beans and spices not usually associated with chili make this a deliciously different variation."

•

Yield: 6 servings
Preparation time: 2-2½ hours, plus soaking time

•

1½ cups	black beans
1 tsp.	salt
2 lbs.	lamb shoulder, cut in ½" cubes
2 Tbsp.	oil
1 Tbsp.	butter
1	large onion, chopped
1 clove	garlic, minced
1 cup	red wine
1-1½ Tbsp.	chili powder
1 Tbsp.	minced fresh ginger
½ tsp.	thyme
1 tsp.	marjoram
1	small dried hot pepper, chopped
1 tsp.	freshly ground black pepper
½ tsp.	cayenne
½ tsp.	allspice
28-oz. can	Italian plum tomatoes, chopped, liquid reserved
	rice

In a flameproof casserole dish, bring beans, covered with water, to a boil. Boil 1 minute. Cover and let stand off heat for 1 hour. Drain; discard liquid. Cover beans with water, add salt and bring to a boil; cook until tender but not mushy, 1½ to 2 hours. Drain, reserving liquid, and set aside.

In a skillet, brown lamb in batches in the butter and oil. Remove meat to the casserole dish. Sauté onion and garlic in the skillet until transparent and add to the lamb. Deglaze the skillet with red wine and add it and the remaining ingredients to the casserole dish. Bring to a boil. Cover, lower heat and simmer for about 1 hour. Add beans and some of their cooking liquid if necessary and continue cooking for another 30 minutes, Serve with rice.

Carolyn Gregson ♦ *Underhill Center, Vermont*

Braised Lamb Stew

"I had never cooked lamb before moving to Vermont four years ago. The first winter, we were given half of a two-year-old ram, and I found myself reading cookbooks and experimenting with recipes to find ways to use it. Since that time, we have raised our own lamb, and every fall I make sure our freezer is stocked with enough to take us through the winter. Spoon this over rice or couscous."

◆

Yield: 4 servings
Preparation time: 1½ hours

◆

2 Tbsp.	vegetable oil
2 lbs.	lamb stew meat, shoulder or leg
2 tsp.	wine vinegar
1 tsp.	dry mustard
2 large cloves	garlic, chopped
1 tsp.	rosemary
2 Tbsp.	soy sauce

Heat oil in a heavy pot and brown meat in it over high heat. Stir together remaining ingredients and 2 Tbsp. hot water, and pour over meat. Stir the mixture, cover and simmer over low heat for about 1 to 1½ hours more. Water may have to be added during cooking.

Irene Leush ◆ Underhill Center, Vermont

Khoreshe Bademjan

(Lamb & Eggplant Stew)

"Maria, the Chinese wife of our Iranian friend Fee, prepared this delicious stew for us and kindly shared the recipe. Since we live in Vermont, with many sheep-raising neighbors, we have substituted lamb for the beef. Maria used shortening to sauté the eggplant, but I prefer a mixture of olive and vegetable oils."

◆

Yield: 4-6 servings
Preparation time: 1½-2 hours

◆

1½ lbs.	lamb shoulder, cut in 1" cubes
1 Tbsp.	butter
1 Tbsp.	olive oil
1	onion, chopped
½ tsp.	salt
¾ tsp.	cinnamon

¼ tsp.	nutmeg
¼ tsp.	pepper
1 cup	tomato puree
	juice of 1 lemon
2	medium eggplants, peeled and cubed
	salt
	vegetable oil and additional olive oil
	rice

In a Dutch oven, brown lamb in batches in butter and oil and remove. Sauté onion until transparent. Add spices and cook 1 minute longer. Return meat to the Dutch oven, and add tomato puree, ½ cup water and lemon juice. Bring to a boil, cover, lower heat and simmer for about 1 hour, adding more water if sauce becomes too thick.

While the meat is simmering, salt the eggplant cubes and let drain for about 20 minutes. Pat dry and sauté in vegetable and olive oils. Add to lamb mixture and simmer for 15 minutes. Serve over rice.

Carolyn Gregson ◆ *Underhill Center, Vermont*

Lamb with String Beans

Variation: This stew may also be made with beef.

"This is a popular family dish in the Middle East. In Middle Eastern cooking, vegetables and meat are usually cooked until very tender."

◆

Yield: 4 servings
Preparation time: 2 hours

◆

2 lbs.	fresh string beans
4 Tbsp.	olive oil
2	medium onions, finely chopped
¼ tsp.	grated nutmeg
½ tsp.	ground cinnamon
	juice of one lemon
2 lbs.	lamb, cut into stewing cubes
3 Tbsp.	tomato paste
1 tsp.	salt
½ tsp.	black pepper

Wash and string the beans and cut them in half. Heat olive oil in a large, heavy skillet. Fry onions in the oil over medium heat until translucent and soft. Add spices and lemon juice. Dry the meat with paper towels to avoid splattering in the oil, then add the meat, a few cubes at a time, to the skillet. Increase the heat and sear the meat.

Add beans and fry very gently until slightly softened. Stir in the tomato paste and season the mixture with salt and pepper. Taste, and adjust seasonings. Add 1 cup water to the skillet, adding a little more to cover the mixture if necessary, and bring to a boil. Cover the skillet and simmer gently for about 1½ hours, or until meat and vegetables are very tender and the sauce is quite thick. More water may be added if necessary during the cooking time.

Ina Fitzhenry-Coor ◆ Burlington, Vermont

Yellow Split Pea & Lamb Soup

"This delicious combination of lamb, yellow split peas, mint, dill and yogurt is Middle Eastern in flavor. We were surprised by its rich flavor the first time we tasted it."

◆

Yield: 4-6 servings
Preparation time: 2 hours

◆

2 tsp.	oil
1 lb.	ground lamb
1	onion, diced
1 stalk	celery, diced
1	carrot, diced
1 tsp.	salt
2 cups	chicken stock
1 cup	yellow split peas
1 tsp.	dried dill
½ tsp.	dried mint
1 cup	yogurt

In a casserole dish, heat oil and brown lamb. Pour off excess fat. Add vegetables and sauté until onion is transparent. Add salt, 3 cups water and chicken stock. Bring to a slow boil, skimming foam as necessary. Boil for 5 to 10 minutes. Add split peas, dill and mint. Cover, lower heat, and simmer until split peas are cooked, about 1½ hours.

Slowly add several tablespoons of the hot soup to the yogurt, stirring constantly, then pour yogurt mixture slowly into the soup. Heat through but do not boil or the yogurt will separate.

Carolyn Gregson ◆ Underhill Center, Vermont

POULTRY & GAME

"Who soothes you when you are ill? Who refuses to leave you when you are impoverished and stretches to give you a hearty sustenance and cheer? Who warms you in winter and cools you in summer? You don't catch steak hanging around when you're poor and sick, do you?"

Judith Martin, a.k.a. Miss Manners

The best chicken soup I ever made was with a couple of old hens who were working their way toward a third winter by foraging across the lawn, without so much as a single egg to their credit. They were horrible to pluck, for their feathers hung on grimly even after they had been dipped in boiling water, and bits of stubbly black pinfeathers remained beneath the skin. The birds were so unappetizing-looking that I almost tossed them into the garbage. But ashamed to waste them, and on the theory that an old-fashioned cookbook could solve the problem of what to do with an old fowl, I consulted my great-grandmother's *The Southern*

Cookbook of Fine Old Dixie Recipes, vintage 1902, for a gumbo recipe.

The hens simmered for several hours in the stewpot. The broth turned a rich yellow, for the chickens had acquired a layer of fat to protect them against the onslaught of winter. I cooled the broth, skimmed off the three inches or so of fat and removed the skin. By that time, the meat was tender but still firmly textured and could be cut into large chunks rather than falling off the bone in mushy slivers. For a frigid winter evening, it is hard to imagine anything more warming or soul-satisfying.

Chicken is the most versatile and popular of meats, adapting to a multitude of seasonings and ingredients: red wine and mushrooms in the traditional French stew Coq au Vin; tomatoes and shrimp in Chicken Marengo; or fruit and chilies in Mexican Chicken. Food-trend observers have lately fixed their sights on the "comfort food" phenomenon, and our contributors have provided us with a wonderful array of homey old favorites, including Chicken Fricassee with Dumplings, harkening back to many of our childhoods.

For those who cannot get free-range chicken, stewing fowl over a year old and weighing 3 to 7 pounds are the next best thing, since their flesh has sufficiently developed to impart flavor to the cooking liquid, whereas 9-to-12-week-old broilers and fryers lack the necessary character. When they are unavailable, roasting chickens or capons, which are usually less than 8 months old, are likely alternatives. The younger the bird, of course, the shorter the cooking time. Fresh birds are preferable to frozen, because their skin is less likely to lift away from the flesh and become an unsightly, free-floating mass in the stewpot.

Like chicken, turkey is versatile, low in fat—most of it unsaturated—and high in protein, with the added advantage that it has a higher ratio of meat to bone. Because it has more character than chicken, it can be played to good advantage in spicy dishes like Turkey Chili with Bitter Chocolate, a traditional Mexican dish in which a small portion of unsweetened chocolate serves to mellow the heat of the chili spices.

Game, with its muscular flesh and low fat ratio, is an ideal candidate for the stewpot. For those without a ready source of moose, venison, pheasant or bear, domestically raised rabbit is a readily available alternative; it is all white meat, low in fat and mild in flavor. The sweet richness of this meat is set off nicely by piquant sauces containing mustard or red wine and prunes.

If one is lucky enough to be on good terms with a hunter, Bill Chappell's Burmese Wild Goose Curry may be just the thing to keep the domestic fires burning, if the testimonial we received from his wife is any indication. (You may have his recipe, but she serves notice that its originator does not go with it.)

—Rux Martin

Mexican Chicken with Prunes & Bananas

"Enticingly delicious" is how our tester describes this dish, which is properly spicy and sweet at the same time. Our Vermont staff gave it exceptional ratings the day it was served in our test kitchen.

◆

Yield: 4 servings
Preparation time: 1½ hours

◆

¾ cup	flour
2 tsp.	salt
1 tsp.	white pepper
1 tsp.	paprika
3 lbs.	boneless chicken breasts
2 Tbsp.	butter
4 Tbsp.	olive oil
2	large onions, chopped
2 cloves	garlic, crushed
28-oz. can	whole Italian tomatoes, drained, juice reserved
3	carrots, thinly sliced
½ tsp.	oregano
½ tsp.	crushed red chilies, or to taste
½ tsp.	whole thyme
1 cup	chicken stock, boiling
¾ cup	dry white wine
18	pitted prunes
3	firm bananas, peeled, split lengthwise and cut in half

Place flour seasoned with salt, white pepper and paprika in a plastic bag. Shake chicken pieces in flour. Brown in a Dutch oven in butter and oil. Set aside.

In the same pot, sauté onion and garlic. Stir in juice from tomatoes and remaining seasoned flour. Add tomatoes, carrots and seasonings. Place browned chicken on top. Combine stock and wine and pour over. Bake, covered, at 350 degrees F for 35 minutes. Add prunes and cook, covered, for 20 minutes longer. Add bananas and cook, covered, 15 minutes more.

Louise Routledge ◆ *Port Coquitlam, British Columbia*

The creamy richness of this traditional chicken stew comes from the roux, which is cooked slowly to a golden brown.

Chicken Fricassee

Accompaniment:
Cheese-Herb Dumplings,
page 223.

◆

Yield: 6 servings
Preparation time: 1 hour 35 minutes

◆

4½-5 lb.	chicken, split and jointed
	ground nutmeg
	white pepper
	paprika
2½ Tbsp.	vegetable oil
3 Tbsp.	flour
1 cup	dry white wine
2	large shallots, cut into slivers
1	medium onion, finely chopped
3	leeks, cut into ½" pieces
4	carrots, cut into ½" pieces
1 cup	celery, cut into ½" pieces
2 Tbsp.	butter
½ tsp.	thyme
1 Tbsp.	chervil
1 tsp.	salt
½ tsp.	paprika

Sprinkle chicken on both sides with seasonings. Heat oil in heavy pot and brown chicken in batches. Set aside. Reduce heat, and add flour, scraping up browned bits with spoon. Cook the roux until it colors to a light brown, mashing lumps. Be careful not to burn. Whisk in 3 cups water and the wine and return chicken to pot. Simmer 45 minutes to 1 hour, covered.

In Dutch oven, sauté vegetables in butter until softened. Strain chicken stock through a colander, add to vegetables, and continue simmering. Skim fat as it rises. Stir in seasonings.

Meanwhile, cool chicken in colander over a bowl and prepare the dumplings. Remove meat from bones and add to Dutch oven, along with any drippings. Spoon in dumplings, cover and cook for 15 minutes, keeping stew at a slow boil. Cook, uncovered, for 5 minutes longer.

Rux Martin ◆ *Underhill Center, Vermont*

Chicken Fricassee with Dill

Dill and lemon add pleasant sharpness to this rich chicken fricassee. Low-fat sour cream may be used.

◆

Yield: 6 servings
Preparation time: 2 hours

◆

4½-5 lbs.	chicken, cut up
	salt & pepper
¼ cup plus 3 Tbsp.	butter
3 Tbsp.	vegetable oil
1	carrot, peeled and halved lengthwise
1	leek, washed and quartered
	bouquet garni
6 cups	chicken stock
⅓ cup	flour
2	egg yolks
½ cup	sour cream
½ cup	snipped dill
1 Tbsp.	lemon juice
	salt & white pepper

Sprinkle chicken with salt and pepper. Brown chicken in large skillet over moderately high heat in 3 Tbsp. butter and oil. Transfer with slotted spoon to Dutch oven.

Add carrot, leek, bouquet garni and stock to chicken. Bring to a boil, skim froth that rises to the surface, and simmer, covered, for 1¼ hours, or until the chicken is tender. Transfer chicken with slotted spoon to a dish and keep warm. Strain stock into a bowl.

In the same Dutch oven, melt ¼ cup butter and stir in flour. Cook roux over low heat, stirring, for 3 minutes. Remove from heat and whisk in 4 cups of stock, saving remaining stock for another use. Cook sauce over moderate heat for 10 minutes.

In a small bowl, whisk egg yolks together with sour cream. Stir some sauce into the egg mixture, then whisk into the sauce in the Dutch oven. Add dill, lemon juice and chicken, heat but do not boil. Season with salt and white pepper.

Veronica Green ◆ *Beausejour, Manitoba*

BOUQUET GARNI: 2 stalks celery, 3 sprigs parsley, 1 small bay leaf, 6 white peppercorns.

Wrap in cheesecloth or lettuce leaf and tie ends with string.

Chicken Stew with Mushrooms

"This chicken stew is a great favorite of my children. The pecans sprinkled over the cooked dish were a last-minute addition one night and were received with such enthusiasm that they have become a permanent part of the recipe."

◆

Yield: 6 servings
Preparation time: 3 hours

◆

14 Tbsp.	butter
1	medium onion, finely chopped
6	whole chicken breasts, boned, skinned and cut into stewing cubes
½ cup	flour
½ cup	milk
1 tsp.	paprika
¼ tsp.	nutmeg
1 tsp.	salt
½ tsp.	white pepper
8 oz.	small mushrooms, wiped clean and sliced
½ cup	pecans, broken into pieces
	rice

Preheat oven to 350 degrees F. Melt 4 Tbsp. butter over moderate heat in a large flameproof casserole dish. Add onion and fry, stirring occasionally, for about 5 minutes, or until it is soft and translucent but not brown. Dry chicken pieces with paper towels and add them to the onions; fry, stirring occasionally, for 6 to 8 minutes or until the meat is lightly browned.

To make sauce: Melt 8 Tbsp. butter in a small saucepan, then gradually add flour, stirring to form a roux. Slowly whisk in milk and cook, stirring constantly for a few minutes until the sauce is thick and creamy. Pour over the chicken mixture. Add paprika, nutmeg, salt and pepper. Stir until well mixed. Cover casserole dish and bake for about 2 hours.

Melt the remaining 2 Tbsp. butter in a small skillet. Add mushrooms and fry, stirring constantly, for about 3 minutes. Add mushrooms to the casserole dish. Bake, covered, for 30 minutes more, or until the chicken is very tender when pierced with a fork. Remove the casserole dish from the oven and sprinkle pecans over the stew. Serve on plain, boiled rice.

Ina Fitzhenry-Coor ◆ Burlington, Vermont

Coq au Vin

The red wine tenderizes the chicken and produces a rich, full-bodied sauce.

◆

Yield: 4 servings
Preparation time: 1¼ hours

◆

3½ lbs.	frying chicken, cut up
2 Tbsp.	vegetable oil
½ lb.	mushrooms
½ lb.	small white onions
¼ cup	minced shallots
1 clove	garlic, minced
1 cup	dry red wine
½ tsp.	thyme
⅛ tsp.	pepper
1	bay leaf
	parsley to taste
2 Tbsp.	butter, softened
2 Tbsp.	flour

Brown chicken in oil, and remove from skillet. Discard all but ¼ cup of the fat. Sauté mushrooms, onions, shallots and garlic in the skillet until browned. Stir in wine, ¾ cup water, thyme, pepper, bay leaf and parsley. Add chicken and bring to boiling over high heat. Reduce heat to low, cover, and simmer 20 to 30 minutes, or until chicken is tender.

Remove chicken and vegetables to a platter and keep warm. Blend butter and flour in a cup and and stir into the pan juices; heat to boiling, stirring constantly. Pour over chicken and vegetables, and serve.

Cheryl Veitch ◆ *Bella Coola, British Columbia*

Chicken Marengo

See photo page 78.

Brandy and white wine complement the savory herbs and shrimp adds elegance to this colorful dish.

◆

Yield: 8-10 servings
Preparation time: 1½ hours

◆

2 3-lb.	frying chickens
¼ cup	vegetable oil
1	onion, thinly sliced
3 Tbsp.	brandy
2 1-lb. cans	Italian tomatoes, drained

½ cup	dry white wine
2 cloves	garlic, pressed
½ tsp.	dried thyme
1	bay leaf
4 sprigs	fresh parsley, plus 2 Tbsp. minced
1 cup	chicken stock
1 tsp.	salt
½ tsp.	ground pepper
1 cup	small, cleaned shrimp
½ lb.	fresh mushrooms, sliced
¼ cup	butter
2 Tbsp.	lemon juice
	croutons

Cut chicken into 8 to 10 serving pieces. Heat oil over medium heat in a large, heavy skillet. Add onion, and sauté until golden brown. Remove and set aside. Add chicken to remaining oil and cook until browned on all sides. Remove chicken from pot, skin, and return to pot. Discard skin.

Heat brandy and pour over chicken. Carefully averting face, ignite brandy with a match and flame, shaking skillet until flame dies. Place tomatoes in a blender or food processor, and puree. Add to skillet. Add wine, garlic, thyme, bay leaf, parsley sprigs, stock, salt, pepper and sautéed onions. Cover the skillet and simmer for 1 hour, or until chicken is tender.

Remove chicken from sauce and keep warm. Strain sauce if desired. Add shrimp to sauce, and simmer for 5 minutes. Sauté mushrooms in butter in a saucepan until tender, then stir in lemon juice. Add to the sauce, and heat through. Arrange chicken pieces on a heated serving platter and pour sauce over chicken. Sprinkle with 2 Tbsp. minced parsley. Garnish with croutons.

Francie Goodwin-Rogne ◆ *Sherwood Park, Alberta*

Olivier's Moroccan Chicken

"**P**assed along by a French friend who had grown up in Morocco, this dish was a staple during the year my friend and I lived in Paris studying medieval art in the smallest room known to man, with only a double-burner hot plate as our kitchen. This stew satisfied all our requirements: it was delicious, inexpensive and didn't require an oven."

◆

Yield: 4 servings
Preparation time: 1½ hours

◆

¾ cup	golden raisins
2 Tbsp.	brandy
6-8	medium onions, sliced
4 Tbsp.	butter
4-lb.	chicken, cut into serving pieces
1 Tbsp.	oil
	salt & pepper

Preparation Hint: The "goldening" of the onions is the key to the flavor of this dish.

Soak raisins in 1 cup hot water and the brandy for 30 minutes to 1 hour. In a heavy skillet, sauté onions in 3 Tbsp. butter over medium heat until golden, about 30 minutes. Be sure to stir frequently, especially when the onions begin to caramelize. Pour liquid from raisins in with onions, stirring to loosen browned bits.

In a separate casserole dish or Dutch oven, brown chicken in oil and remaining 1 Tbsp. butter, and add salt and pepper. Smother chicken with contents of skillet and raisins. Bring to a boil, cover, lower heat, and simmer for about 45 minutes, or until chicken is tender. Serve with rice.

Carolyn Gregson ◆ Underhill Center, Vermont

Garden Patch Chicken

Preparation Hint:

Thoroughly browning the chicken and potatoes adds lots of flavor to this dish.

"**A** lovely all-in-one dinner that is easy to fix and takes advantage of the summer garden or market." Fresh rosemary adds a softly aromatic touch.

◆

Yield: 4 servings
Preparation time: ¾ hour

◆

3-lb.	fryer, cut into pieces
1 lb.	new potatoes, washed, with a 1"-wide strip peeled around the center
6 Tbsp.	butter, melted
	salt & pepper to taste
2	green onions, sliced
¼ cup	chopped fresh parsley
1 tsp.	minced fresh rosemary, or ¼ tsp. dried, crushed
1 cup	peas, preferably fresh
½ cup	sliced celery
1 cup	sour cream
1 tsp.	thyme

Brown chicken and potatoes slowly in the melted butter until nicely browned. Add salt and pepper. Reduce heat and simmer, covered, 30 minutes. Stir in onions. Sprinkle parsley and rosemary over chicken, and add peas and celery. Cover, and simmer about 10 minutes, or until peas are tender.

Remove vegetables and chicken to a deep platter and keep warm. Pour off the excess fat from pan. Add sour cream, thyme and salt and pepper to taste. Stir to loosen browned bits from the pan. Turn heat to low and heat the sour cream mixture briefly, but do not boil. Pour over chicken.

Irene Louden ◆ *Port Coquitlam, British Columbia*

Marinated Chicken Niçoise

Frozen small white onions work well in this recipe.

There is hardly a trace of fat in this well-marinated chicken stew with black olives. The marinade works better when it is thoroughly chilled.

◆

Yield: 4 servings
Preparation time: 7 hours

◆

1 cup	dry white wine
	juice of 1 lemon
2 cloves	garlic, minced
½ tsp.	dried basil
1	bay leaf
4	boned, skinned chicken breasts, cubed
1 cup	small white onions
½ lb.	sliced mushrooms
2 Tbsp.	olive oil
28-oz. can	Italian tomatoes, chopped
1 cup	pitted black olives, halved
	salt & pepper to taste
	rice

Mix wine, lemon, garlic, basil and bay leaf and chill at least 1 hour. Marinate chicken in the liquid 3 to 6 hours, refrigerated, in a covered, shallow dish, stirring occasionally.

Sauté onions and mushrooms in olive oil in a stewpot. Add chicken and marinade liquid (discarding bay leaf), tomatoes and olives. Boil gently ½ hour. Season with salt and pepper. Serve over rice, if desired.

Melissa McClelland ◆ *Burlington, Vermont*

Chicken with Vegetables & Elephant Garlic

See photo page 71.

Elephant garlic, so called because of its size, is less potent than ordinary garlic and much easier to peel. After the baking, it will be sweet enough to eat right alongside the vegetables.

◆

Yield: 4 servings
Preparation time: 1¼ hours

◆

3-lb.	whole chicken, small enough to fit in baking pot
	salt & pepper
10 cloves	elephant garlic, peeled, not crushed
2	carrots, sliced
1½ cups	white onions
8	whole new potatoes, or 1½ cups cubed
1 Tbsp.	dried tarragon, or fresh sprigs

Preparation Hint: If you remove the skin from the garlic without crushing the clove, it will taste mellow rather than stinging.

Preheat oven to 350 degrees F. Fill top and bottom of unglazed clay pot with water, let sit 5 minutes. Rinse chicken, pat dry, remove excess fat, lightly salt and pepper inside and out.

Discard water, place chicken in pot. Add garlic, carrots, onions and potatoes, placing some of the vegetables inside the cavity. Sprinkle tarragon over (or place fresh sprigs in cavity), cover, and bake 1 hour, turning halfway through.

Melissa McClelland ◆ *Burlington, Vermont*

Chicken with Figs

Figs make a wonderful addition to this chicken stew, combining with the sherry to give a rich but not overly sweet taste.

◆

Yield: 4 servings
Preparation time: 1½ hours

◆

2	onions, chopped
8 oz.	mushrooms, sliced
2 Tbsp.	olive oil
3-lb.	chicken, skinned, cut into serving pieces
3 cups	chicken stock

2 cups	cubed turnips (about 3 medium)
½ cup	black olives, pitted, sliced
½ cup	dried Mission figs, chopped
½ cup	cooking sherry
4 Tbsp.	lemon juice
	salt & pepper to taste

Sauté onions and mushrooms in oil. Add chicken. Brown for 5 minutes on both sides. Add stock and remaining ingredients. Heat to boiling, reduce heat, cover, and simmer 1 hour.

Melissa McClelland ◆ *Burlington, Vermont*

Lemon Chicken on Spinach

A main-course variation on the famous Greek egg-lemon soup.

◆

Yield: 4 servings
Preparation time: ¾ hour

◆

4	chicken breasts, boned, skinned, cubed
2 cups	chicken stock
2	eggs
1	lemon, juiced
4 cups	spinach, chopped

Simmer chicken in stock until cooked, about ½ hour, skimming foam and grease. Set aside 1 cup of stock to cool. Mix eggs with lemon juice until smooth, and whisk in the cup of warm (not hot) stock. Add to remaining stock and chicken, and simmer 10 minutes more. In a small saucepan, lightly steam spinach; divide and place in bottom of 4 shallow bowls. Spoon chicken over and serve.

Melissa McClelland ◆ *Burlington, Vermont*

Health Tip: Be sure to simmer the soup for 10 minutes after adding the egg mixture in order to kill salmonella, which is sometimes present in raw eggs.

Chicken with Lemon & Onions

Suggested Accompaniments:
Pita bread and Raita (page 222).

The chicken remains tender and succulent, while the wedges of whole lemons wilt and soften so they can be eaten rind and all.

•

Yield: 8 servings
Preparation time: 2 hours

•

8	whole chicken breasts, skinned, boned, cut into large pieces
2	large onions, 1 chopped, 1 sliced lengthwise
1"-long piece	fresh ginger, peeled and coarsely chopped
4 cloves	garlic, peeled and coarsely chopped
8-9 Tbsp.	vegetable oil
1 Tbsp.	ground coriander
1 tsp.	ground cumin
½ tsp.	ground turmeric
4 Tbsp.	plain yogurt
4 Tbsp.	tomato sauce
1 tsp.	salt
¼ tsp.	cinnamon
¼ tsp.	ground cloves
⅛ tsp.	cayenne pepper
2	whole, juicy, ripe lemons, each sliced into 8-10 wedges and seeded
1 Tbsp.	sugar
⅛ tsp.	freshly ground pepper

Wash chicken pieces and dry them with paper towels. Set aside. Put the chopped onion, ginger, garlic and 6 Tbsp. water into a food processor and puree until it becomes a thick paste. Heat 8 Tbsp. oil in a large, heavy skillet over high heat, and fry sliced onion until dark brown and limp. Do not burn. Remove and set aside to drain on paper towels.

In the same pan, brown chicken pieces in batches, adding another Tbsp. of oil if necessary. Do not overcook. Set them aside on a plate. Pour the paste from the food processor into the skillet, taking care not to let it splatter. Fry paste on medium heat, stirring for a few minutes until it becomes golden brown.

Add coriander, cumin and turmeric, and continue to stir. Add yogurt and tomato sauce a tsp. at a time, continuing to stir. Stir in salt, cinnamon, cloves, cayenne and 1½ cups water. Bring to a boil, cover, and reduce heat; simmer for about 10 minutes.

Add lemon wedges, chicken pieces, fried onions, sugar and ground pepper to the sauce, stirring. Bring to a boil, cover, lower heat, and simmer for 20 minutes. Stir occasionally. If the mixture becomes too dry, add a little water. (If you wish, you may bring the mixture to a boil, then set it aside. Just before serving time, cook it the remaining 20 minutes.)

Ina Fitzhenry-Coor ◆ *Burlington, Vermont*

Curried Chicken with Cashews

"This recipe can also be prepared as a completely vegetarian meal, and it's just as good that way."

◆

Yield: 4 servings
Preparation time: 1½ hours

◆

2 Tbsp.	oil
2 Tbsp.	whole wheat flour
2-3 cups	vegetable or chicken stock
2	onions, chopped
3 cloves	garlic, chopped
4	boned, skinned chicken breasts, cubed
2	apples, diced
½ head	cauliflower, cut into pieces
2 cups	peas
2	carrots, sliced
2 cups	halved green beans
1 Tbsp.	curry powder
1	lemon, juice and peel
1½ tsp.	salt
½ cup	chopped cashews
½ cup	toasted unsweetened coconut
	rice
	chutney
	yogurt

Unsweetened coconut can be found in health food stores.

In a heavy pot, heat oil and stir in flour over medium heat. Add 2 cups stock, stirring constantly. Add remaining ingredients except cashews and coconut. Simmer gently until vegetables are tender, about 1 hour, adding a third cup of stock if the stew seems dry. Just before serving, stir in nuts and coconut. Serve over rice with chutney and yogurt.

Melissa McClelland ◆ *Burlington, Vermont*

Smoked Chicken with Cilantro & Rice Noodles

Smoked chicken is available in some specialty stores, but if you have a smoker, you can smoke your own. Rice noodles can be found in the Oriental section of many supermarkets.

"I developed this recipe after being introduced to Malaysian and Chinese cooking practices." Cilantro is available at Oriental groceries and some supermarkets.

◆

Yield: 4 servings
Preparation time: 1½ hours

◆

1 gal.	chicken stock
	bones and skin from 1 smoked chicken
½ oz.	chopped fresh cilantro
1 tsp.	fennel seed
1 tsp.	whole thyme
2	bay leaves
2 cloves	crushed garlic
½ lb.	carrots, diced
½ lb.	Spanish onions, diced
½ lb.	green peppers, diced
4 oz.	rice noodles, broken into 2" pieces
1½ cups	diced smoked chicken
	salt & pepper

Place stock, chicken skin and bones, and cilantro in a large pot. Tie fennel seed, thyme, bay leaves and garlic into a cheesecloth bag and add to pot. Bring to a boil, reduce heat and simmer, uncovered, 15 to 20 minutes.

Remove bones, fat and cheesecloth bag, and discard. Add carrots, onions and peppers, and cook until tender, about 5 to 10 minutes. Add noodles and chicken, and cook 5 minutes more. Add salt and pepper to taste.

John Weir, Chef/Manager ◆ *Soho Grill, Maritime Center, Halifax, Nova Scotia*

Turkey with Spinach & Yogurt

Raw or cooked turkey serves equally well for this recipe.

◆

Yield: 2 servings
Preparation time: 1 hour

◆

1 clove	garlic
½ tsp.	salt
2 Tbsp.	oil
1 tsp.	paprika

1 lb.	turkey meat, cubed
½ lb.	tomatoes, chopped
1	small cucumber, chopped
4 cups	chopped spinach
1 cup	plain low-fat or nonfat yogurt

Mince garlic and blend with salt, oil and paprika. Spoon over meat, turning cubes to cover completely, and set aside to marinate for ½ hour.

Place turkey and marinade in a heavy casserole dish, sauté for a few minutes. Add tomatoes, cover tightly and simmer 15 minutes. Add cucumber and simmer 15 minutes longer. Stir in spinach; cook just until spinach wilts, 30 seconds to 1 minute. Serve topped with yogurt.

Melissa McClelland ◆ *Burlington, Vermont*

Variation: This recipe also can be made with chicken.

"**P**lenty of stewed onions give a melting sweetness to this comforting hash that uses leftover turkey. Raw turkey breast or legs may also be used. Leftover bread stuffing that is seasoned with sage and thyme may be added as well, but not fruit or corn bread stuffing. Serve over rice."

Dods's Turkey Hash

Variation: This hash is delicious served on buttered toast for breakfast.

◆

Yield: 4 servings
Preparation time: 1 hour 10 minutes

◆

3 cups	onions, sliced into rings
3 stalks	celery, coarsely chopped
2 Tbsp.	butter
2 cups	turkey, cut into bite-sized pieces
1 cup	stuffing (optional)
2 cups	turkey or chicken stock, or enough to cover
½ cup	white wine
½ tsp.	thyme
1 tsp.	salt
	freshly ground black pepper
3 Tbsp.	flour, dissolved in 5 Tbsp. cold water

Sauté onions and celery in butter until soft. Add turkey and stuffing, if desired, and cover with stock. Stir in wine, thyme, salt and pepper, and simmer, covered, for 45 minutes. Stir in flour mixture and cook 10 minutes more.

Mrs. Frederick Smyth ◆ *New Preston, Connecticut*

Turkey Chili with Bitter Chocolate

See photo page 80.

Variation: 3 cups of cooked turkey, cut into cubes, and 2½ cups stock may be substituted for uncooked turkey thighs. Preparation time will be reduced to ½ hour.

D on't shy away from the chocolate in this adaptation of a traditional Mexican dish, originally reserved for royalty. It adds smoothness and depth to the spices. And while the list of ingredients is long, the dish is easily made.

◆

Yield: 6 servings
Preparation time: 2 hours if using uncooked turkey

◆

4-5 lbs.	uncooked turkey thighs
1 Tbsp.	oil
1 Tbsp.	butter
1	onion, studded with clove
1	carrot, cut in fourths
1 stalk	celery, cut in fourths
	salt & pepper
1 clove	garlic, crushed

1	medium onion, chopped
1 clove	garlic, minced
1 Tbsp.	butter
1 Tbsp.	hot Mexican chili powder
¼ cup	sesame seeds
½ tsp.	coriander seed
½ tsp.	aniseed
4	cloves
1½"	cinnamon stick
1 cup	almonds
2 cups	tomato puree
2 4-oz. cans	mild green chilies, chopped
3 Tbsp.	golden raisins
1 oz.	unsweetened chocolate
	rice

If using uncooked turkey thighs, brown in 1 Tbsp. each oil and butter. Pour out excess fat, and add whole onion, carrot, celery, salt, pepper, crushed garlic and 2 qts. water. Bring to a boil, lower heat, and simmer for 1 to 1½ hours, until tender. Cool and remove meat from bones. Strain stock and set aside.

In a casserole dish, sauté chopped onion and minced garlic in butter until transparent. Add chili powder and sesame seeds, and continue cooking 1 minute longer.

In a food processor, finely grind together coriander seeds, aniseed, cloves and cinnamon stick. Then add almonds and continue processing until uniformly pureed. Add tomato puree and process until smooth. Add tomato-spice mixture to the casserole dish along with green chilies, raisins, turkey and enough turkey stock to thin as necessary.

Bring to a boil, reduce heat, cover, and cook for 10 minutes. Add chocolate, and cook until chocolate is melted, about 5 minutes. Serve over rice.

Carolyn Gregson ◆ *Underhill Center, Vermont*

Wild French Duck

"Come to the table with an appetite, for this is a rich dish. A light, green salad with a simple vinaigrette, bread and a good French Burgundy will make this meal an exercise in debauchery."

◆

Yield: 2-4 servings
Preparation time: 2-2½ hours

◆

3-4 lbs.	duck, quartered
6 Tbsp.	butter
3	carrots, finely chopped
1	medium onion, finely chopped
1-2	large shallots, finely chopped
¼ cup	Spanish sherry vinegar
2½ cups	dry French Burgundy
4-6	tomatoes, chopped
1 Tbsp.	fresh horseradish, or 2 Tbsp. prepared
1 Tbsp.	dried rosemary
1 cup	whipping cream
½ lb.	button mushrooms
	salt & pepper
	wild rice or noodles

Place quartered duck on a roasting rack and cook in a 350-degree F oven for 45 minutes to 1 hour.

Melt butter in a Dutch oven and sauté carrots, onions and shallots. Cover and cook for 10 minutes, stirring once or twice. Add vinegar and reduce by half. Add Burgundy, tomatoes, horseradish and rosemary. Bring to a slow boil, add duck, and simmer for 1 hour.

Remove duck and keep warm. Add cream and mushrooms to Dutch oven, and reduce sauce by boiling until it coats the back of a spoon. Salt and pepper to taste. Serve with wild rice or buttered noodles.

R. Kent Cummings ◆ *North Ferrisburg, Vermont*

Preparation Hint: The duck may be roasted the day before and the stew prepared later.

Burmese Wild Goose Curry

"I can't think of a nicer thing to happen to a Canada goose than to be cooked in this Burmese fashion. This is not a curry for those with meek taste buds."

◆

Yield: 2 servings
Preparation time: 2½ hours plus overnight

◆

MARINADE

2 heaping Tbsp.	whole coriander seeds
2 Tbsp.	whole cumin seeds
2 tsp.	ground turmeric
3	whole, small, round, dry, chili peppers
½ tsp.	ground fenugreek
¼ tsp.	cinnamon
4 large cloves	garlic
3-4 Tbsp.	dark soy sauce

Variation: Domestic goose may be substituted, and will yield 4 servings.

3-lb.	wild goose, cut into small serving pieces
1	medium onion, chopped
⅓ cup plus 2 Tbsp.	butter
1 can	chicken stock
3	bay leaves
2 Tbsp.	flour

Toast coriander and cumin seeds at 250 degrees F for 20 to 25 minutes, or until a light golden color. In a blender, grind coriander, cumin, turmeric, chili peppers, fenugreek and cinnamon. Set aside. Using blender, blend garlic with 3 Tbsp. soy sauce, and mix in powdered spices. Add enough additional soy to make a smooth paste. Smear paste all over the meat and marinate in the refrigerator overnight.

In a Dutch oven, brown onion in 2 Tbsp. butter and set aside; brown meat in batches, adding more butter as needed, up to ⅓ cup. Put all meat back into the Dutch oven, along with the onion, stock, 1 cup water and bay leaves. Simmer, covered, for about 2 hours, or until the goose is very tender. Skim fat. If necessary, thicken by melting some butter in a separate pan, stirring in flour, and adding to the pot.

Bill Chappell ◆ *North Battleford, Saskatchewan*

Pheasant in Juniper Sauce

"We have pheasant for dinner often. This is our favorite recipe, and it can be used for chicken and other poultry, especially leftover turkey." Gin or juniper berries add a snappy flavor.

◆

Yield: 2 servings
Preparation time: 2 hours

◆

	breast meat from 1 pheasant per person (up to 4 per recipe)
⅓ cup	flour, seasoned with pepper
1	large onion, sliced
2 Tbsp.	butter
1 Tbsp.	oil
⅔ cup	red wine
1¼ cup	chicken stock
1 tsp.	basil
1 tsp.	rosemary
½ cup	gin, or 6 juniper berries
1½ cups	sliced mushrooms

Coat meat with flour. In a casserole dish, fry meat and onion in butter and oil until browned. Stir in remaining flour. Stir in wine, stock, basil, rosemary and gin or berries. Cover, and simmer 1 hour. Add mushrooms, simmer ½ hour more.

Nancy Lange ◆ Metamora, Michigan

Juniper berries, small blue-black berries from a European evergreen, are the principal flavoring in gin, and are used to flavor game marinades. They are available in the spice section of many supermarkets. Toasting them briefly in a skillet brings out their flavor.

Rabbit in Mustard Sauce

"My friend Pam often made this deliciously rich dish when we were living in Paris. The mustard flavor is subtle after the slow cooking, and the bacon adds a hint of smokiness. For a different texture and flavor, you may use grainy Dijon mustard."

◆

Yield: 4 servings
Preparation time: 1 day plus 1½-2 hours

◆

1	rabbit, cut in 5-6 pieces
6 Tbsp.	Dijon mustard
	flour
1 Tbsp.	butter
1 Tbsp.	oil
2 slices	bacon, cut into 4 pieces
1	onion, chopped

"Use an authentic French Dijon mustard that is slightly hot to taste."

1 clove	garlic, minced
½ cup	chicken stock
5	potatoes, quartered and partially cooked
½ cup	cream
	salt & pepper

Coat rabbit with mustard and refrigerate several hours, preferably 12 to 24.

Roll rabbit in flour and sauté in butter and oil. Remove rabbit to a casserole dish. Sauté bacon until crisp, adding onion and garlic part way through the cooking and sautéing them until transparent. Add to casserole dish with chicken stock. Bring to a boil, cover, reduce heat, and simmer for 1 hour.

Add partially cooked potatoes and cream, and continue cooking for 15 minutes. Remove rabbit and potatoes to a warm serving platter. Whisk the sauce and reduce by boiling if sauce seems too thin. Season with salt and pepper. Spoon sauce over rabbit and potatoes, and serve.

Carolyn Gregson ◆ *Underhill Center, Vermont*

Lapin en Pot

Plenty of onions, garlic and savory herbs counter the sweetness of the currant jelly in this rich French one-pot.

◆

Yield: 6 servings
Preparation time: 2¾ hours

◆

4-lb.	rabbit, cut into serving pieces
¼ cup plus 2 Tbsp.	flour
1 tsp.	salt
¼ tsp.	freshly ground pepper
1 tsp.	brown sugar
1 tsp.	thyme
1 tsp.	summer savory
4 Tbsp.	butter
2 cloves	garlic, finely chopped
3	onions, cut in quarters
6 slices	bacon or salt pork
1	onion, stuck with 3 cloves
1	bay leaf
2 Tbsp.	parsley
1½ cups	dry red wine
3 Tbsp.	red currant jelly

Roll rabbit pieces in ¼ cup flour seasoned with salt, pepper, sugar, thyme and savory. Fry in butter with garlic and onion quarters until rabbit is browned on all sides.

Line a casserole dish with bacon or salt pork. Add rabbit, sautéed onion and garlic, whole onion, bay leaf and parsley. Pour wine over all. Cover, and cook at 325 degrees F for about 2 hours, or until rabbit is tender.

Remove the cloved onion and, using a slotted spoon, transfer the other ingredients to a warmed dish. Thicken the sauce with 2 Tbsp. flour, a dash more red wine and currant jelly. Simmer until well blended, then pour over the rabbit.

Helen Campbell ◆ Loughborough Inlet, British Columbia

Stewed Rabbit

"**H**aving raised rabbits for our own consumption for 18 months, I'm always on the lookout for new recipes for this delicious and often overlooked meat." Lemon pepper contributes nicely to the flavor of this simple stew.

◆

Yield: 4 servings
Preparation time: 2¼ hours

◆

3-3½ lbs.	rabbit
1-2 tsp.	lemon pepper
1-2 tsp.	garlic powder
7-8 Tbsp.	butter
4	medium carrots, peeled and cut in 1" chunks
2 stalks	celery, cut in ½" chunks
4	medium potatoes, peeled and quartered
4-5	small onions, peeled and left whole
5 cups	chicken stock
3-5	wild leeks (optional)
1-3 cloves	garlic, left whole
½ lb.	button mushrooms
¼ cup	diced, mixed green and red peppers
4 Tbsp.	flour

Variation: Omit the leeks and potatoes, and stir in 6 to 7 oz. of drained frozen or canned crabmeat during the last 15 minutes of cooking time.

Cut rabbit into serving pieces. Sprinkle with lemon pepper and garlic powder. In a large pan, melt 3 to 4 Tbsp. butter, and brown rabbit. Add carrots, celery, potatoes and onions. Add chicken stock, leeks, garlic, mushrooms and peppers. Simmer, covered, 1 to 1½ hours, stirring at 15-to-20-minute intervals to prevent sticking.

Combine flour and 4 Tbsp. melted butter, and add to hot liquid to thicken, stirring frequently, about 10 to 15 minutes.

Valerie & Gregory R. Brown ◆ Chatsworth, Ontario

Chicken Letter Soup

"I have two young children and they quite enjoy this chunky soup full of letters."

◆

Yield: 4 servings
Preparation time: 40 minutes

◆

4 cups	chicken stock
¼ cup	barley
1 large stalk	celery with leaves, diced
1	large carrot, cut into thin coins
1	small onion, diced
1 tsp.	salt
	freshly ground pepper
¼ tsp.	dried summer savory
¼ tsp.	dried basil
1 cup	diced cooked chicken
¼ cup	alphabet noodles

Place all ingredients except chicken and alphabet noodles into a pot. Bring to a boil and simmer for 20 minutes. Add chicken and alphabet noodles, and simmer 10 minutes more.

Connie Green ◆ Langham, Saskatchewan

Matzo Ball Soup

"When Harry fell out of love, in the old days, he went to bed 'sick' for two days. I brought this soup and he always recovered, never realizing that there was a correlation." The matzo balls are the surprise, remaining feather-light while soaking up the flavor of the soup.

◆

Yield: 6 servings
Preparation time: 2½ hours

◆

3-4-lb.	chicken, quartered
1	large onion, chopped
2 stalks	celery, minced
1	parsnip, chopped (optional)
1-2 Tbsp.	salt
2	carrots, minced
½ cup	dry baby lima beans
	minced parsley

Wash chicken and remove excess fat. Put into a large kettle with water to cover. Add remaining ingredients except parsley. Cover, and simmer until the chicken is tender, about 1½ hours.

Remove chicken, and simmer another 30 minutes. Take meat from bones and add to soup. Refrigerate, skim fat, and reheat. Add parsley. Add matzo balls to the soup to cook.

MATZO BALLS

5	eggs, separated
1 tsp.	salt
⅛ tsp.	pepper
1½ Tbsp.	melted schmaltz (chicken fat)
1 cup	matzo meal

Beat egg whites until stiff. Beat yolks until lemon-colored. Add 1 tsp. cold water, salt, pepper and fat to yolks. Fold yolk mixture into whites, and gradually add matzo meal. Refrigerate.

With wet hands, shape dough into balls about the size of a walnut, and drop into boiling soup. Cover, and simmer 30 minutes before serving.

Cary Elizabeth Marshall ◆ *Thunder Bay, Ontario*

FISH & SEAFOOD

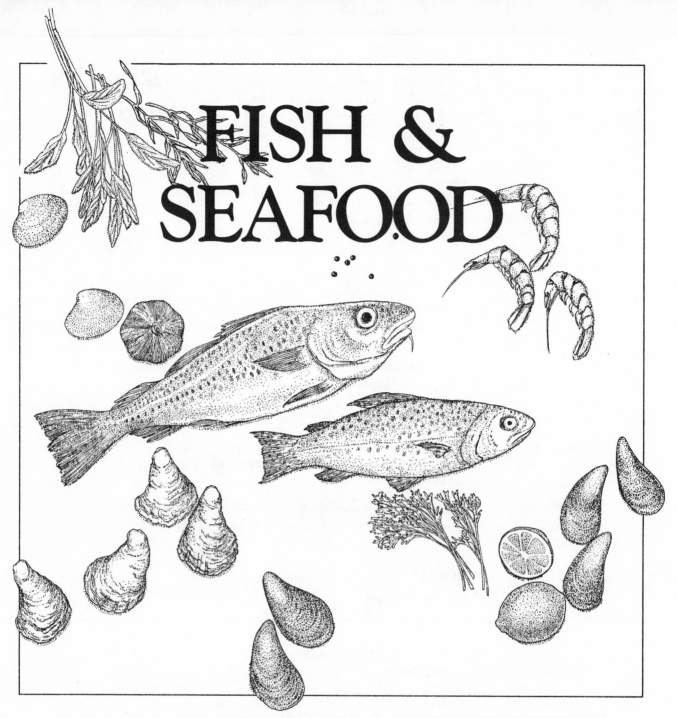

"I could not restrain a wistful sigh. 'Jeeves is a wonder.' 'A marvel.' 'What a brain!' 'Size nine-and-a-quarter, I should say.' 'He eats a lot of fish.'"

P.G. Wodehouse, *Thank You, Jeeves*

Two years ago," contributor Carol Simpson of Fulford Harbour, British Columbia, writes, "my neighbor Bernie, a fisherman, brought me 90 pounds of coho salmon. Being delighted with the price, but not the timing, I put the fish into the freezer for dealing with 'later,' and suggested that if he had another good run and could get them for me at the same price, I would like another 90 pounds, 'whenever.' Late in August, I had a few free days and I decided it would be a good time to bottle the fish. I put them in my mother's utility sink (she lives next door) so they would be thawed and ready for use Sunday morning.

Mom was helping me cut and bottle the fish when Bernie showed up with not only my additional 90 pounds, but also 100 pounds for my mother.

"After we finished bottling the fish, we had to decide what to do with all the heads, fins and skeletons in the bucket, so we made soup. Three large canning kettles were needed to simmer all the bones and heads in enough water to cover them, and to accommodate the thyme, onions, celery and carrots and other things necessary to make a good stock. When the fish was just cooked, we strained off the liquid and set it all aside. The next day, we picked all the fish off the bones."

According to the letter, there was more to these preparations, including the arrival of five 30-pound cases of peaches in the middle of the soup-making, but eventually, all the chowder was put up into jars. If all this salmon—not to mention the hours of work—boggles the mind, we should be quick to state that single meal quantities of fish chowders and stews are among the simplest and quickest of one-pot meals. Many can be prepared in under 30 minutes, though they can benefit by steeping for a bit in their own juices after they are made.

Fish soups and stews have traditionally taken shape spontaneously from what is fresh and available. The recipes that follow, too, are more creations of expediency rather than long shopping lists and didactic rules. Particularly inland, where sources of fish can be capricious, it is unwise to adopt too firm a view of what will enter the chowder pot until one is at the market.

Fresh fish should be clean and fresh-smelling, with no "fishy" smell, and their eyes should be bulging, not sunken. Especially for soups and stews, frozen fish is often the best buy, since the fish is often frozen on the boat just after being caught, with only a small loss of flavor and texture. Canned clams, however, are quite another thing and contribute little flavor. Choose frozen fish, shrimp or squid instead.

The connecting tissues of fish are thin and delicate, accounting for only 3 percent of the total anatomy; overcooking is fish's mortal enemy. In addition, because fish contains relatively little fat, long cooking causes it to shrink and disintegrate.

Fish broth, or fumet, strained and either used immediately or frozen for future use, adds a rounder flavor to soups than does water. Although canned clam broth may be substituted, the gelatinized saline fullness of the real thing is well worth the effort and only slightly more time-consuming, provided, of course, that one does not, as our contributor did, start with 280 pounds of coho salmon.

Fresh Salmon & Corn Chowder

"**D**ill and fresh salmon add a delicate twist to the classical corn chowder base of this pretty yellow-and-pink-speckled soup."

◆

Yield: 6 servings
Preparation time: ¾ hour

◆

5 Tbsp.	sweet butter
1	large shallot, finely chopped
5 Tbsp.	flour
6 cups	chicken stock
2 cups	whole kernel corn, fresh or frozen
2	potatoes, diced into ½" pieces
1 cup	dry white wine or vermouth
1 lb.	fresh salmon
½	lemon, juice and grated rind
4 Tbsp.	fresh dill, or 2 tsp. dried
	salt & pepper to taste

Melt butter in a soup pot, add shallot and cook until softened. Add flour and cook, stirring, while the mixture sizzles for about 5 minutes. Whisk in chicken stock and cook until smooth and slightly thickened. Add corn and diced potatoes to the pot. Let simmer until tender, about 15 minutes.

Meanwhile, put wine or vermouth in a skillet and bring to a gentle simmer. Add fresh salmon to the wine and poach it for 10 to 15 minutes, or until almost done. Remove the piece of salmon to a dish, flake and separate the flesh from the bones and skin. Discard wine and bones. Add salmon, lemon juice and rind, and dill to the soup pot. Heat the soup thoroughly and finish cooking the salmon gently. Taste and then add salt and pepper. Serve immediately.

JoAnne B. Cats-Baril ◆ *Charlotte, Vermont*

Salmon Chowder

The chowder base—stock, salmon and vegetables—may be frozen in quart containers and reheated with the milk or light cream added at this point. Do not add water to thin the stock.

◆

Yield: 4 servings
Preparation time: 1-1½ hours

◆

1	whole salmon, up to 5 lbs., or heads, tails, fins and skeletons of approximately 5 salmon
4	carrots, cut into large chunks
1	large onion, peeled and quartered
4 stalks	celery, cut into large chunks
	salt, pepper, thyme, rosemary, basil to taste
4 cups	diced potato
2 cups	diced carrots
2 cups	diced celery
1 cup	diced onion
1 cup	peeled, diced tomato
	salt & pepper to taste
	light cream or milk

Place salmon, chunked vegetables and herbs in a large soup kettle and add cold water to cover. Simmer on medium heat until fish falls from bones. Remove from heat and strain. Cool. Separate fish from bones; put meat in a bowl, reserve stock, and discard bones, pot vegetables and herbs.

Place stock in a large kettle and add the salmon meat. Add diced potato, carrots, celery, onion and tomato and simmer until vegetables are tender. Season with salt and pepper. Measure liquid, and stir in an equal amount of milk or light cream (or less if you like a thicker soup), and heat but do not boil.

Carol Simpson & Ellen Bennett ◆ Salt Spring Island, British Columbia

Variation: To bottle soup for canning, place approximately 1 cup stock in quart jars and divide salmon meat between jars. Add seasonings, diced vegetables and 1 tsp. coarse salt. Process in a pressure canner, following instructions for fish. The colorful jars make great gifts.

Cape Cod Corn & Fish Chowder

Evaporated skim milk makes this mild chowder nutritious and low in fat.

◆

Yield: 4 servings
Preparation time: 1 hour

◆

2 Tbsp.	safflower oil
1 cup	onion, chopped
4 cups	potatoes, peeled and diced
½-1 tsp.	basil
1 tsp.	salt
¼ tsp.	pepper
1 lb.	frozen haddock fillets
10 oz.	kernel corn, frozen or canned
12-oz. can	evaporated skim milk

Heat oil in a medium-sized soup pot and sauté onion until limp but not browned. Add potatoes, basil, salt, pepper and 2 cups water. Bring to a boil, reduce heat and simmer for 15 minutes. Add fish, corn and milk and simmer until fish is flaky, about 10 to 15 minutes.

Nancy Hill ◆ Greensboro, Vermont

New England Chowder

This classic New England chowder is augmented with corn. "Traditionally, each bowl is topped with a pat of butter and a grinding of fresh pepper just before serving."

◆

Yield: 4-6 servings
Preparation time: 65 minutes

◆

¼ lb.	bacon, diced
1 large or 2 medium	onion(s), chopped
1 lb.	any white-fleshed fish: cod, haddock, pollack, etc.
4	medium potatoes, scrubbed well and diced, or peel first if you prefer
16-oz. can	whole-kernel corn, or 10 oz. frozen, or 1 cup fresh
1 pt.	light cream
15-oz. can	evaporated milk (substitute regular milk if you prefer, but the chowder will be thinner)
	salt & pepper to taste

Fry bacon over medium heat in a heavy cast-iron Dutch oven, or other deep pan, until crisp. Remove with slotted spoon and set aside. Add onion and sauté 5 minutes. Pour off any remaining fat and return bacon pieces to pan.

Cut fish into bite-sized pieces and remove any bones. Add to pan. Add potatoes (and corn, if using fresh). Barely cover with water. Cover pan, bring to boil, reduce heat, and simmer for 15 minutes or until potatoes are barely tender. Add undrained can or package of corn now if not using fresh.

In separate saucepan, heat cream and evaporated milk until hot, but not boiling. Add hot cream mixture to fish. Do not let boil. Season to taste.

Donna L. Herlihy ◆ Ashland, New Hampshire

Seafood Chowder with Tomatoes

Chunks of haddock and scallops and whipping cream give this chowder richness. It's even better when made the night before.

◆

Yield: 6-8 servings
Preparation time: 1 hour 50 minutes

◆

8 slices	bacon, cut into 1" squares
3	medium onions, chopped
3 medium stalks	celery, chopped
3 lbs.	potatoes, peeled and diced
3 cups	fish stock, or 16 oz. bottled clam juice diluted with 1 cup water
2 sprigs	thyme, or ¼ tsp. dried
2 Tbsp.	chopped fresh parsley
2½ cups	milk
½ cup	whipping cream
	salt & freshly ground pepper
2 lbs.	haddock, cod or other firm-fleshed white fish, cut into 1½" cubes
1¼ cups	canned tomatoes, drained and coarsely chopped
½ lb.	whole bay scallops or sea scallops, cut in half
	paprika

Preparation Hint: Be careful not to cook scallops longer than a minute, or they will toughen.

Cook bacon in heavy Dutch oven over medium heat until golden brown, about 10 minutes. Transfer to paper towel. Pour off all but 3 Tbsp. bacon fat. Add onions and celery. Sauté over low heat for 6 to 8 minutes, until vegetables have softened. Add potatoes, and fish stock or clam juice to cover the vegetables. Bring to a boil. Tie thyme and parsley in a piece of cheesecloth. Add to soup. Reduce heat, cover and simmer until potatoes are tender, 15 to 20 minutes.

Transfer half the vegetables to a blender or processor and puree until smooth. Return to pot. Add the milk, cream, and salt and pepper to taste. Bring soup to boil, stirring until smooth. Add fish. Cover and simmer gently for 4 to 5 minutes. Discard cheesecloth bag. Add tomatoes, scallops and bacon to soup, stir gently. Cover and simmer until fish and scallops are just opaque, about 1 minute.

To serve, ladle into soup bowl and sprinkle each serving with paprika.

Maureen Parker ◆ *Victoria, British Columbia*

Clam & Fish Chowder

"A healthy chowder with no added salt; to my taste, there is enough in the natural ingredients. I cook for myself and can eat a bowl of it every other evening for a week or more."

◆

Yield: 4 servings
Preparation time: ¾ hour

◆

1 Tbsp.	oil
1	onion, chopped
2 stalks	celery, cut into 1" pieces
1	potato, cut into 1" cubes
1 pt.	tomatoes with juice, chopped
2	bay leaves
1-2 cloves	garlic, finely chopped
4-6	large fresh clams, shucked and finely chopped
1 lb.	ocean white fish — cod or haddock — cut into 1" cubes
	freshly ground black pepper to taste

Heat oil in soup pot and sauté onion until wilted. Add celery and sauté until soft. Add remaining ingredients except clams and fish. When potatoes are almost soft, about 30 minutes, add clams and fish. Thin with water, if desired, and simmer until cooked, about 10 to 15 minutes. Season with pepper.

Max Brubaker ◆ Bedford, Pennsylvania

Manhattan-Style Clam Chowder

"This recipe was handed down from my father to me verbally in the kitchen while cooking it. Its flavors are rich and briny. I am not blowing my own horn, but this chowder is one of the best that I have ever had."

◆

Yield: 6 servings
Preparation time: 1 hour

◆

Preparation Hint: Wash clams well in cold running water, scrubbing them with a brush. Cook them just to heat through or they will toughen.

2-3 strips	bacon
2 medium cloves	garlic, finely minced
1 cup	chopped onion
3 cups	chopped carrot
3 cups	diced potato
3 cups	chopped celery with leaves

1 qt.	bottled clam juice
28-oz. can	tomatoes with juice, chopped
2 tsp.	thyme, or to taste
	salt & pepper
2 dozen	raw chowder clams (quahogs), chopped, juice reserved

Fry bacon, remove from fat and discard. Sweat garlic and vegetables in fat, covered, for 5 to 10 minutes. Add clam juice and tomatoes with juice. Add thyme, salt and pepper. Allow chowder to simmer for a while to let flavors develop. Add chopped clams; heat through. Adjust seasonings; serve.

George Sprague ◆ *Islip, New York*

Mussel Potato Chowder

The inspiration for this creamy, aromatic mussel soup was a delicious potato salad with mussels made by a friend.

◆

Yield: 4 servings
Preparation time: 30 minutes

◆

4 lbs.	mussels
1	small onion, chopped
1 clove	garlic, minced
1 Tbsp.	olive oil
4	potatoes, peeled and cut into 1" cubes
2	carrots, peeled and grated
pinch	saffron
	freshly ground black pepper
½ tsp.	salt, or to taste
1 cup	light cream
3 Tbsp.	chopped fresh parsley

Shopping Tip: Cultivated mussels, which are grown on ropes suspended from rafts, are larger and meatier than their wild counterparts and are grit-free.

Wash and debeard mussel shells. Place in heavy pot and add cold water to about halfway up the shells. Cover and steam just until the shells open. Do not overcook. Cool and shell mussels and set aside, reserving 2½ to 3 cups mussel liquid.

In a heavy skillet, sauté onion and garlic in olive oil until soft. Add mussel liquid, potatoes, carrots, saffron, pepper and salt and cook until potatoes are soft. Add mussels and cream and heat but do not boil. Sprinkle with parsley and serve.

Rux Martin ◆ *Underhill Center, Vermont*

Lough-borough Chowder

Variation: Our tester, who regrets that she did not have sea cucumbers "on hand," nonetheless reports that this chowder tastes very good without them.

"I invented this recipe for serving a crowd from what was on hand. Prawns and sea cucumbers make it rich and special. Sea cucumbers do not look appetizing when caught, but their muscles are delicious, and when finely cut up, they resemble noodles."

◆

Yield: 12 servings
Preparation time: 1¼ hours

◆

1 cup	chopped onion
4 Tbsp.	butter
3 cups	diced potatoes
½ cup	chopped celery
½ cup	celery leaves, chopped
1 qt.	canned tomatoes
2 cups	steamed clams
2 cups	clam liquor
1 cup	sea cucumber (optional)
2 lbs.	shelled prawns
1 tsp.	thyme
1 tsp.	salt
	freshly ground pepper

Cook onions in butter until just golden. Add remaining vegetables and 6 cups boiling water. Cook until potatoes are soft. Meanwhile, steam clams by placing them in a heavy pot and adding water to about halfway up shells. Cover and steam just until shells open. Remove meat, add to chowder pot with remaining ingredients, and simmer gently until well heated.

Helen Campbell ◆ *Loughborough Inlet, British Columbia*

Bass Cheek Chowder

"The cheeks of a largemouth bass can be quite sizable and are known as the fish's 'filet mignon' by those in the know." The chervil should be added at the last moment to get the benefit of its delicate anise flavor. This soup is best made a day or two ahead.

◆

Yield: 4 servings
Preparation time: 1 hour

◆

Variation: Substitute sole or scallops for bass cheeks.

1 cup	chicken stock
2	potatoes, diced
½ tsp.	tarragon
1 tsp.	paprika
	salt & pepper
¼ cup	butter
1 cup	largemouth bass cheeks (other fish cheeks can be used)
2	onions, chopped
1 stalk	celery, chopped
3 slices	bacon, chopped
½ cup	dry white wine
2 cups	milk
1 cup	light cream
pinch	cayenne pepper
	chopped fresh chervil

In a large soup pot, heat chicken stock, potatoes, tarragon, paprika, salt and pepper.

Melt butter in a skillet, and lightly sauté bass cheeks (or sole or scallops), onions, celery and bacon. Add to stock mixture. Stir in wine and simmer until potatoes are cooked. Do not boil. Add milk and cream slowly, stirring constantly; do not boil or it will curdle. Add cayenne. Garnish with chervil.

Helen Shepherd ◆ Lyndhurst, Ontario

White Fish-Bean Soup

"In this dish, you have the best of both worlds: health and flavor. Fresh tomatoes enhance it, but canned ones will do in a pinch. For best results, use fresh herbs."

◆

Yield: 6 generous servings
Preparation time: ¾ hour

◆

1 bunch	leeks (you may substitute onions)
¼ cup	olive oil
1 cup	dry white wine
1 qt.	bottled clam juice (or your own fish stock)
1 lb.	peeled tomatoes (drain if canned)
1 lb.	canned white beans (navy or great northern)

1 tsp.	fresh thyme, or ½ tsp. dried
1 tsp.	minced fresh basil, or ½ tsp. dried
½ tsp.	salt
¼ tsp.	freshly ground black pepper
1 lb.	red snapper or other mild white fish
	juice of ½ lemon
¼ cup	minced parsley

Remove and discard green tops and roots of leeks. Slice in half lengthwise and rinse out any grit. Chop leeks. Heat olive oil in 3-qt. saucepan. Add leeks and cook over high heat, stirring often, until soft. Add white wine, simmer about 5 minutes, then add clam juice. Chop tomatoes into small pieces and add along with beans, thyme, basil, salt and pepper. Bring to a boil. Cut fish into 1-inch pieces and add to soup along with lemon juice. Simmer 8 to 10 minutes. Pour into hot bowls, then sprinkle with parsley.

Sarah Fritschner ◆ Louisville, Kentucky

Mexican-Style Red Snapper

"To most North Americans, Mexican food means tacos and burritos and little else, partially because most of us avoid recipes calling for exotica. This recipe for Mexican-Style Red Snapper is at least partly traditional and can be executed with chilies that are easily found in the average supermarket."

◆

Yield: 6 servings
Preparation time: 1 hour

◆

2	medium onions, diced
3	Anaheim chili peppers (pale green, large California peppers), or 3 4-oz. cans, chopped
1	jalapeño pepper, chopped
¼ cup	olive oil
1½ lbs.	fresh tomatoes, or canned ones drained
1 Tbsp.	fresh oregano, or 1 tsp. dried
6 or 8 sprigs	fresh coriander
2 lbs.	red snapper, or other fish or shrimp
	salt & pepper to taste

Heat oil in a large skillet. Add onions and peppers, and cook until soft.

Meanwhile, dip tomatoes in boiling water for 10 seconds; remove their peels and cores. Chop tomatoes roughly and add to skillet along with herbs. Bring to a boil, add fish, and simmer 20 to 30 minutes, until fish is opaque and flakes easily. Add a little salt and pepper. Serve with hot rice, if desired.

Note: If you like, instead of boiling the fish, place it in a baking dish in a single layer, cover with sauce, and bake 25 to 35 minutes at 400 degrees F.

Sarah Fritschner ◆ *Louisville, Kentucky*

Fresh Tuna-Tomato Stew

"We like this substantial soup-stew stingingly hot, preferably made with a fresh red serrano pepper. Spicy or mild, this Spanish peasant stew, served with bread and cheese, leaves everyone satisfied."

◆

Yield: 6 servings
Preparation time: 1¼ hours

◆

2 lbs.	fresh tuna, cut into bite-sized chunks
	salt
2	onions, chopped
4 cloves	garlic, minced
¼ cup	olive oil
2	large green peppers, chopped
1	fresh chili pepper, chopped
1-lb. can	crushed tomatoes, or 1 lb. fresh tomatoes
½ tsp.	paprika
3	potatoes, peeled and thinly sliced
¼ tsp.	cayenne pepper

Variation: Mackerel may be substituted for tuna.

Salt fish lightly and set aside. In a Dutch oven or other heavy pot, sauté onions and garlic in olive oil until soft. Add green peppers and chili pepper and sauté for a few minutes.

If fresh tomatoes are used, peel by placing them in boiling water until the skins pucker. Dip in cold water and skin. Cut into quarters. Add tomatoes to the pot with paprika and simmer 20 minutes.

Add potatoes and 2 cups water. Cover and cook until potatoes are soft, about 20 minutes. Add cayenne pepper and fish, cover, and simmer 10 minutes more.

Rux Martin ◆ *Underhill Center, Vermont*

Curried Fish Soup

Tomato and curry powder, rather than cream, form the base of this fish-scallop-clam-filled chowder.

◆

Yield: 6 servings
Preparation time: 1 hour

◆

1 Tbsp.	butter
2	large onions, chopped
1 Tbsp.	curry powder
2 28-oz. cans	tomatoes with juice
1 tsp.	dried basil
½ tsp.	thyme
¼ tsp.	cayenne pepper
pinch	salt
2 10½-oz. cans	baby clams, or 2 6½-oz. cans minced clams
1-1½ lbs.	fresh white fish, such as cod
½ lb.	mixed seafood, such as scallops or shrimp

Melt butter in large pot, add onion and sprinkle with curry. Sauté over medium heat for 5 minutes. Stir in tomatoes, breaking them up with a fork. Add seasonings and bring to a boil. Drain and rinse clams with cold water and stir into soup. Simmer for 10 minutes. Add bite-sized pieces of fish and mixed seafood. Simmer for 10 more minutes.

Marney Allen ◆ Edmonton, Alberta

Saucy Fish Stew

At the outset, there is little liquid in this leek- and lemon-flavored stew. But just as its name promises, it creates its own ample sauce when covered and simmered. Fresh or frozen fish may be used.

◆

Yield: 4-6 servings
Preparation time: ¾ hour

◆

Leeks usually conceal lots of sand: wash them well under running water, fanning out the folds of their stalks. If you can't get leeks, substitute ⅓ cup onion.

1 lb.	sole fillets, frozen or fresh
1 lb.	haddock fillets, frozen or fresh
1 cup	thickly sliced yellow onions
½ cup	thinly sliced leek leaves
2 Tbsp.	vegetable oil

1 cup	white wine (or chicken or fish stock)
¼ cup	diced potatoes
1 cup	pureed tomatoes
1	bay leaf
1 tsp.	salt
¼ tsp.	pepper
1 tsp.	grated lemon rind
1 Tbsp.	chopped fresh parsley

Thaw frozen fillets just enough to ease cutting, about 30 minutes. Cut into bite-sized pieces. In a Dutch oven, sauté onion and leeks until golden in vegetable oil. Add remaining ingredients, except parsley. Bring to a boil, cover and simmer 20 minutes or until fish is cooked and tender. Sprinkle with parsley before serving.

Donna Jubb ◆ Fenelon Falls, Ontario

Portuguese Fish Soup

Variation: When funds are low, substitute 2 lbs. inexpensive white fish for the cod (hake, pollack, ocean catfish) and omit the shrimp.

"**I** used to serve this swiftly prepared soup as an appetizer, until I found that guests insisted on making a meal of it. I use the side of a cheese grater to slice the potatoes."

◆

Yield: 4 servings
Preparation time: 25 minutes

◆

2-3	hot red peppers, such as red serranos
¼ cup	olive oil
1	large onion, thinly sliced
3 cloves	garlic, minced
3	large potatoes, peeled and grated as thinly as possible
1	bay leaf
½ tsp.	salt
1 Tbsp.	red wine vinegar
1 lb.	fillet of cod, skinned
1 lb.	raw shrimp, peeled
¼ cup	chopped fresh parsley
sprinkling	Old Bay seasoning (optional)

Sauté 2 red peppers in olive oil until they are lightly browned; discard peppers. Sauté onion and garlic until softened. Add potatoes and bay leaf and cover with 2 cups water. Add salt and vinegar. (For a hotter soup, add the remaining pepper.) Cover pan and simmer for about 15 minutes, or until the potatoes are almost cooked. Lay fish and shrimp on top of potatoes and simmer for 5 to 10 minutes longer, until fish is done and shrimp are pink. Sprinkle with parsley, and Old Bay seasoning, if desired.

Rux Martin ◆ *Underhill Center, Vermont*

Vermont Cheddar & Crab Soup with Broccoli

Gentle simmering is essential to the making of this well-balanced soup.

◆

Yield: 6-8 servings
Preparation time: 1 hour

◆

½ cup	diced onions
¼ cup	butter
½ tsp.	white pepper
1 tsp.	sage
1 tsp.	Worcestershire sauce
½ tsp.	nutmeg
3-6 drops	Tabasco
2 Tbsp.	chopped fresh parsley
4 cups	chicken stock
¼ cup	cornstarch dissolved in ¼ cup water
½ cup	dry white wine
2 cups	milk
2 cups	grated Cheddar, sharp or extra-sharp
1 lb.	crabmeat, preferably fresh or frozen
1 cup	broccoli florets, blanched and chilled

Sauté onions in butter until soft. Whisk in all seasonings and chicken stock; simmer 30 minutes. Add cornstarch mixture, whisking until smooth. Add wine and milk. Bring just to a boil and then simmer, gently. Add grated Cheddar and continue to simmer until all is smooth, stirring frequently to prevent scorching. Do not boil. Add crabmeat and broccoli, simmering to heat through.

R. Kent Cummings ◆ *North Ferrisburg, Vermont*

The addition of Cheddar cheese takes this chowder beyond the realm of soup. Almost a casserole, it is thick, creamy and filling.

Seafood Chowder au Gratin

◆

Yield: 4-6 servings
Preparation time: 1-1½ hours

◆

2 cups	diced onion
3 cups	diced celery
3 Tbsp. plus ½ cup	butter
1 tsp.	salt
½ tsp.	pepper
½ tsp.	garlic powder
¼ tsp.	paprika
5 cups	milk
¾ cup	flour
1 lb.	Cheddar cheese, shredded
10 oz.	lobster meat
½ lb.	crabmeat
¾ lb.	shrimp, peeled and de-veined
1 lb.	scallops, cooked and quartered

Sauté onion and celery in 3 Tbsp. butter. Add spices. In another pan, bring milk almost to a boil. Melt remaining butter in a separate saucepan, and stir in flour. Stir butter-flour mixture into milk and add onion mixture and cheese. Cook until cheese is melted and sauce is slightly thickened. Add seafoods and place in a large casserole dish or individual casserole dishes. Heat in 350-degree F oven until bubbly and brown.

Debbie Simon ◆ Lakeview, Nova Scotia

Seafood Gumbo

Variations: "Suit your taste by adding spicy hot sausage or chunks of ham and chicken."

"The popularity of blackened redfish may wane, but the Cajun-food craze has left us a delicious legacy of gumbos and jambalayas. This gumbo is not entirely traditional, in that it skips the lengthy process of browning a roux of flour and butter. This recipe makes quite a bit; you can count on leftovers or a freezer stash."

◆

Yield: 8-10 servings
Preparation time: 2½ hours

◆

5 Tbsp.	butter
1	medium onion, chopped
1	green pepper, chopped
1	red bell pepper, chopped
1 bunch	green onions, finely chopped
1 rib	celery, finely chopped
½-¾ lb.	okra
	Old Bay or other Creole seasoning
1 qt.	white wine
3 qts.	seafood stock, or 1½ qts. each bottled clam juice and water
2	fresh tomatoes, peeled, seeded and chopped
3 oz.	tomato paste
2 Tbsp.	flour
10-20	oysters
1 lb.	shrimp
1 lb.	grouper or snapper
	cooked rice

Melt 3 Tbsp. butter in large soup pot and add onion, peppers, green onions and celery. Cook over medium heat until soft, stirring occasionally. Slice okra and add to vegetables; stir over heat until it becomes gummy. Sprinkle generously with Old Bay or other Creole seasoning to coat vegetables lightly.

Add wine and simmer to reduce by about half, then add stock (or clam juice and water), tomatoes and tomato paste. Simmer 1 to 2 hours, uncovered. Melt remaining butter, stir in flour, add to pot, and simmer 20 minutes. This is the basic gumbo base and it can hold a day or so in the refrigerator. Bring to a boil before adding fish and seafood.

If you add about 2 pounds of seafood, bring the mixture back to a boil and cook 15 or 20 minutes, or until fish has just turned opaque. Serve in large bowls over cooked rice.

Sarah Fritschner ◆ Louisville, Kentucky

A tasty mélange of meats and seafood awaits those who make this jambalaya. Adding the hot sauce at serving time gives a choice to those who love this spicy topping and those who don't.

Creole Jambalaya

See photo page 73.

◆

Yield: 6-8 servings
Preparation time: 1½ hours

◆

4 slices	bacon, chopped
3	sweet Italian sausages
1	medium onion, chopped
2 cloves	garlic, crushed
1	green pepper, diced
1½ cups	raw rice
½ lb.	ham or boneless chicken breast, cubed
2½ cups	canned tomatoes, drained and diced
½ cup	liquid from tomatoes
2 cups	chicken stock
1 tsp.	salt
½ tsp.	thyme
2 Tbsp.	chopped fresh parsley
¼ tsp.	cayenne pepper
1 lb.	raw shrimp, peeled and deveined, or 12 oz. frozen shrimp, peeled
	hot pepper sauce to taste

In a heavy 3-qt. pot that can be heated on top of the stove and then set in the oven, fry bacon until fat is transparent. Fry sausage with bacon until it is no longer pink. Drain all but 2 Tbsp. fat.

Add onion and sauté until transparent. Add garlic and green pepper and sauté, stirring, for 2 to 3 minutes, or until soft. Stir in rice and sauté, stirring, for 2 to 3 minutes more. Add ham or chicken, tomatoes, tomato liquid, chicken stock, salt, thyme, parsley and cayenne. Cover and bring to a boil. Transfer to a preheated 350-degree F oven and bake for 20 minutes.

Add shrimp and poke them into the rice so they are covered. Cover with lid and cook for 10 to 15 minutes longer, cooking frozen shrimp for the longer time. Serve when moisture is absorbed and shrimp are cooked. Pass the hot sauce to the Cajun-food fanciers.

Lynne Roe ◆ *Orangeville, Ontario*

Preparation Hint: Leftover ham or chicken can be frozen in plastic bags for jambalaya.

Shellfish Stew, Chilean Style

A rich, complex, creamy stew, which pleases the palate with its range of tastes and textures: green chili peppers, hard-cooked eggs, slivered almonds and abundant shellfish. Serve with French rolls.

◆

Yield: 6 servings
Preparation time: 1 hour

◆

6 Tbsp.	butter
1	onion, chopped
4 Tbsp.	flour
1 qt.	fish stock or clam juice, heated
2 cups	dry white wine
½ tsp.	white pepper
1 lb.	medium-sized shrimp, shelled, deveined and halved lengthwise
1 lb.	scallops, halved or quartered
1 or more	fresh green chili peppers, seeded and minced
1 cup	heavy cream
2	hard-cooked eggs, chopped
½ cup	slivered blanched almonds
	salt & freshly ground pepper to taste

Melt butter in a Dutch oven, and sauté onion until transparent. Blend in flour and cook 2 minutes. Add stock, wine and white pepper and simmer 20 minutes. Add shrimp, scallops and chili peppers and cook 5 to 7 minutes, or until seafood is done. Add cream and eggs; heat through. Stir in almonds, salt and pepper.

Lucia Cyre ◆ *Logan Lake, British Columbia*

Shrimp Gumbo

In true Southern style, the thickener for this simple gumbo is okra; its sticky juices provide body and flavor. Its slightly crunchy, slippery seeds provide a delightful contrast in texture.

◆

Yield: 6 servings
Preparation time: 1 hour

◆

2 cups	sliced fresh okra

¼ cup	vegetable oil
⅔ cup	chopped green onions, with tops
3 cloves	garlic, chopped finely
1½ tsp.	salt
½ tsp.	pepper
1 lb.	shrimp, peeled and deveined
1 cup	canned tomatoes
2	whole bay leaves
6 drops	Tabasco
1½ cups	hot, cooked rice

Stirring constantly, sauté okra in vegetable oil about 10 minutes, or until okra appears dry. Add onion, garlic, salt, pepper and shrimp. Cook about 5 minutes; add 2 cups hot water, tomatoes and bay leaves. Cover and simmer 20 minutes. Remove bay leaves. Add Tabasco. Place ¼ cup rice in the bottom of 6 soup bowls; fill with gumbo.

DeLois Sims ◆ *Crockett, Texas*

Okra in its fresh state is crunchy, while frozen okra is somewhat gooier. Avoid old pods that are darkened and spotted with black. Okra, incidentally, is high in vitamin A and potassium.

Cape House Inn Iced Buttermilk with Shrimp Soup

We think this soup is out of this world, and we offer it here again to readers who do not have *The Harrowsmith Cookbook Volume II*. It was originally discovered by a contributor vacationing in Nova Scotia.

◆

Yield: 12 servings
Preparation time: 25 minutes

◆

3 cups	shrimp
3 qts.	buttermilk
1½	English cucumbers, coarsely chopped
3 Tbsp.	fresh dillweed
2 Tbsp.	dry mustard
3 Tbsp.	chopped dill pickle
1 tsp.	pepper
	cayenne
	salt to taste

English cucumbers are long and virtually seedless; they are found in the produce section wrapped in plastic. Ordinary cucumbers, seeded, may be substituted.

Cook shrimp in boiling water until tender. Peel and chop into 1-inch pieces. Combine all ingredients, adding cayenne to taste. Mix well and chill. Serve garnished with thin cucumber slices.

Billie Sheffield ◆ *North Gower, Ontario*

Swamp Mull

Partly soup, partly stew, mull is a traditional Southern combination dish, and like jambalaya, lends itself to quick improvisations. The ingredients, too, are almost identical to those of jambalaya, except that it contains mushrooms but no rice.

◆

Yield: 6-8 servings
Preparation time: 50 minutes

◆

2 cups	small shrimp, boiled and peeled
2 cups	cooked, diced ham
2 cups	cooked, diced chicken
1 cup	sliced mushrooms
¼ cup	chopped celery
½ cup	chopped onion
½ cup	chopped green pepper
	salt, pepper, Tabasco to taste
1 large can	tomatoes, chopped
1 Tbsp.	flour
1 Tbsp.	butter
1 cup	chicken stock
½ cup	olive oil (optional)
	brown rice

Simmer shrimp, ham, chicken, mushrooms, celery, onion, pepper, seasonings and tomatoes in Dutch oven until mixture thickens. Add flour, butter, chicken stock and olive oil. Cook 5 more minutes. Serve over a bed of brown rice.

Sandra K. Bennett ◆ Richmond, Virginia

New Orleans Shrimp

"I served this dish at a rehearsal dinner the night before my October wedding. I had made the sauce with vegetables from the garden in August and put it in the freezer. My in-laws spent the morning of the rehearsal peeling shrimp. When we returned from the church, I put the sauce in big pots and reheated it as the rice cooked. At the last minute, I added the shrimp, which cooked to perfection in a very short time."

◆

Yield: 8 servings
Preparation time: 1 hour 35 minutes

◆

⅔ cup	vegetable oil
½ cup	flour
1¾ cup	sliced green onions
1 stalk	celery, including leaves, diced
2	medium onions, peeled and diced
1	green pepper, diced
6 large cloves	garlic, peeled and minced
¼ cup	minced fresh parsley
1 qt.	tomatoes
8 oz.	canned tomato sauce
¼ cup	red wine
4	bay leaves
6	allspice berries
2	whole cloves
	salt & pepper
½ tsp.	cayenne pepper, or more to taste
¼ tsp.	chili powder
½ tsp.	thyme
	juice of ½ lemon
2 lbs.	shrimp, peeled
	rice
	hot sauce

Heat oil and flour slowly in the bottom of a large pot. It should gradually turn a medium brown—this takes 15 minutes or more. Stir constantly, or nearly so.

Add onions, celery, green peppers, garlic and parsley, and simmer, stirring occasionally, about 20 minutes. Add tomatoes, chopping them roughly, and their juice, tomato sauce, wine, seasonings and lemon juice. Bring to a boil and reduce heat. Simmer 45 minutes, uncovered. Add shrimp, return to the boil, reduce heat and cook until shrimp are done—about 10 minutes for medium shrimp. Serve on boiled rice. Pass the hot sauce at the table.

Sarah Fritschner ◆ *Louisville, Kentucky*

Shrimp Stew with Feta

"Greece is the origin of this lively, full-bodied stew and its secret is in the feta cheese."

◆

Yield: 4 generous servings
Preparation time: 1 hour

◆

Suggested Accompaniments:
"Bread and a Greek salad of cucumber, tomato, onion, feta and Romaine lettuce. Unlike most seafood dishes, this one takes well to a light, young red wine."

6 Tbsp.	olive oil (Greek if possible)
½ cup	onions sliced lengthwise
1 clove	garlic, chopped
1	red (or green) sweet bell pepper, sliced lengthwise
1½ lbs.	raw shrimp, peeled and de-veined
1 tsp.	dried oregano, crumbled (Greek if possible; otherwise from a new jar, so that the flavor is strong)
1 tsp.	salt
	freshly ground black pepper
1½ cups	canned tomatoes, peeled, chopped and drained (reserve the liquid)
4 oz.	feta cheese (do not substitute), chopped into ¼" cubes
3 Tbsp.	coarsely chopped fresh parsley
	rice

Heat olive oil in a large heavy skillet and when it is moderately hot, add onions to brown. Add garlic, taking care not to burn it. Add bell pepper and mix the ingredients, cooking until they are soft.

Add shrimp and sprinkle with oregano, salt and pepper, cooking shrimp until they begin to curl. Do not overcook them. Add chopped tomatoes and reduce the heat. Add tomato liquid. Create a stewlike consistency by bringing the mixture to a boil to thicken it slightly. Cook for about 5 minutes, then add feta and sprinkle the mixture with the fresh parsley. Do not stir needlessly, so that the feta pieces can retain their cubelike shapes. Serve with plain boiled rice.

Ina Fitzhenry-Coor ◆ *Burlington, Vermont*

"This soup, filled with pieces of chicken, shrimp, corn, rice and ripe olives, will put you in mind of a Southern gumbo."

◆

Yield: 5-6 servings
Preparation time: 1 hour

◆

Prawn & Chicken Soup

Prawns are large shrimp.

2	small whole chicken breasts, boned, skinned and halved
⅓ cup	flour
3 Tbsp.	vegetable oil
1	medium onion, sliced
1	small zucchini, sliced
1 cup	chopped tomato
½ cup	pitted ripe olives, drained
1 clove	garlic, chopped fine (optional)
2½ cups	chicken stock
pinch	cayenne
¼ tsp.	thyme
	salt & pepper to taste
½ lb.	raw prawns, peeled and deveined (leave tails on)
1 cup	cooked rice
¾ cup	whole kernel corn, cooked
	parsley and lemon slices

Cut each chicken breast into 3 pieces and roll in flour. Heat oil in a heavy saucepan. Brown chicken, remove and set aside.

Add onion, zucchini, tomato, olives and garlic to saucepan and sauté until onion is tender, but not brown. Add chicken stock, cayenne, thyme, salt, pepper and chicken. Simmer for 20 minutes. Add prawns, rice and corn, cook another 4 or 5 minutes or until prawns are cooked. Do not boil.

Garnish with parsley and a lemon slice.

Irene Louden ◆ Port Coquitlam, British Columbia

Italian Fish Stew

Squid, fresh or frozen, is a little-known delicacy that is a bargain.

To clean, cut the head and tentacles in one piece from the body. Cut off the tentacles just below the eyes and throw out the head. Save the tentacles, which are pretty and delicious in stew.

Under running water, remove the cellophanelike cartilage from the body along with the ink sac and discard them.

Wash the body and pull off the purplish skin. Cut the body into rings.

"Lobster in the shell will make this rustic fish stew more elegant, but it is less expensive and almost as good without it. In consistency, this is thinner than tomato sauce but chunkier than a soup."

♦

Yield: 4 servings
Preparation time: 1½ hours

♦

SAUCE

3 cups	clam juice
1 lb.	crushed Italian plum tomatoes packed in puree
1 clove	garlic, minced
1 tsp.	dried oregano, or 1 Tbsp. fresh
1 tsp.	dried basil, or 1 Tbsp. fresh
1 tsp.	dried thyme, or 1 Tbsp. fresh
¼ tsp.	red pepper flakes
½ tsp.	fennel seed

STEW

1 lb.	fusilli (corkscrew pasta)
1	live lobster (optional)
1 cup	flour
	salt & pepper
	oregano
1 lb.	skinless, boneless, firm fish, such as red snapper
¼ cup	olive oil
¼ lb.	shrimp, peeled
½ lb.	squid, cleaned and sliced into rings
½ lb.	scallops
8	mussels, scrubbed, with beards removed
1	tomato, peeled, seeded and diced

Combine sauce ingredients with 1 cup water in a large pot and simmer 15 minutes. (If using fresh herbs, wrap them in cheesecloth and let them stay in the sauce until ready to serve.)

Cook pasta in boiling water until just barely tender. Drain in colander, rinse with cold water and set aside.

Drop lobster into boiling water and cook 5 minutes. Plunge into ice water. Cut off tail and cut in half widthwise. Remove claws. Discard lobster body.

Season flour with salt, pepper and oregano. Cut fish into 4 pieces and dredge in flour. Shake to remove excess. Heat olive oil in a large skillet, brown fish on both sides and set aside.

Add shrimp, squid and scallops to red sauce and simmer 5 minutes. Add lobster tail halves and claws, still in shell, mussels and tomato pieces, and simmer 2 minutes. Add pasta and stir. Place fish in the bottom of large bowls or soup plates. Top with seafood mixture. Garnish with lobster pieces, if desired, and keep nutcrackers handy to break lobster shells.

Sarah Fritschner • Louisville, Kentucky

Italian Fish Soup with Fettuccine Nests

"**I** stole the idea of putting fettuccine nests in seafood soup from a Boston chef I once worked for who used to hurl knives and pots at me whenever he got angry." The nests are sold in larger supermarkets, but ordinary fettuccine may be used in their stead. Serve with homemade coriander-seasoned hot sauce.

◆

Yield: 4 servings
Preparation time: ½-¾ hour

◆

12	clams in shell
12	mussels in shell
3 cloves	garlic, minced
2	medium onions, chopped
2 Tbsp.	olive oil
2 cups	white wine
2 cups	bottled clam juice
6	Italian tomatoes, chopped
2 lbs.	firm-fleshed fish fillets
12	fettuccine nests (4 egg, 4 tomato, 4 spinach)
	salt & pepper to taste
	hot sauce (recipe follows)

Scrub clams and mussels, steam over 2 cups of water until they open, strain and reserve liquid. Keep clams and mussels warm.

In a Dutch oven, sauté garlic and onion in olive oil until golden, add liquid from steamed shellfish, wine, clam juice and tomatoes. Boil water for pasta. Cut fish into pieces, add to broth, simmer 10 minutes. Cook pasta at a gentle boil to avoid breaking up nests, and drain.

Add clams and mussels to broth, season with salt and pepper. Place 3 pasta nests in bowl (one of each type) and ladle soup on top. Serve with crusty bread and hot sauce.

HOT SAUCE

2 Tbsp.	cayenne pepper
1 Tbsp.	olive oil
1½ tsp.	coriander

Boil cayenne and 3 Tbsp. water briefly, then add oil and coriander.

Melissa McClelland ◆ *Burlington, Vermont*

One-Dish Fish with Sun-Dried Tomatoes

Variation: Substitute thin slices of chicken breast for the fish.

See photo page 69.

T here's nothing stodgy about this dish, bursting with the combined flavors of red-skinned potatoes, oyster mushrooms and the intense tang of sun-dried tomatoes. It is a good choice for winter but also convenient in summer because of its short cooking time.

◆

Yield: 2 servings
Preparation time: ¾ hour

◆

3-4	sun-dried tomatoes soaked in marinade *(recipe follows)*
2	medium red-skinned potatoes, sliced ⅛" thick
1 Tbsp.	safflower oil
¾ Tbsp.	margarine
1¾ Tbsp.	unsalted butter
	pinch dried tarragon
1 tsp.	dried parsley
¾-1 lb.	white fish fillets
1	medium yellow onion, sliced very thin
3 oz.	oyster mushrooms (button mushrooms may be substituted)
	freshly ground black pepper
2 pinches	dried dillweed
	juice ½ medium lemon
½ cup	dry white wine
2	scallions, chopped

TOMATO MARINADE

1 heaping tsp.	Dijon mustard
½ pinch	salt
pinch	freshly ground black pepper
1 tsp.	olive oil

Marinate sun-dried tomatoes for at least several hours in marinade. (If marinating for longer, stir every day.)

Fry potatoes over medium heat in cast-iron skillet in oil and margarine until brown. Set aside on an oven-proof platter and keep warm. Turn up heat slightly under the skillet, add 1 Tbsp. butter, tarragon and parsley. Add fish and cook 1 to 2 minutes on each side, depending on the thickness of fillets. Place fish over potatoes on the platter and keep warm.

Sauté onion in remaining ¾ Tbsp. butter until translucent. Chop sun-dried tomatoes finely and add them to onions with mushrooms, pepper and dillweed. Stir and cook 2 minutes. Add lemon juice and wine, and simmer slowly until somewhat thickened. Drizzle over fish and potatoes, cover platter with foil and heat briefly in a 350-degree F oven. Garnish with scallions.

Richard Thomasy ◆ *Watertown, Massachusetts*

North American Bouillabaisse

Monkfish, a firm, white fish readily available in the winter, takes on the flavor of shellfish in this fennel-scented stew.

◆

Yield: 6 servings
Preparation time: 50 minutes

◆

4 large cloves	garlic, crushed
1	medium onion, chopped
1	green pepper, cut into 1" chunks
1	red pepper, cut into 1" chunks
2 Tbsp.	olive oil
¼ cup	chopped fresh parsley
¼ tsp.	red pepper
½ tsp.	dried thyme
½ tsp.	salt
¼ tsp.	black pepper
2 qts.	fish stock (*recipe follows*)
3	canned plum tomatoes, drained and chopped
2 lbs.	monkfish fillets, cut into 1½" pieces
1½ lbs.	mussels, washed and de-bearded
1½ lbs.	shrimp, peeled and deveined
6 slices	French bread fried in olive oil
	garlic mayonnaise seasoned with Tabasco
	Parmesan cheese

Optional Garnish: This stew is immeasurably better topped with a slice of crisply fried French bread, a spoonful of garlic mayonnaise generously seasoned with Tabasco, and a sprinkling of Parmesan cheese.

See photo page 66.

Sauté garlic, onion and peppers in oil in a heavy stockpot until softened. Stir in seasonings and sauté briefly. Add fish stock, tomatoes and monkfish, and simmer until monkfish pieces are opaque.

Steam mussels in 1 cup water, and add water to stockpot. When monkfish is done, add shrimp and simmer just until they turn pink. Stir in mussels in their shells, and serve. Top with bread, garlic-Tabasco mayonnaise and grated cheese.

FISH STOCK

2	medium onions, chopped
2 stalks	celery, chopped
4 cloves	garlic, crushed
1 tsp.	fennel seeds
½ cup	chopped fresh parsley
¼ cup	olive oil
1	canned plum tomato
	shrimp shells (from shrimp used in bouillabaisse)
2	fish heads from nonoily fish
1	bay leaf
½ tsp.	dried thyme
1 strip	orange peel
2 cups	dry white wine
	salt & pepper

Sauté onions, celery, garlic, fennel seeds and parsley in oil in a stockpot. Stir in remaining ingredients and 6 cups water. Simmer 30 minutes and strain.

Makes 2 quarts.

Rux Martin ◆ Underhill Center, Vermont

Spinach-Oyster Stew

This "stew" takes just minutes to prepare. Bottled chili sauce adds a touch of piquancy.

◆

Yield: 6 servings
Preparation time: 35 minutes

◆

2 Tbsp.	unsalted butter
2	large shallots, minced
¼ cup	finely chopped celery
1½ tsp.	lemon juice
1 lb.	shelled oysters, with liquid
2 Tbsp.	bottled chili sauce
3 cups	chopped spinach, tough stems removed

2	large potatoes, peeled and diced into ¾" cubes
5 cups	milk
1 cup	heavy cream
1 tsp.	paprika
¼-½ tsp.	cayenne pepper
	salt & pepper

Preparation Hint: The secret of this dish is to cook the oysters just until their edges curl; they should be hot but still limpid.

Melt butter in skillet and sauté shallots and celery until softened. Whisk in lemon juice, oyster liquid and chili sauce. Add spinach and cook until slightly wilted. Set aside. Boil potatoes until just cooked, drain, and place in stewpot along with contents of skillet. Add remaining ingredients including oysters. Heat on low flame just until liquid is hot and edges of oysters begin to curl. Do not overcook.

Rux Martin ◆ *Underhill Center, Vermont*

Cream of Tomato Soup with Oysters

Oysters are a wonderful addition to this homemade tomato soup. Be careful with the cayenne, as it becomes piquant quickly.

◆

Yield: 4 servings
Preparation time: ¾ hour

◆

2 cups	tomatoes, preferably fresh, or canned
2	onions, sliced
1 tsp.	salt
¼ tsp.	pepper
1 tsp.	sugar
dash	cayenne
3 Tbsp.	butter
2 Tbsp.	flour
2 cups	milk
dash	baking soda
1 pt.	oysters, with liquid

Cook tomatoes, onions, salt, pepper, sugar and cayenne together for 15 minutes. Cool. Melt 2 Tbsp. butter in a pan and whisk in flour. Add milk gradually and simmer. When tomato mixture is cool, puree in a food processor or blender. Add baking soda to tomato mixture, and gradually add tomatoes to milk, stirring constantly. Simmer 10 minutes. Heat oysters in 1 Tbsp. butter just until edges curl, and add to soup.

Rhonda Barnes ◆ *Fulford Harbour, British Columbia*

VEGETABLES

Pray for peace and grace and spiritual food,
For wisdom and guidance, for all these are good,
But don't forget the potatoes.

John Tyler Petee

M y appreciation of the power of vegetables was awakened during Lent, in a small taverna outside of the Agora in Athens, Greece. By the time my husband and I emerged from exploring the site of the ancient market, we were famished, but most of the tavernas, the small, inexpensive and invariably spotless restaurants that serve the traditional food of Greece, had stopped serving lunch. Finally, we stumbled on a tiny one crowded with workers, tucked out of reach of the tourist section. Because of the religious season, all the dishes on display were vegetarian. Disappointed at the prospect of a meatless meal after all the walking, I made my selection by pointing dolefully at a stew of potatoes, carrots and whole baby artichokes in a long pan.

It is difficult to say what made this simple combination superlative. The vegetables were bathed in a light liquid produced by their own combined juices, augmented by olive oil, lemon juice and some chopped parsley. There may have been a bit of garlic and perhaps oregano, but only a hint. The broth was rich and full. Nothing intruded upon the clear, uncomplicated flavors of the vegetables.

It was a dish so complete and satisfying that I felt guilty for having greeted it with such pessimism. It called to mind the words of a nineteenth-century French nobleman who had a similar reaction to food of the religious fast: "Are the meatless meals of our Lenten enthusiasts really meals of abstinence?" Prompted more by health concerns than by religious mandate, today's enthusiasm for vegetables has produced a variety of substantial, vibrant dishes to satisfy the staunchest carnivore.

The most common source of failure in the vegetable stews we tasted was watery broth and insufficient flavor. Because vegetables have only negligible amounts of fat, an important contributor of flavor, one must take steps to ensure that the soup will be full-bodied. Strong-tasting vegetables like turnip and kale generally need no stock, but milder vegetables require it. The most expedient way to boost flavor and add richness is to use a base of chicken broth, but a properly made vegetable stock will do as well, without interfering with the subtle identity of the vegetables.

Sautéing onion is a good beginning to most soups and stews, since cooking makes onion molecules 50 to 70 times as sweet as sugar. Likewise, some of the other vegetables in the soup may be finely diced and sautéed to release their flavors early in the cooking. Cut the rest of the vegetables into large pieces whenever possible to minimize the loss of flavor, juices and nutrients. Vary your treatment of them, creating a variety of shapes by chopping, slicing, dicing them into thick or thin rounds, or cutting them on the diagonal. Aggressive vegetables like broccoli and cabbage will take over the cooking pot and annihilate delicate vegetables like peas and asparagus, so choose their companions with care.

Staggering the cooking time is crucial so that the vegetables will retain their individual textures. Potatoes, onions and carrots can endure and even benefit from long cooking times, but spinach becomes drab and grassy. Members of the cabbage family—including broccoli, cauliflower and Brussels sprouts—release acrid mustard oil (a natural form of the wartime chemical scourge, mustard gas) that becomes more pungent as the cooking time lengthens.

The best way to thicken the vegetable one-pot and unite its flavors is to blend a portion of the cooked vegetables until they are smooth, and return the puree to the pot. A finishing touch can be provided with a dab of pesto, a spoonful of garlic-infused mayonnaise, or a sprinkling of Parmesan cheese.

—*Rux Martin*

Sorrel Soup with Doughboys

Sorrel may be gathered wild or cultivated. It is available in many supermarkets. Its mouth-puckering tang comes from oxalic acid.

The arrowhead-shaped green leaves of sorrel have a sweet-sour taste that is perfect for cream soups. With the inventive addition of tiny doughboys, this one becomes a full meal.

◆

Yield: 4 servings
Preparation time: 50 minutes

◆

1 cup	diced potatoes
½ cup	diced onions
½ cup	diced carrots
1 tsp.	salt
1 Tbsp.	butter
2 cups	finely chopped young sorrel leaves
½ cup	sour or sweet cream (your preference)
2 Tbsp.	chopped fresh dill

Gently simmer potatoes, onions, carrots, salt and butter in 1½ cups water for 15 minutes. Add sorrel and 3 additional cups water, simmer for 10 minutes more.

DOUGHBOYS

1	egg, beaten
	flour

Make doughboys by beating egg with 2 Tbsp. warm water. Stir in enough flour to make a stiff dough.

Pinch off tiny pieces of dough and drop onto boiling soup. Cook, covered, for 10 minutes. Remove from heat, add cream. Sprinkle with fresh dill.

Rose Strocen ◆ Canora, Saskatchewan

Soupe au Pistou

"I learned to make this Provençal soup while living in Aix-en-Provence, France, for six years. It is wonderful in summer when one can get fresh basil and fresh, large, white shelling beans. Place a generous tablespoon of pesto in the bottom of a soup bowl and ladle on the colorful soup."

◆

Yield: 10-12 servings
Preparation time: 1¼ hours

◆

1	onion, chopped
4	tomatoes, peeled, seeded and chopped
1 Tbsp.	oil
¼ lb.	salt pork
10-12 oz.	frozen lima beans or fresh white shelling beans
1 lb.	fresh or frozen green beans, chopped
4	zucchini, chopped
4	carrots, chopped
1 stalk	celery, chopped
4	potatoes, chopped
1 cup	large egg noodles
	salt & pepper

Fry onions and tomatoes in oil until cooked, about ½ hour. Add remaining ingredients—except noodles, salt and pepper—plus 1½ qts. water. Simmer for ½ hour. Add noodles and cook for 15 minutes longer. Season with salt and pepper.

SAUCE AU PISTOU

1 handful	fresh basil
½ cup	olive oil
1 clove	garlic
½ cup	Parmesan cheese

Make sauce by placing all ingredients in a blender or food processor and pureeing until smooth.

To serve, put 1 Tbsp. pistou in the bottom of a soup bowl and ladle soup over top; stir. Pass more grated Parmesan at the table.

Gladys Carleton ◆ *Cremona, Alberta*

Fresh basil is mandatory for this summer soup. The word *pistou* comes from the Niçoise word *pista*, "to pound" the basil.

"This recipe came into being the day my kitchen cabinets were installed. When it got to be suppertime and the crew was still working, I realized I had to feed them without the use of my kitchen. The garden was at its best, I had running water outside and a fire pit to cook over. I call it 'August Stew,' but in warmer parts of the country it might have to be called 'July Stew.' It's one of the few ways that my kids really like zucchini."

◆

Yield: 4-6 servings
Preparation time: ¾ hour

◆

August Stew

Suggested Accompaniment: Mom's Popovers, page 232.

1	onion
2 cloves	garlic, minced
1	medium zucchini
¼ cup	butter
6-8	ripe tomatoes
3	carrots, sliced
3 stalks	celery, chopped
1 cup	cut-up green beans
1 cup	cut-up wax beans
1 cup	peas or cut-up sugar-snap peas
	salt & pepper to taste
a few	fresh basil leaves, or 2 tsp. dried
¼ cup	chopped parsley
2 cups	grated mozzarella cheese

Sauté onion, garlic and zucchini in butter until translucent. Add tomatoes and cook slowly until tomatoes are stewed, about ½ hour. Add the other vegetables and cook over medium heat for 10 to 15 minutes until lightly cooked. Season with salt and pepper, basil and parsley. Serve topped with grated cheese.

Anne C. Morrell ◆ *Margaree Valley, Nova Scotia*

Garden Vegetable Chowder

Suggested Accompaniment:
Drop Biscuits, page 224.

This rich, creamy chowder drew rave reviews from the Vermont staff the day it was served. "Wonderful eye-appeal and even better on the tongue," said our tester.

◆

Yield: 6 servings
Preparation time: ½ hour

◆

1	zucchini, 6-8" long
¼ cup	butter
1	small onion, chopped
1 Tbsp.	snipped fresh parsley
2 Tbsp.	chopped fresh basil, or ½ tsp. dried
2 Tbsp. plus 1 tsp.	flour
½ tsp.	salt
dash	pepper
⅛ tsp.	Hungarian hot paprika (optional)
1½ cups	chicken or vegetable stock
½ tsp.	lemon juice

1 cup	fresh corn, scraped from the cob, or 1 cup frozen
1 pt.	light cream
3	medium tomatoes, peeled, seeded and finely chopped
½ cup	shredded Cheddar cheese
2 Tbsp.	grated Romano cheese
	parsley for garnish

Cut zucchini lengthwise in half; chop into ⅜-inch slices. Melt butter in a heavy 3-qt. pot. Cook and stir zucchini, onion, parsley and basil in butter for 6 to 8 minutes.

Stir flour, salt, pepper and paprika into vegetable mixture. Cook over low heat, stirring constantly, until bubbly. Remove from heat. Stir in stock and lemon juice. Heat to boiling, stirring constantly.

Add corn to chowder. Return to boiling; reduce heat and cover. Simmer, stirring occasionally, until corn is cooked, about 5 minutes. Stir in cream and tomatoes. Heat just to boiling. Stir in cheeses. Cook and stir over low heat until cheeses are melted. Garnish with fresh parsley.

Judy Sheppard-Segal ◆ *Falmouth, Maine*

Italian Zucchini Stew

A fresh-tasting vegetable soup that brings the garden to the table. Fresh mint and basil add spark to this Italian recipe.

◆

Yield: 8-10 servings
Preparation time: 1¼ hours

◆

Suggested Accompaniment: Gougère, page 230.

1½-2 lbs.	zucchini, cut into rounds (about 6 cups)
2	large onions, sliced
1	large green pepper, cut into chunks
3 Tbsp.	oil
2	basil leaves, chopped
1 tsp.	oregano
2 cloves	garlic, crushed
1 tsp.	thyme
2 leaves	mint, chopped, or to taste
	salt & pepper to taste
5	large tomatoes, chopped (about 6 cups)
4 cups	fresh greens: spinach, Romaine lettuce, endive, beet tops and/or dandelion greens

Sauté zucchini, onions and pepper in a large pot with oil. Add herbs, tomatoes and water to cover. Simmer, covered, for 30 to 40 minutes. Add greens and simmer another 10 minutes.

Arlene Low ◆ *Norwood, Ontario*

Ratatouille

Vine-ripened tomatoes are essential for ratatouille — no substitutes allowed.

"This ratatouille may be served cold, accompanied by lemon wedges, or hot, topped with Parmesan cheese and placed under the broiler until golden."

◆

Yield: 8-10 servings
Preparation time: 2¼ hours

◆

6 Tbsp.	olive oil
1	medium-sized eggplant, unpeeled, cut into 1½" cubes
3	medium-sized zucchini, cut into 1½" cubes
	salt & pepper to taste
3	onions, coarsely chopped
2	green peppers, peeled, seeded and coarsely chopped
4 cloves	garlic, minced
1	bay leaf
2 lbs. (about 12)	medium-sized, well-ripened tomatoes, preferably plum, peeled and cut into 1" cubes
½ cup	finely chopped parsley
2 tsp.	finely chopped fresh thyme, or ½ tsp. dried
1 Tbsp.	finely chopped fresh basil, or 1 tsp. dried

Preheat oven to 250 degrees F. Heat 3 Tbsp. oil in a large skillet and sauté eggplant, zucchini, salt and pepper, stirring constantly, for about 5 minutes. Remove to a large casserole dish.

Add remaining 3 Tbsp. oil to skillet and sauté onions and green peppers until soft. Add garlic and bay leaf. Add tomatoes and simmer, stirring occasionally, for about 10 minutes.

Add tomato mixture to the casserole dish along with parsley, thyme and basil. Mix all ingredients well. Cover casserole dish and bake for 1¼ to 2 hours. Remove bay leaf before serving.

Helen M. Abrahams ◆ *Toronto, Ontario*

Minestrone

A deep-flavored, robust vegetable and beef minestrone. Beans, peas and bits of spaghetti are added at the end so they retain their freshness.

◆

Yield: 10 servings
Preparation time: 4 hours

◆

Suggested Accompaniment:
Focaccia, page 232.

1 lb.	shin beef with bone
1-2 Tbsp.	salt, or to taste
1 cup	dried kidney beans
2 cloves	garlic, peeled, whole
1 Tbsp.	olive or other oil
½ cup	minced onion
½ cup	minced parsley
⅛ tsp.	pepper
¾ cup	diced celery
2 cups	finely shredded cabbage
1 cup	diced carrots
1 cup	canned tomatoes
1 cup	cut string beans
⅔ cup	peas
½ cup	spaghetti, broken up finely
	Parmesan cheese

Place shin in large heavy pot. Add 3½ qts. water, salt and dried beans. Cover and bring to boil. Skim foam. Cover and simmer 3½ hours.

Brown garlic in oil in skillet. Discard garlic. Add onion and parsley and sauté until onions are tender but not brown. Remove bones and meat from stock. Add onion, parsley, pepper, celery, cabbage, carrots and tomatoes to stock. Cover and simmer for 20 minutes. Add string beans and cook for 10 minutes, then add peas and spaghetti and cook 10 minutes longer. Serve, passing the cheese to sprinkle on top.

Donna Jubb ◆ Fenelon Falls, Ontario

Tomato Gumbo

"Fresh okra adds texture and flavor to tomato-based soups and stews." Measure okra before slicing and wipe clean rather than washing, since water makes okra slimy.

◆

Yield: 4 servings
Preparation time: 1 hour

◆

2 Tbsp.	butter
1	large white onion, finely chopped
2 cups	canned tomatoes, with juice, or equivalent ripe, fresh tomatoes, peeled
4 cups	okra, wiped clean and stems removed, sliced cross-wise thinly
1	bay leaf
¼ tsp.	dried thyme
4 cups	chicken stock
	salt & pepper
	Tabasco sauce

Melt butter. Cook onion for a few minutes. Add tomatoes and mash them until they are broken up. Add okra, herbs and chicken stock. Bring to a boil, cover and simmer gently for 30 minutes. Add seasonings to taste.

Karen Kadlec ◆ *Toronto, Ontario*

Corn Chili

Suggested Accompaniment:
Rosemary Biscuits, page 226.

"This chili is very versatile; it can be made entirely from fresh ingredients, or it can be made from frozen or canned ingredients if time is short."

◆

Yield: 4 servings
Preparation time: 1 hour, plus overnight and 45 minutes for beans

◆

1	onion, chopped
2 cloves	garlic, chopped
1	green pepper, chopped
3 Tbsp.	oil
28-oz. can	Italian tomatoes, or chopped fresh
4 cups	cooked pinto beans
2 cups	corn kernels
1 tsp.	chili powder, or to taste
1½ tsp.	salt
	pepper

To cook pinto beans: Soak overnight; drain soaking water, cover with fresh water, and simmer for 45 minutes, or until tender.

Sauté onion, garlic and pepper in oil in stewpot. Place tomatoes and 2 cups of the beans in blender or food processor, and puree. Add to sautéed vegetables, then stir in remaining beans, corn and seasonings. Simmer ½ hour.

Melissa McClelland ◆ *Burlington, Vermont*

Corn Chowder Bisque

This traditional northern recipe for corn chowder is particularly sweet with fresh corn, though canned or frozen may also be used.

◆

Yield: 6-8 servings
Preparation time: 1½ hours

◆

2 slices	salt pork, cut into ¼" cubes
4	small onions, finely minced
6	medium potatoes, peeled and cubed
4	medium tomatoes, peeled and sliced
2 tsp.	salt
¼ tsp.	pepper
6 ears	corn
1 Tbsp.	butter
1 Tbsp.	flour
1 qt.	hot milk
¼ tsp.	baking soda

Fry salt pork until crisp and light brown in a Dutch oven. Remove from heat and add onions, potatoes and tomatoes, arranging them in layers. Sprinkle with salt and pepper. Cover with 1 pt. boiling water and simmer until vegetables are almost cooked. Add corn that has been cut from the cob and cook for 30 minutes.

In another pan, melt butter, stir in flour and gradually stir in hot milk. Add to Dutch oven. Stir in baking soda, stirring rapidly. Simmer for 10 minutes.

Elsie P. Willett ◆ *Lake Charlotte, Nova Scotia*

Red Pepper & Corn Soup

Roasting peppers gives them a deliciously mellow sweetness. Once you try them, you'll be reluctant to have them any other way. Accompany this soup with Mexican Corn Bread (page 228) and hot pepper sauce.

◆

Yield: 4 servings
Preparation time: ¾ hour

◆

To roast peppers: Cut peppers in half lengthwise; remove seeds and stem. Place on broiler pan, skin side up. Broil until skin is charred and blistered, flattening them as they soften. Let cool until you can handle them. Place under cold running water and peel off charred skin. Slice in strips.

Peppers can also be roasted by placing them, whole, on an inverted burner grate of a gas stove, with the flame turned to medium high.

1	onion, chopped
2 Tbsp.	butter
1 cup	fresh tomatoes, peeled and chopped before measuring, or 1 cup canned, drained
2	large red bell peppers, roasted
2 cups	chicken stock
2 cups	cooked fresh, frozen or canned corn
	salt & pepper
	hot pepper sauce (optional)
½ cup	sour cream
½ cup	grated cheese (brick, white Cheddar or Monterey Jack)

In a large pot, sauté onion in butter for 5 minutes. Puree tomatoes and red pepper strips in a blender or food processor. Add to pot with chicken stock. Coarsely chop corn in blender or food processor, add to pot, and bring to a boil. Reduce heat and simmer 20 to 30 minutes.

Season to taste, adding a few drops of hot pepper sauce if desired. Remove from heat. Whisk in sour cream, a few spoonfuls at a time. Pour into warmed bowls. Garnish with grated cheese.

Karen Kadlec ◆ *Toronto, Ontario*

Cream of Summer Squash Soup

"**I** learned to make this Hungarian soup by watching my mother cook. By Hungarian standards, it is not considered fancy or out-of-the-ordinary, but is a good, hearty soup that is filling and nutritious."

◆

Yield: 4 servings
Preparation time: 1½ hours

◆

8-10	yellow summer squash
2 tsp.	salt
1	medium onion, finely chopped
1 Tbsp.	oil
1 tsp.	sweet Hungarian paprika
4-5 cups	chicken stock
1 Tbsp.	finely chopped fresh dill, or ½ tsp. dried
	salt & pepper
1 Tbsp.	white vinegar
⅓ cup	flour

1 cup	milk
1 cup	half-and-half
	sour cream or yogurt
	fresh dill or chives

Variation: "If more flour is used in the thickening, this soup can double as a creamed vegetable and be served alongside roasts."

Peel and grate squash. Place in a large bowl and combine with salt. Set aside for ½ hour, drain in colander and press out as much water as possible. (There should be about 5 cups of drained squash.)

Sauté onion in oil until transparent. Remove from heat and stir in paprika, squash, chicken stock and dill. Bring soup to a boil, stirring constantly, reduce heat and simmer for 30 to 40 minutes. Adjust seasoning, adding salt, pepper and more dill if needed. Add vinegar and thicken with a smooth mixture of flour, milk and half-and-half. Simmer, stirring occasionally, for 15 minutes longer on low heat. Garnish with sour cream or yogurt and a sprinkling of dill or chives.

Maria Breton ◆ *Addison, Ontario*

A refreshing alternative to gazpacho—well suited to imaginative substitutions during the gardening season. Yogurt may be substituted for buttermilk.

◆

Yield: 4-6 servings
Preparation time: ½ hour

◆

Chilled Buttermilk Soup

Preparation Hint: This dish is ideal for summer, since it is cooling but does not need to be made in advance.

2	medium potatoes, un-peeled, finely diced
	salt
4	green onions, coarsely chopped, white and green parts separated
1	cucumber, peeled and diced
2	large ripe tomatoes, diced
1 qt.	buttermilk
3 large cloves	garlic
	juice of 1-2 lemons, to taste
2 Tbsp.	chopped fresh dill
1 Tbsp.	dill seeds, or to taste
	freshly ground pepper
	alfalfa sprouts, croutons and/or sunflower seeds

Place 2 cups water and potatoes in a saucepan and simmer 15 minutes, adding the white part of the onions toward the end to poach for a minute or two. Place cucumbers and tomatoes in a bowl or tureen with the green tops of the onions.

Remove half the onions and potatoes with a slotted spoon and add to the bowl of prepared vegetables. Puree until smooth the remaining potatoes and onions in their liquid in a blender, along with 2 cups of the buttermilk, garlic and lemon juice. Pour into the bowl of vegetables and stir in the remaining 2 cups buttermilk, dill and dill seeds. Add pepper, and either chill or serve at once, garnished with sprouts, croutons or sunflower seeds, or a combination of them.

Lucia Cyre ◆ *Logan Lake, British Columbia*

Italian Peasant Soup

A great way to use up stale bread. The bread acts as a thickener, giving this minestrone a stewlike consistency.

◆

Yield: 6 servings
Preparation time: 3 hours

◆

1 cup	dried white beans
8 cloves	garlic, chopped
½	red onion, diced
2 Tbsp.	olive oil
2	carrots, sliced
1 cup	shredded green cabbage
2 ribs	celery, sliced
28-oz. can	crushed Italian tomatoes with puree
1	bay leaf
1 loaf (about 8 oz. when fresh)	day-old Italian bread, crust removed
½ lb.	fresh spinach, washed, chopped
	salt & pepper to taste
½ cup	grated Romano cheese

Put beans in 2 cups water, bring to boil and simmer until beans are tender, about 2 hours.

Sauté garlic and onion in oil, add carrots, cabbage and celery, fry for a few minutes. Add tomatoes, beans, bay leaf and 2 cups water. Crumble bread into soup. Cover pot, simmer until vegetables are tender, approximately 45 minutes. When vegetables are almost done, add spinach. Season with salt and pepper. Serve topped with Romano.

Melissa McClelland ◆ *Burlington, Vermont*

Greek Artichoke Stew with Garlic Mayonnaise

The flavors of the Mediterranean permeate this light but sturdy vegetable stew, a favorite in Greece during Lent. A pressure cooker can speed the cooking of the vegetables.

◆

Yield: 6 servings
Preparation time: 1¼ hours

◆

4 large cloves	garlic, crushed
⅓ cup	olive oil
8	medium artichokes
2½ tsp.	salt
	juice of 1 lemon
1 cup	dry white wine
8	medium russet potatoes, cut into 2" wedges
12	carrots, peeled and cut into 2" lengths
1	bay leaf
1 Tbsp.	dried oregano
2½ Tbsp.	cornstarch, mixed with 1 cup cooled artichoke water
½ cup	chopped fresh parsley
	pepper
6 slices	good French bread
	olive oil
	garlic mayonnaise

In a stockpot, sauté garlic in oil until golden. Let stand. Parboil artichokes in 12 cups water and 1½ tsp. salt for 20 minutes, or until softened. Reserve water.

Remove leaves from artichokes and set aside for another use. Remove stems and spiny "chokes." Quarter hearts and place in a little water mixed with 2 tsp. lemon juice; set aside. Discard garlic from stewpot, add wine, and heat until vapors have evaporated. Add 4 cups artichoke water, potatoes, carrots, bay leaf, oregano, 1 tsp. salt and remaining lemon juice. Simmer 20 to 30 minutes, or until vegetables are tender. Add artichoke hearts, and simmer a few minutes longer. Thicken with cornstarch mixture, stir in parsley and adjust seasonings.

Fry bread lightly in oil and place a slice in the bottom of each soup bowl. Ladle stew over bread and top with garlic mayonnaise.

Rux Martin ◆ Underhill Center, Vermont

Garlic Mayonnaise

1 egg
½ tsp. salt
½ cup olive oil
¼ cup vegetable oil
4 cloves garlic, crushed
2 Tbsp. lemon juice

Beat egg with salt, using a whisk or a food processor. Beat in ¼ cup olive oil drop by drop, until mixture is thickened. Add remaining olive oil gradually. Add vegetable oil in a thin stream, beating continuously. Beat in garlic and lemon juice. Serve immediately, or chill for later use.

Ghivetch

Suggested Accompaniment:
Gougère, page 230.

"The only rules for success in this Rumanian stew are don't stint on the seasonings and don't overcook it, or the vegetables will become too blended. They should remain fresh-tasting and colorful." It should be served immediately after making.

◆

Yield: 6 servings
Preparation time: 50 minutes

◆

2	small potatoes
1	small yellow squash
3 cups	cubed rutabaga
3-4	medium carrots
1 cup	green beans, fresh or frozen
1 stalk	celery
1	large onion
2	medium tomatoes
½ cup	green pepper, cut in strips
2 cups	beef stock
⅓ cup	olive oil
2 small cloves	garlic, crushed
2 tsp.	salt
½	bay leaf
¼ tsp.	tarragon

Wash and prepare all vegetables. Peel and dice potatoes and place in water until needed. Cut squash in half, remove seeds and slice thinly. Peel rutabaga and cut in ½-inch cubes; cut carrots into ¼-inch-thick rounds. Slice green beans into 1-inch diagonals; cut celery in ¼-inch diagonal slices; slice onion thinly; core and cut tomatoes into quarters; cut green pepper into strips. Place stock, oil, garlic, salt, bay leaf and tarragon into soup pot.

Heat to boiling. Drain potatoes; add to stock along with carrots and rutabaga. Cover and cook 10 minutes. Add squash, green beans, celery and onion. Mix lightly and cook another 10 minutes. Stir lightly and add tomatoes and green peppers. Cook 5 minutes longer.

B. Gillies ◆ *Estevan, Saskatchewan*

French Onion Soup Camembert

A simple version of French Onion Soup with creamy Camembert replacing Gruyère cheese.

◆

Yield: 2-3 servings
Preparation time: ¾ hour

◆

2	large white onions (about ½ lb. each)
2 Tbsp.	butter
2½ cups	beef stock
1	small bay leaf
pinch	dried thyme
2-3 slices	French bread
4 oz.	Camembert or Brie
	salt & pepper

Peel onions and slice lengthwise thinly. Melt butter over moderate heat in large saucepan. Add onions and cook, stirring occasionally, for 10 to 15 minutes, or until they are soft and golden. Do not allow them to become too brown. Add stock, bay leaf and thyme. Bring to a boil, cover, lower heat and simmer for 30 minutes.

Spread bread with Camembert or Brie. Place on a baking sheet and toast under broiler until cheese is melted. Remove bay leaf from soup; taste and add salt and pepper if needed. Ladle soup into 2 or 3 bowls and float bread, cheese side up, in each.

Karen Kadlec ◆ *Toronto, Ontario*

Preparation Hint: "The onions should be sliced lengthwise rather than into rings to retain their texture."

French Onion Soup

"The secret ingredient in this onion soup is honey, which gives the broth a velvety texture without making it noticeably sweet. Our tester, who is trained in Cordon Bleu and knows a good onion soup when she tastes one, cries "Bravo!"

◆

Yield: 4-6 servings
Preparation time: 1½ hours

◆

4 Tbsp.	butter
6	medium onions, peeled and sliced
1 clove	garlic, minced
2	shallots, finely chopped
2 tsp.	honey
4 Tbsp.	dry white wine
2 Tbsp.	flour
2½ cups, or 2 cans	beef stock
1¼ cups, or 1 can	chicken stock
	salt & pepper to taste
6 slices	French bread, toasted
1½ cups plus 6 slices	Gruyère cheese
6 Tbsp.	Parmesan cheese

"It's important to cook the onions over low heat, sweating them until they are soft."

In a 4-qt. saucepan, heat butter and sauté onions, garlic and shallots with honey over very low heat, stirring frequently, until onions are golden and soft, approximately 30 minutes. Add wine and cook until it has evaporated. Add flour and heat through for a few minutes. Add stocks, and 1 cup water if using canned stock, and seasonings, and heat through, stirring occasionally.

Place 6 ovenproof soup bowls on a cookie sheet. Place 1 slice French bread in each bowl. Place ¼ cup grated Gruyère and 1 Tbsp. grated Parmesan on the bread. Fill each bowl with soup. Heat in a 350-degree F oven for about 20 minutes. Place 1 slice Gruyère over each bowl and continue baking until cheese is melted.

J. Baxter ◆ *London, Ontario*

Red Cabbage with Black-Eyed Peas

Kombu is an edible seaweed, found in health food stores and Oriental markets.

The seasonings—garlic, anise and fennel—add a nice warmth to this simple cabbage dinner, which is loosely inspired by the traditions of the South.

◆

Yield: 4-6 servings
Preparation time: 1-1½ hours

◆

1½ cups	black-eyed peas
1 piece	kombu, chopped
2 stalks	celery, sliced
2	onions, sliced
2	potatoes, chopped
2	carrots, sliced
½ head	red cabbage, chopped
2 cloves	garlic, minced
1 tsp.	anise seed
2 tsp.	fennel seed
1	bay leaf
1-2 tsp.	salt, or to taste
	chopped parsley

Simmer peas in 2 qts. water with kombu for 30 minutes. Add celery, onions, potatoes and carrots and simmer 15 minutes. Add remaining ingredients; simmer 15 minutes more. Garnish with chopped parsley.

Diane Barlau ◆ *Duluth, Minnesota*

Cream of Vegetable Soup

"This soup can be made in the late summer when the garden is at full tilt, and it freezes well so that it can also be enjoyed in the fall." Our tester pronounced it "just like the cream of vegetable soups in France—bright-tasting."

♦

Yield: 6 servings
Preparation time: 1 hour

♦

¼-¾ cup	butter
¾ cup	chopped onion
1½ cups	diced potato
¾ cup	peeled, diced tomato
¾ cup	diced carrot
¾ cup	diced green beans
¾ cup	chopped broccoli
¾ cup	chopped leek
¾ cup	chopped zucchini
1 clove	garlic, minced
6 cups	chicken stock
	salt & pepper to taste
½ cup	cream
	chopped parsley

Melt butter in large pot over medium heat. Add onion and sauté 1 to 2 minutes. Reduce heat and add remaining vegetables. Cook until vegetables are soft but not browned, about 20 minutes.

Add stock and bring to boil over medium heat. Reduce heat and simmer about 10 minutes. Let cool a bit. Transfer to blender and puree until smooth. Taste and add salt and pepper as needed. Return to pot and gradually add cream. *Do not boil.* Garnish with parsley.

Barbara Alguire ♦ *Delta, Ontario*

Kohlrabi Soup

"Should anyone ever ask, 'What do you do with kohlrabi?', pass on this wonderful recipe." The turniplike vegetable that looks like a spaceship becomes buttery in this soup, which is scented with caraway. With a slice of rye or whole-grain bread, it makes a filling meal.

♦

Yield: 6-8 servings
Preparation time: 3 hours

♦

1½-2 lbs.	meaty beef shinbones
1	medium onion, chopped
1	bay leaf
1 Tbsp.	caraway seed
1 tsp.	salt
6	whole peppercorns
3-4	kohlrabi, with tops
1	large potato, diced
2	large carrots, diced
3 Tbsp.	butter
4 Tbsp.	flour

Bring 3 qts. water to a boil in a 6-qt. pot. Add beef, onion, bay leaf, caraway seed, salt and peppercorns. Cover, lower heat, and cook for about 2 hours.

Peel and dice kohlrabi, coarsely shred the young tender leaves, discarding stems and yellow or tough outer leaves. When the meat is cooked, add the vegetables except kohlrabi leaves, and continue cooking for another ½ hour, or until vegetables are tender. Remove from heat, cut meat from bones, and return meat to the soup with kohlrabi leaves, discarding bone.

In a saucepan, melt butter, add flour and sauté until golden. Immediately remove from heat. Add approximately 1 cup of broth from soup, stirring quickly to prevent lumps. Add to soup, stirring. Reheat and adjust seasonings.

Helen Wedgwood ◆ *Wildwood, Alberta*

Not-That-Authentic Portuguese Kale Soup

Linguica is a milder sausage than chorizo; either may be used.

Perhaps not, but it was a hit with our tester, who reports that it is "simply good food."

◆

Yield: 6-8 servings
Preparation time: ¾ hour, longer if dried beans are used

◆

1 lb.	linguica or chorizo sausage
1 cup	finely chopped onion
1 tsp.	finely chopped garlic
3 Tbsp.	olive oil
2 qts.	chicken, beef or vegetable stock
4	medium potatoes, scrubbed and diced
1 cup	carrots, scrubbed and cut into rounds

9	plum tomatoes, chopped
1 cup	red or white kidney beans, cooked and drained
½ lb.	fresh kale, cut in ½" slices
	vinegar

Prick sausage in several places with a fork. Cover with water and simmer for 15 minutes. Drain, slice thinly and set aside.

In a Dutch oven, sauté onions and garlic in olive oil for 5 minutes. Add stock, potatoes and carrots. Simmer for 15 minutes. If tomatoes are canned, drain and chop them. Add tomatoes, beans, kale and sausage to the pot, and simmer for 15 minutes more. Add ½ tsp. vinegar to each bowl just before serving.

Donna Herlihy ◆ *Ashland, New Hampshire*

Hearty Cabbage Soup

"I usually make this soup in the fall, using up the extra cabbage and tomatoes in the garden. A food processor is an invaluable tool in making it." The vegetables maintain a pleasing crispness, while blending nicely with the beefy base.

◆

Yield: 6-8 servings
Preparation time: 3¾ hours

◆

1 lb.	lean ground beef
1-2	large onions, chopped
2 cloves	garlic, minced
½ cup	diced celery
1	green pepper, chopped
2 Tbsp.	oil
28-oz. can	tomatoes, or 2 lbs. fresh, or 2 cups frozen
2 5½-oz. cans	tomato paste
2 cups	raw, diced potatoes
2 cups	diced carrots
4 cups	beef stock
	salt & pepper to taste
	paprika
6-7 cups	coarsely chopped cabbage

Sauté beef, onions, garlic, celery and pepper in oil. Add remaining ingredients except cabbage. Simmer, uncovered, for 1 hour. Add cabbage. Simmer for 1 hour more, adding more water, up to 3 cups, if necessary.

Susan Cox ◆ *Waterloo, Ontario*

Turnip-Cheese Soup

This harvest soup has a creamy texture and a distinctive flavor that melds when chilled and reheated.

◆

Yield: 6 servings
Preparation time: ½ hour

◆

1	large potato, peeled and diced
3 cups	diced yellow turnip
1 cup	fresh or frozen peas
2 Tbsp.	butter
2	medium onions, finely chopped
	salt & pepper
2-3 cups	milk
1 cup	grated sharp Cheddar cheese (preferably white)
	dillweed

Simmer potato and turnip in 1½ cups water for 5 minutes. Drain, reserving liquid. Cook peas and set aside.

Melt butter in a Dutch oven. Add onion and cook over medium heat until soft, about 4 minutes. Add 1 cup of reserved cooking liquid, potato, turnip, salt and pepper. Cover pan and simmer until vegetables are very tender, about 10 minutes.

Cool slightly, and pour into blender or food processor and process until smooth. Thin to desired consistency with milk. Return soup to pot and add cheese and peas. Heat over low heat, stirring until cheese has melted. Spoon into bowls and garnish with dill and a little additional grated cheese, if desired.

Ann Budge ◆ Belfountain, Ontario

Curried Butternut Squash Soup

Suggested Accompaniment:
Oatmeal Biscuits, page 225.

Butternut squash, curry and apple juice blend perfectly in this refreshing soup, garnished with Granny Smith apples.

◆

Yield: 4-6 servings
Preparation time: 1¼ hours

◆

4 Tbsp.	sweet butter
2 cups	finely chopped onion
4-5 tsp.	curry powder

2	medium-sized butternut squash (3 lbs.), peeled and cubed
3 cups	chicken stock
2	apples, peeled and chopped
1 cup	apple juice
	salt & pepper to taste
	Granny Smith apples, unpeeled, grated

Melt butter, add onions and curry powder and simmer, covered, on a low heat for about 25 minutes. Add squash, stock and chopped apples. Bring to a boil, lower heat and simmer for 25 minutes. Puree soup, add apple juice, season and reheat. Garnish with grated apple.

Diana Williams ◆ *Lethbridge, Alberta*

Cream of Pumpkin Soup

Hearty and quickly put together, this soup acquires satisfying depth from brandy and tomatoes.

◆

Yield: 6-8 servings
Preparation time: 25 minutes

◆

4 cups	cubed potatoes
½ cup	finely sliced onion
1 Tbsp.	chopped green pepper
¼ cup	butter
2 Tbsp.	flour
2½ cups	milk
½ cup	brandy (optional)
1½ cups	canned tomatoes
¾ cup	pumpkin puree
1½ tsp.	salt
dash	pepper
1 cup	grated sharp cheese
	fresh parsley

Preparation Hint: This soup freezes well; use a double-boiler to reheat it.

Cook potatoes, onion and green pepper in ¼ cup water in a Dutch oven for 10 minutes. Add butter. Blend flour and 1¼ cups cold water and add gradually, stirring. Add remaining ingredients except cheese and parsley. Bring just to a boil, lower heat and simmer 20 minutes. Sprinkle with cheese and parsley.

Helen Keillor ◆ *Berwyn, Alberta*

Savory Pumpkin Soup

See photo page 76.

"**A** savory, bright and cheerful fall soup, livened with chicken broth, orange juice and a hint of ginger. This is a newcomer, but one we like."

♦

Yield: 4 servings
Preparation time: 25 minutes

♦

2 Tbsp.	butter
1	small onion, finely chopped
2 cups	orange juice
1½ cups	cooked, pureed pumpkin, fresh or canned
1 cup	milk
1¼ cups	chicken stock
1 tsp.	grated orange rind
1 tsp.	ground ginger
½ tsp.	salt
pinch	pepper
¼ cup	pumpkin or sunflower seeds
4	orange slices

In a large saucepan, melt 1 Tbsp. butter, and sauté onion until soft. Stir in remaining ingredients except pumpkin seeds and orange slices. Simmer, covered, for 10 minutes.

In the meantime, in a small saucepan melt the remaining butter and sauté the pumpkin seeds until lightly toasted. Drain on paper towels. Ladle soup into warmed bowls. Garnish with an orange slice and pumpkin seeds.

Irene Louden ♦ Port Coquitlam, British Columbia

Smoked Ham & Pumpkin Soup

Pumpkin, smoked ham, cumin and Marsala wine make this soup rich, smooth and pleasantly smoky. Don't limit it to harvesttime; canned pumpkin may be substituted for fresh, with considerable savings in preparation time.

♦

Yield: 6 servings
Preparation time: ¾-1¼ hours

♦

4 Tbsp.	butter
6 cups	peeled, chopped, fresh pumpkin, or 29-oz. canned
6 cups	chicken stock

½ cup	Marsala wine
1 tsp.	cumin
	salt & pepper
½ lb.	smoked ham, cut into small pieces
	toasted pumpkin seeds

Melt butter in a large pot over medium heat. Add pumpkin and cook approximately 15 minutes to soften. Add chicken stock, cover, and continue cooking about 30 minutes, or until pumpkin is tender (if using canned pumpkin, omit this step).

Add wine, cumin and salt and pepper to taste. Puree soup in the blender until smooth. Return to pot and add ham. Simmer another 10 minutes. Garnish with toasted pumpkin seeds. Serve immediately.

TOASTED PUMPKIN SEEDS

	pumpkin seeds
2 Tbsp.	peanut oil
	sea salt

Scoop all the seeds out of pumpkin. Wash them to remove the pulp and dry with paper towels. Spread on a cookie sheet and dry for 2 hours. Sprinkle oil and sea salt over the seeds. Toast in oven, stirring every few minutes, until they are golden brown—approximately 25 minutes. Let cool. Add more salt if necessary.

Lucia Cyre ◆ *Logan Lake, British Columbia*

Leek & Potato Pressure Cooker Soup

Using a pressure cooker distributes the flavors in this colorful soup and speeds its making.

◆

Yield: 4-6 servings
Preparation time: 1 hour

◆

2 cups	leeks, well washed and finely chopped
2 cups	potatoes, washed and chopped into ½" cubes
1 cup	chopped or sliced carrot
1-2 tsp.	marjoram
1-2 tsp.	savory
1-2 tsp.	rosemary
1-1½ tsp.	salt
½ tsp.	pepper
2 Tbsp.	flour
1-2 cups	milk or stock from soup

Place vegetables, herbs, salt and pepper into pressure cooker. Cover with water. Cook under pressure, with top rocking slowly, for 7 to 10 minutes. Mix flour and milk and shake together in a jar to remove any lumps. Add to cooker. Cook over medium heat, stirring gently, until heated through.

Jeanne Lambert ◆ *Bishops Mills, Ontario*

Australian Leek & Carrot Soup

Suggested Accompaniment:
Honey-Mustard & Cheddar Muffins, page 229.

"This soup was given to me by Australian friends and quickly became a favorite with our family." Although pureed, it is substantial.

◆

Yield: 6 servings
Preparation time: 1¼ hours

◆

½ cup	chopped celery
4 or 5	leeks, sliced
4 Tbsp.	butter
1 cup	thinly sliced carrots
1 tsp.	salt
¼ tsp.	white pepper
3 cups	milk
1½ Tbsp.	flour
2 Tbsp.	minced parsley
	grated raw carrot

Sauté celery and leeks in 2 Tbsp. of butter for 10 minutes in a heavy pot. Add carrots and sauté 5 minutes longer. Sprinkle with salt and pepper. Add milk and simmer, covered, for 30 minutes, stirring occasionally.

Cool slightly, puree in a food processor or blender. Melt remaining 2 Tbsp. butter in pot, add flour and cook, stirring, for a few minutes. Stir in pureed vegetables and simmer for a few minutes more. Thin with milk if necessary, and adjust seasonings. Garnish with parsley and grated carrot.

Mary E. Bailey ◆ *Lethbridge, Alberta*

This authentic Ukrainian borscht is soured the old-fashioned way with the liquid from fermented beets, which is added at the last minute to maintain its brilliant color. Our tester, whose mother was born and raised in the Ukraine, said this soup put her in touch with her heritage and persuaded her to renounce her mother's less traditional recipe.

Borscht with Beet Kvas

◆

Yield: 8-10 servings
Preparation time: 2½ hours plus 5-6 days for kvas

◆

Lemon juice may be substituted for kvas.

BEET KVAS

12	medium-sized beets, washed and peeled
1 slice	sour rye bread

Cut the beets into eighths. Place in a crock and cover with boiled water cooled to lukewarm. Add a slice of sour rye bread to aid fermentation. Cover and keep at room temperature for several days.

When the liquid is sour, pour it off into jars, discarding beets. Put lids on the jars and keep refrigerated.

Preparation Hint: "Add the kvas to the borscht during the last few minutes of cooking. Too much boiling destroys its brilliant color."

BORSCHT

1½ lbs.	beef soup meat with bone
1 small piece	lean pork
1 small piece	smoked pork (optional)
1 tsp.	salt
2	large beets
1	carrot
1	medium onion, chopped
1	large potato, diced
1 stalk	celery, sliced
½ cup	diced string beans
2 cups	shredded cabbage or sauerkraut
¾ cup	strained tomatoes or tomato juice
½ clove	garlic, crushed
1 Tbsp.	flour
	beet kvas and/or lemon juice
	salt & pepper
	chopped dill
½ cup	sour cream or thick sweet cream

Cover meats with 3 qts. water, add salt, bring to a boil and skim fat. Cover and simmer for 1½ hours. Remove bones.

Cut beets and carrots into julienne strips or grate. Add vegetables, tomato juice and garlic to broth and simmer until tender. Blend flour with a bit of cold water and add to the borscht. Add a small amount of beet kvas or lemon juice. The borscht should be slightly tart but not sour. Add salt and pepper and dill.

Before serving, stir in sour cream or thick sweet cream, or serve with a dollop of sour cream.

Cary Elizabeth Marshall ◆ Thunder Bay, Ontario

Fast Russian Borscht

See photo page 70.

Easy and quick, this soup is welcome in winter. It can be made in the fall and frozen, with sour cream added during the reheating.

◆

Yield: 6 servings
Preparation time: 1 hour

◆

2 cups	shredded fresh beets
1 cup	shredded carrots
1 cup	shredded cabbage
1 cup	chopped onion
2 cups	beef stock
1 Tbsp.	butter
1 Tbsp.	lemon juice
	sour cream

Cook beets, carrots, cabbage and onions in 2½ cups boiling salted water for 20 minutes. Add beef stock and butter. Simmer 15 minutes. Stir in lemon juice. Serve hot or chilled topped with sour cream.

Wendy Hobsbawn ◆ Golden Lake, Ontario

Borscht with Broad Beans

Young rhubarb, broad beans and beets make this vegetable soup tart and robust.

◆

Yield: 8 servings
Preparation time: 3 hours, plus overnight

◆

½ cup	broad beans
1	medium onion, diced
1 clove	garlic, finely diced
1	tomato, chopped
4 Tbsp.	butter
1 lb.	beef soup bones
1 lb.	pork neck bones or spareribs
3-4	large beets, cut into thin strips
1	carrot, diced
1	potato, peeled and diced
¼ cup	chopped celery leaves
2 stalks	young rhubarb, diced (lemon juice may be substituted)
¼ cup	chopped parsley
2 Tbsp.	finely chopped dill
¼ cup	chopped chives
2	bay leaves
3	whole peppercorns
1 cup	shredded cabbage
1 cup	peas
½ cup	mushrooms
½ cup	sour cream
	salt & pepper

Wash beans and soak them overnight. Drain.

In a Dutch oven, sauté onions, garlic and tomato in butter. Wash beef and pork bones and add them to the pot with beans, beets, carrot, potato, celery leaves, rhubarb, seasonings. Cover with 8 to 10 cups of water, and simmer, covered, for 2 to 3 hours. Remove bones and add cabbage, peas and mushrooms. Stir in sour cream, and cook briefly but do not boil. Adjust seasonings.

Anne Mychajluk ◆ Calgary, Alberta

Preparation Hint: "The tartness of this soup may be increased by adding more rhubarb or lemon juice."

BEANS & GRAINS

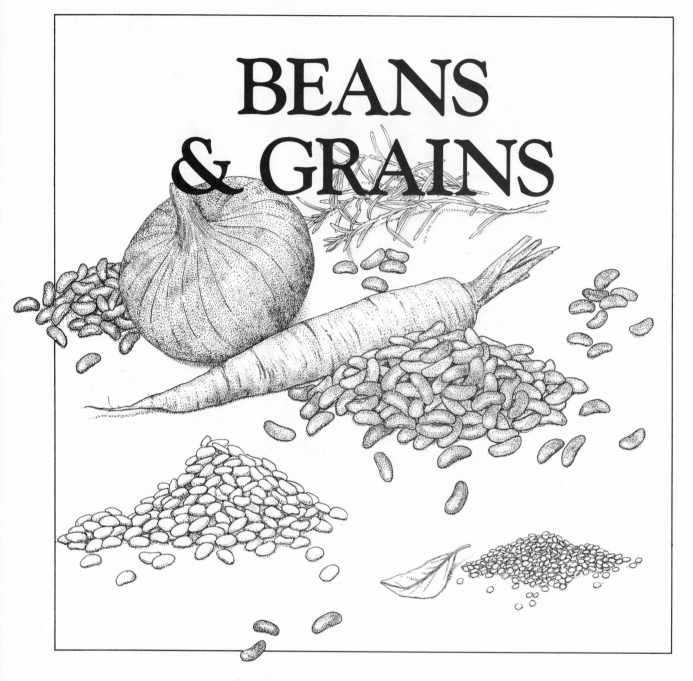

"I wish I had time for just one more bowl of chili . . ."

Kit Carson
His (alleged) last words

Mary North Allen lived in the Wisconsin country-side and tended to a large tract of land, a rambling house, three children and an ever-changing number of domestic animals. Her solution to the demands of country life was to throw seasonal "work parties" and invite some 25 able-bodied friends from the nearby university for a Sunday of wood-stacking or canning in exchange for country air and a good meal. While we worked, Mary played general contractor and cook.

Though my friend could tease a whole dinner out of beans and grains, bulgur pilaf was her trademark and the foundation of her work-party suppers. Nutty and persistently fluffy, it represented the changing seasons with combinations of snap peas and asparagus, broccoli and tomato, turnips and carrots, or apples and sausage. In addition to the pilaf, a fall dinner at Mary's might include mushroom-barley soup, lemony lentil salad, warm, whole-grain breads and bottles of Chianti, followed by flats of oatmeal-and-apple crisp. Such a meal would have been impossible without the dozens of glass jars lining the pantry: bulgur, barley, oats, lentils, wheat berries, rice and a variety of dried beans.

Because they can be stored in cool, dry places for long periods of time, dried beans, peas and grains are convenience foods of very high quality. Moist-heat methods of cooking, of course, are not only ideal but mandatory for them. In risottos, pilafs, Tex-Mex chilis, baked beans and cassoulets, beans, rice and other grains provide substantial nourishment at a negligible caloric price. Eaten together, in dishes like Aromatic Lentils & Rice or Couscous with Chick-peas & Summer Vegetables, beans and grains supply completely balanced protein.

Legumes—dried beans and peas—in particular are held in the highest esteem by nutritionists. According to recent findings, they contain substances that dissolve fat globules in the veins and arteries and are credited with lowering blood cholesterol.

Unfortunately, though, dried beans and peas are also high in complex sugars called olio-saccharides, which break down in the digestive tract and are eaten by bacteria that generate carbon dioxide gas. Navy beans and dried limas are the worst offenders in producing gas, but if some simple steps are taken, much of the gas can be eliminated. All beans, except lentils, black-eyed peas and split peas, should be soaked for at least four to five hours, or preferably overnight, and the soaking water should be changed several times. Before cooking, the beans should be rinsed and brought to a boil and the cooking water discarded.

If necessary, the soaking time may be shortened by washing the beans and boiling them for 10 minutes, then draining and soaking them in fresh water for 30 minutes to an hour, or longer if time permits. Black beans, it should be emphasized, are especially slow to absorb water and should be soaked at least overnight.

The cardinal rule when cooking beans is to have patience: a rushed bean is a hard, flavorless, gaseous bean. Salt and acidic ingredients like tomatoes, pineapple, lemon juice and vinegar should not be added to the pot until the beans are tender, because they can toughen the skins and prevent the absorption of water. Contrary to popular mythology, baking soda should never be added to beans: it makes them mushy and destroys their nutrients.

Among the rices, brown is the most nutritious, for it contains large reserves of B-complex vitamins—riboflavin, B_6, thiamine and niacin—as well as abundant fiber. Brown basmati rice, a long-grained variety, which is imported from India, has a delicate, nutty flavor and a dry texture that makes it a perfect choice for vegetable pilafs. As it cooks, it sends up inviting clouds of steam with the scent of new-mown hay and nuts.

"Converted" (an Uncle Ben's trademark), or parboiled, rice is the most nutritious of the white rices and is also a good choice for pilafs, in which the grains should remain firm and separate. Before the bran of converted rice is milled, the rice is steamed under pressure, a process that leaves it raw but drives the B vitamins deep into the grain.

For risottos, the creamy Italian rice dish in which the liquid is incorporated gradually by stirring, and for Spanish paellas, Arborio rice, a short-grain variety imported from the Mediterranean, is the traditional choice. It has stubby grains, a compact texture and a cereal-like flavor.

Despite the differences in their preparation and textures, pilafs, paellas and risottos are versatile dishes, accommodating almost infinite combinations of vegetables, seafood and meat, according to the demands of the season, the pantry and one's own appetite.

—JoAnne B. Cats-Baril

Fruited Chili

Prunes and apples add sweetness to this mellow chili garnished with almonds.

◆

Yield: 6 servings
Preparation time: 1 hour

◆

2	large onions, chopped
3 stalks	celery, thinly sliced
2	green, red or yellow sweet peppers, chopped
2 cloves	garlic, finely chopped
3 Tbsp.	oil
2 lbs.	lean ground beef
2 14-oz. cans	kidney beans
26-oz. can	tomatoes
5½-oz. can	tomato paste
2 Tbsp.	chili powder
1 cup	quartered, pitted prunes
2	unpeeled green apples, chopped
½ tsp.	freshly grated nutmeg
½ cup	toasted slivered almonds

In a Dutch oven, sauté onions, celery, peppers and garlic in oil until just tender. Remove from pan and brown ground beef, stirring. Drain fat, if necessary. Combine onion mixture and meat. Add beans, tomatoes, tomato paste, chili powder and prunes, and simmer for 30 minutes. Stir frequently to prevent prunes from sticking to bottom. Add apples and nutmeg. Simmer for 10 minutes. Just before serving, add almonds.

Lori Messer ◆ *Sooke, British Columbia*

Jackie's Homemade Chili

Cashews and raisins take the place of meat in this chili.

◆

Yield: 12 servings
Preparation time: 3½ hours plus overnight

◆

4 cups	dry kidney beans
2 Tbsp.	olive oil
1½ cups	chopped celery
1½ cups	chopped green pepper
1 cup	chopped onion

3-4 cloves	garlic, chopped
½ cup	raisins
2 qt.	tomatoes, undrained
1 qt.	tomato juice
1 pt.	tomato sauce
¼ cup	red wine
2-3 Tbsp.	chili powder
1 Tbsp.	snipped parsley
2 tsp.	salt
2 tsp.	chopped fresh basil, or 1½ tsp. dried
2 tsp.	chopped fresh oregano, or 1½ tsp. dried
1½ tsp.	ground cumin
1 tsp.	ground allspice
¼-½ tsp.	pepper
1	bay leaf
¼-½ tsp.	bottled hot pepper sauce, or to taste
¾ cup	cashew nuts
1 cup	shredded Swiss, mozzarella or Cheddar cheese

Soak beans overnight; cook and set aside.

Heat oil in 4½-qt. Dutch oven. Add celery, green pepper, onion and garlic, and sauté, covered, until vegetables are tender but not brown. Stir in drained beans, raisins, tomatoes, tomato juice, tomato sauce, wine, and seasonings, including hot sauce. Bring to a boil, reduce heat and simmer, covered, for at least 2 hours.

Stir in cashews, return to boiling; simmer, uncovered, 30 minutes longer, or until chili is desired consistency. Remove bay leaf. Sprinkle cheese atop each serving.

Jackie Darrow ◆ Iowa City, Iowa

"This soup has everything to recommend it: it is delicious, nourishing, inexpensive, easy to make, has plenty of vitamins and fiber, and it freezes beautifully." The lentils dissolve during the cooking, thickening the soup nicely.

◆

Yield: 8 servings
Preparation time: 1 hour

◆

Brown Rice & Lentil Soup

Lentils do not need to be soaked before cooking.

1½ cups	diced carrots
1 cup	chopped onion
½ cup	chopped celery
1 cup	sliced mushrooms
3 cloves	garlic, chopped
8 cups	chicken or vegetable stock
14-oz. can	tomatoes, coarsely chopped
1½ cups	red lentils
1 cup	uncooked brown rice
1½ tsp.	dried basil
1½ tsp.	dried thyme
1½ tsp.	dried oregano
½ tsp.	dried hot red pepper flakes
2	bay leaves
	salt & pepper to taste
½ cup	chopped parsley

In a large kettle, combine vegetables, stock, tomatoes, lentils, rice and herbs except for the parsley. Bring to a boil and simmer, stirring occasionally, for about 35 minutes, or until the lentils and rice are tender. Season with salt and pepper, remove the bay leaves, add the parsley and serve.

Bernice Moir ◆ *West Vancouver, British Columbia*

Quebec Pea Soup with Red Lentils

Variation: Adzuki or lima beans may be added.

Lentils and barley make this pea soup a sturdy supper.

◆

Yield: 12 servings
Preparation time: 3 hours

◆

	meaty ham bone
3 cups	mixed yellow and green split peas
¾ cup	red lentils
¾ cup	barley or rice
2 cups	grated winter squash
1	large onion, diced
2 stalks	celery, diced
½ tsp.	ground cumin
¼ tsp.	ground marjoram
½-1 tsp.	salt, or to taste
	pepper

Place bone in 4 qts. water, bring to a boil and cook until meat is tender.

Strip meat from bone and return meat to pot. Add peas, lentils, barley or rice, vegetables and seasonings. Bring to boil, reduce heat and simmer about 2½ hours. Adjust seasonings.

Allison Harding ◆ *Ormstown, Quebec*

Italio-Lentil Soup

Hot Italian sausages give this soup proper zip.

◆

Yield: 10-12 servings
Preparation time: 2 hours

◆

2-4	Italian sausages
3 Tbsp.	olive oil
2 cloves	garlic, crushed
2	medium onions, chopped
2 tsp.	salt
	freshly ground pepper
2 tsp.	oregano
2 tsp.	basil
¼ cup	red wine vinegar
½-1 tsp.	Worcestershire sauce
1½ cups	lentils
1 cup	chopped celery
1 cup	chopped green peppers
1 cup	chopped carrots
1 cup	chopped zucchini
28-oz. can	tomatoes, or 1½ cups fresh
6-oz. can	tomato paste

Cut sausages into 1-inch pieces, fry in a Dutch oven over medium heat in 1 Tbsp. olive oil until brown. Drain fat. Add remaining 2 Tbsp. oil and fry with garlic and onions. Add 9 cups water, seasonings, wine vinegar, Worcestershire sauce and lentils, and simmer for 20 minutes. Add vegetables, tomatoes and tomato paste. Simmer gently for 1 hour, adding more water if necessary.

Harry & Beth Kope ◆ *Quebec City, Quebec*

Aromatic Lentils & Rice

Suggested Accompaniments:
Pita bread and a spoonful of
plain or spiced yogurt.

This spicy dish brings the lowly lentil to
new heights.

◆

Yield: 6-8 servings
Preparation time: 1½-2 hours

◆

2	onions (1 small, 1 medium)
½	hot red pepper
10	medium-sized fresh mushrooms
1" piece	fresh ginger, peeled
6-8 cloves	garlic
2 Tbsp.	oil
1 Tbsp.	cumin seeds
1 tsp.	cayenne, or to taste
½ tsp.	turmeric
½ tsp.	salt
2 tsp.	ground cumin
2 tsp.	ground coriander
1 tsp.	Hungarian paprika
1 cup	washed brown lentils
⅔ cup	basmati rice (or other long-grain rice)
2 cups	chicken stock
4	medium tomatoes, coarsely chopped
1	small green pepper, diced

SPICED YOGURT

1 Tbsp.	oil
1 Tbsp.	black mustard seeds
1	small onion, diced
pinch	curry powder
2 tsp.	ground coriander
½ tsp.	powdered ginger
1½ cups	plain yogurt

Place small onion, red pepper, 5 mushrooms, ginger, garlic and 3 Tbsp.
water in a blender or food processor, and puree until the mixture is a
paste. Set aside.

In a pot with a tight-fitting lid, heat oil and sauté cumin seeds, remaining
medium onion, coarsely chopped, and remaining mushrooms, coarsely
chopped. Add paste from the food processor along with cayenne, turmeric, salt, cumin, coriander and paprika. Simmer over medium heat 4 to
5 minutes. Add lentils, rice, chicken stock, tomatoes and green pepper.
Simmer about 30 minutes, or until liquid is absorbed. Serve with a dollop
of spiced yogurt.

To make spiced yogurt: In a frying pan, heat oil over medium heat and add black mustard seeds. When seeds begin to pop, add onion, curry, coriander and ginger. Stir, simmer for a few minutes, but do not boil. Remove from heat. Cool 5 minutes, then stir in yogurt. Refrigerate until ready to use.

Bonnie Lawson ◆ *Medicine Hat, Alberta*

Brazilian Black Bean Soup

Ever since I first tasted this sturdy soup at a friend's open house, I've loved its rich South American flavors. Black beans should be soaked for a generous amount of time—preferably overnight.

◆

Yield: 6-8 servings
Preparation time: 4¼ hours, plus soaking time

◆

2 cups	black beans, sorted and washed
3 cloves	garlic
1	large onion, chopped
2	large carrots, chopped
2 stalks	celery, chopped
1 Tbsp.	oil
1 qt.	canned tomatoes
1 tsp.	coriander powder
1½-2½ tsp.	ground cumin
1 Tbsp.	white vinegar
	salt & freshly ground black pepper
1-2 Tbsp.	dry sherry (optional)
	cayenne pepper (optional)
	sour cream

Soak black beans in water to cover for 5 hours or longer. Drain. Bring 5 cups of water to a boil and simmer beans approximately 2 hours. Sauté garlic, onion, carrots and celery in oil until softened. Add them to beans. Add tomatoes, coriander, cumin, vinegar, salt and pepper. Cook 1½ to 2 hours longer. Puree some of the soup in a blender and return to pot. Stir in sherry and cayenne, if desired, heat for a few minutes and serve. Garnish with sour cream.

Rux Martin ◆ *Underhill Center, Vermont*

Lebanese Black Bean Soup

Black beans can be found in health food stores.

This nutritious soup full of black beans, chick-peas, lentils and rice is flavored with caraway seeds.

◆

Yield: 8-10 servings
Preparation time: 3½ hours, plus overnight

◆

1 cup	black beans
1 cup	chick-peas, dried or canned
1 cup	lentils
½ tsp.	caraway seeds
3 qts.	chicken stock or water
2	onions, minced
2-4 cloves	garlic, crushed
¼-½ cup	olive oil
½ cup	brown rice
	salt & pepper to taste

Soak black beans and chick-peas (if dried are used) overnight in water to cover.

In the morning, drain beans and place in a heavy pot along with lentils, caraway seeds and 3 qts. chicken stock or water. Sauté onions and garlic in oil until browned. Add to beans. Bring to a boil, reduce heat and simmer several hours, until beans are tender. Add more water if necessary. Add rice during the last hour. Simmer until rice is cooked, and add salt and pepper to taste.

Cary Elizabeth Marshall ◆ *Thunder Bay, Ontario*

Tuscan Minestrone

"It was a trip to Tuscany that enlightened me about the variety of Italian food." Allow this thick soup plenty of time to simmer.

◆

Yield: 6-8 servings
Preparation time: 3½ hours, plus overnight

◆

3 cups	navy beans
½ cup	olive oil
5 cloves	garlic, peeled
1	onion, peeled and chopped
1	carrot, chopped
1 stalk	celery, chopped
2	leeks
1 tsp.	rosemary, or 1 sprig fresh

¼ tsp.	hot red pepper flakes
1	ham hock (optional)
½ lb.	fresh spinach, stems removed
	salt & pepper to taste
4 slices	dense bread, toasted
8 oz.	Parmesan cheese

Soak beans overnight and drain. Heat 3 Tbsp. olive oil in a large pot. Mince 3 cloves garlic and add to oil along with onion, carrot and celery. Trim roots and green tops from leeks. Slice in half lengthwise and rinse well to remove any grit. Chop and add to pot along with rosemary, red pepper, ham hock, beans and 2 qts. water. Simmer about 2 hours.

Remove ham bone. Strip meat from bone and reserve. In a blender, process half the soup, including broth, until smooth. Return it to pot. Chop spinach leaves and add to soup. Add salt, pepper and ham from bone; cook 10 minutes.

When ready to serve, heat remaining olive oil in small skillet. Add remaining garlic and cook slowly until it begins to brown. Remove garlic and discard. Add half the oil to the soup and stir. Place toast in the bottom of 4 large soup bowls. Top with soup and cheese. Spoon a little garlic oil on top.

Sarah Fritschner ◆ *Louisville, Kentucky*

Maple Baked Beans

"A variation of this dish was served at a Maple Syrup Tour at the Nova Scotia Agricultural College ten years ago and is now the only recipe I use for baked beans. The preparation of dried beans is my own method." The chunks of pork saturated with maple syrup are delicious.

◆

Yield: 1 bean pot
Preparation time: 5½ hours, plus overnight

◆

Suggested Accompaniment: Cabbage Apple Salad, page 222.

4 cups	dried white beans
½ cup	chili sauce
1 cup	maple syrup
1 Tbsp.	dry mustard
1 Tbsp.	salt
1	medium onion, diced
5 or 6 pieces	smoked pork (optional)

Rinse beans and soak in plenty of water overnight.

Drain beans and place in a Dutch oven, and add water to cover. Cover pot, bring to a boil and remove from heat. Let stand for 1 hour. Mix in remaining ingredients. Cover and bake in a bean pot at 300 degrees F for 4 hours, adding more water if needed.

Dianne Baker ◆ *Tatamagouche, Nova Scotia*

Family Reunion Beans

Chick-peas are a crunchy, pleasant change from the usual kidney beans, and are found in health food stores.

"These beans have delighted more than a few hungry crowds."

◆

Yield: 1 large bean pot
Preparation time: 7 hours, plus overnight

◆

2 cups	dried white pea beans
2 cups	dried chick-peas
2 Tbsp.	oil
2	large onions, chopped
6 cloves	garlic, minced
6-8 stalks	celery, chopped
12 slices	bacon (optional)
2 cups	tomato juice
¼ cup	brown sugar
⅓ cup	cider vinegar
⅓ cup	mustard powder
1 Tbsp.	salt, or to taste
1 tsp.	pepper
¼ tsp.	cloves
4	large tomatoes, peeled, seeded and chopped
2	large red peppers, chopped
1	large green pepper, chopped

Wash, pick over and soak beans and chick-peas overnight. The next day, drain, cover with fresh water, and simmer until skins are ready to "pop." Drain.

Put oil in large pot and sauté onion, garlic and celery until tender. Meanwhile, brown the bacon. To the sautéed vegetables add tomato juice, brown sugar, vinegar, mustard, salt, pepper, cloves, tomato, bacon and drained beans. Add enough water or tomato juice to cover beans. Stir, cover, and bake at 300 degrees F for 6 hours, or until beans are tender, adding more liquid if needed. Add chopped peppers during the last hour of cooking. If liquid is too thin, remove cover and bake until thickened.

Laurie Bradley ◆ *Surrey, British Columbia*

This rendition of cassoulet—a substantial bean casserole that is traditionally made with a variety of different meats—is hearty, nourishing country fare. Bread crumbs give a crusty thickness to the finished dish.

Cassoulet with Pork

♦

Yield: 8-10 servings
Preparation time: 3½ hours

♦

Preparation Hint: Cassoulet can be made and served the same day or assembled over a period of days with a final chilling in the refrigerator before baking.

2½-3-lb.	boned pork loin roast
4 Tbsp.	cooking oil
1	carrot, quartered
2	onions, quartered
9 cloves	garlic
3 cups	Great Northern beans
1 Tbsp.	salt
1 lb.	bacon
1 cup	sliced onions
1	bay leaf
3 sprigs	fresh thyme, or 1 Tbsp. dried
2	cloves
1 lb.	sausage meat, in patties or links, fried and drained
4 Tbsp.	tomato puree
2 cups	dry white wine
4 cups	beef stock
¾ tsp.	freshly ground pepper
1¼ cups	bread crumbs
4 Tbsp.	pork fat or melted butter

Dry pork thoroughly and brown on all sides in oil in a small casserole dish. Add carrot, quartered onions and 2 cloves crushed garlic. Cover, and roast at 325 degrees F for 1½ to 2 hours, or until the meat thermometer reads 175 degrees F. Discard vegetables, set meat aside, or refrigerate when finished.

Meanwhile, drop beans into 5 quarts boiling, salted water and boil for 2 minutes. Remove from heat and let sit for 1 hour more. While beans are soaking, cut bacon into 1½-inch pieces and blanch in boiling water for 5 minutes. Drain and return to pot with 1 qt. cold water; bring to a boil and simmer for 10 minutes more. Do not drain; set aside.

Add bacon and water, sliced onion, 4 cloves unpeeled garlic, bay leaf, thyme and cloves to beans and bring the pot back to a simmer. Simmer for 1½ hours. Meanwhile, fry sausage, drain and break or cut into bite-sized pieces. Cut pork roast into bite-sized pieces. Remove bacon from beans. Mix tomato puree, 3 cloves crushed garlic, wine, beef stock, 4 cups bean-cooking juices and pepper; set aside.

To assemble, choose an attractive 8-qt. oven-to-table casserole dish (if you have a glazed pottery ovenproof dish, use it). Put a layer of beans on the bottom of the dish, next a layer of pork and sausage, then beans, and so on, ending with beans. Pour the tomato liquid mixture over top, enough to come to the top layer of beans. Reserve the extra liquid, if there is any, to add as needed during the final baking period.

Mix bread crumbs with pork fat or melted butter and sprinkle over the top of the casserole. Bake for 1 hour in a preheated, 375-degree F oven. Every 20 minutes, stir the crust that forms on the top into the casserole and add a few spoonfuls of reserved liquids if necessary. Serve from the casserole dish with the final crust intact.

JoAnne B. Cats-Baril ◆ *Charlotte, Vermont*

Garden Paella

Arborio rice, such as Tesori, is best for this paella.

This quick and colorful summer meal uses Italian short-grain rice, which absorbs flavors, yet remains firm. Long-grain white rice can be substituted.

◆

Yield: 6 servings
Preparation time: ¾ hour

◆

¼ lb.	fresh green beans, whole or cut into 2" lengths
2	carrots, scraped and cut on the diagonal into ⅜" slices
4 Tbsp.	olive oil
1	large onion, chopped
1	large green or red pepper, chopped into 1½" pieces
1	jalapeño pepper, minced
2 cups	white rice, preferably short-grain
2	large tomatoes, chopped
¼ tsp.	saffron
4 cups	vegetable or chicken stock
1 tsp.	salt
¼ tsp.	cayenne pepper
½ cup	blanched slivered almonds
4 large cloves	garlic
½ cup	minced parsley
⅔ cup	peas, fresh or frozen
2	zucchini, cut into 1" chunks
2	hard-boiled eggs, cut in wedges
1	lemon, cut in wedges

Preheat oven to 350 degrees F. Blanch beans and carrots in boiling water until they are crisp-tender. Refresh in cold water, drain and set aside.

Heat 3 Tbsp. of oil in a skillet and sauté onion and peppers briefly. Add rice and sauté until translucent. Add tomatoes and saffron, and cook 5 minutes, stirring. Add stock, salt and cayenne, and bring to a boil. Cook on medium-high heat, stirring occasionally with a fork, until most of the liquid has been absorbed but the rice is still moist.

Meanwhile, chop almonds and garlic, and mix with parsley. Using a fork, gently stir garlic-parsley mixture, beans, carrots and peas into rice. Bake in the oven, uncovered, for 10 minutes, until the liquid is absorbed.

Sauté zucchini in remaining 1 Tbsp. of oil. Five minutes before the dish is done, place the zucchini on the rice and continue baking. Remove from oven, cover with foil and let stand 5 to 10 minutes.

Garnish with wedges of hard-boiled eggs and squeeze lemon juice on before serving.

Rux Martin ◆ Underhill Center, Vermont

Seafood Risotto

Risotto, an Italian rice dish, goes against everything American cooks have been taught about cooking rice. Made with a short-grain Italian variety called Arborio, and stirred constantly during its preparation, it becomes rich and creamy. A properly made risotto is not only filling but very good for you, for it is chock-full of protein and complex carbohydrates.

◆

Yield: 4 servings
Preparation time: 1½ hours

◆

12	clams, in shells
12	mussels, in shells
4 Tbsp.	olive oil
½ lb.	mushrooms, sliced
½ lb.	skinless, boneless monkfish
4 cups	fish stock, or 2 cups bottled clam juice mixed with 2 cups water
2 Tbsp.	butter
½ cup	minced onion
2 cloves	garlic, minced
2 cups	Arborio rice
½ cup	dry white wine
¼ cup	Parmesan cheese

Arborio rice may be obtained in health food stores or Italian specialty shops.

Scrub clams and mussels well, being careful to remove all grit. Remove beards from the mussels. Place in a colander and rinse under cold water. Transfer shellfish to a large pot with 1 cup water. Cover the pot and bring water to a boil. Simmer about 5 minutes, or until the shells open (large shellfish may take slightly longer). Discard any shells that do not open. Remove meat from shells and strain liquid through a clean dishtowel set in a strainer; set aside.

Heat 2 Tbsp. oil in a skillet. Add mushrooms. Fry over high heat about 3 minutes. Set aside with seafood. Cut fish in chunks and heat in same skillet about 3 minutes. Set aside.

Combine stock with strained liquid from steaming mussels and clams. Simmer on top of stove. Heat butter and remaining oil in large, heavy saucepan; fry onion and garlic until softened.

Add rice and stir to coat all over. Add wine and stir until it is completely absorbed. Add simmering stock, ½ cup at a time, stirring frequently. Wait until the liquid is absorbed before adding another ½ cup. Keep stirring and adding liquid for about 25 minutes. The rice should be tender but still firm. Stir in seafood, mushrooms and cheese.

Sarah Fritschner ◆ Louisville, Kentucky

Basmati Pilaf with Asparagus & Scallions

Basmati rice, which is available from health food stores, should be soaked overnight, or for at least half an hour.

This meal of rice and asparagus, garnished with almonds, gets high marks both for nutrition and taste.

◆

Yield: 4 servings
Preparation time: 1 hour

◆

3 Tbsp.	butter
1	medium onion, chopped
1 cup	brown basmati rice, or other brown long-grain, rinsed, soaked and drained (measure before soaking)
1	bay leaf
¼ tsp.	leaf thyme
2¼ cups	chicken or vegetable stock
½ tsp.	salt
¼ tsp.	white pepper
¼ cup	blanched, slivered almonds
8 spears	asparagus, chopped into 2" pieces
3	scallions, cut into 1" pieces
1 Tbsp.	yogurt

Preheat oven to 350 degrees F. Melt 2 Tbsp. butter in an ovenproof dish and sauté onion until softened. Add rice, bay leaf and thyme, and sauté until rice is whitened, about 5 minutes. Stir in stock, salt and pepper, and bring to boil. Stir lightly with a fork. Discard bay leaf. Cover the skillet tightly with foil and a lid, and bake in oven for 30 minutes.

Remove from oven and let stand, covered, 10 minutes. Toast almonds in a pan in the oven until tan, about 5 minutes. Blanch asparagus in water until just tender. Refresh with cold water and drain. Sauté asparagus and scallions in remaining 1 Tbsp. butter. With a fork, gently stir yogurt, asparagus stems and scallions into the rice. Garnish with asparagus tips and toasted almonds.

Rux Martin ◆ *Underhill Center, Vermont*

Chicken Pilaf with Asparagus & Mussels

This colorful, delicious spring supper contrasts glossy black mussels with saffron-yellow rice, red pepper and spokes of green asparagus.

◆

Yield: 4-6 servings
Preparation time: 50 minutes

◆

4 Tbsp.	olive oil
4	chicken breasts, skinned, cut into serving pieces
1	large sweet red pepper, chopped
1	medium onion, chopped
3 large cloves	garlic, minced
½ tsp.	saffron
2 cups	long-grain white rice
3 cups	chicken stock
½ cup	white wine
2 tsp.	salt
½ tsp.	cayenne pepper
	black pepper to taste
8-10 spears	fresh asparagus
12-18	fresh mussels, in shell (optional)

Saffron, from the stigma of the Spanish mountain crocus, has a rich, delicately spicy flavor and yellow hue and is particularly good in seafood and chicken dishes.

Preheat oven to 325 degrees F. Heat olive oil in large skillet and sauté chicken breasts until brown and nearly cooked through. Set aside.

Add sweet pepper, onion, garlic and saffron, and cook until vegetables are softened. Stir in rice and cook for a few minutes, until translucent. Add stock, wine, salt, cayenne and black pepper, bring to a boil and cook over medium heat, stirring occasionally with a fork, for 5 to 7 minutes, until most of the water has been absorbed but the rice is not dry.

Blanch asparagus in boiling water until just tender. Refresh in cold water. Bury chicken in the rice, and place mussels around the outside of the pan, half-buried in rice, with the edge that will open facing up. Bake, uncovered, for 18 minutes, or until mussels have opened. During the last 5 minutes, place asparagus on top of the rice, tips pointing outward. Cover with foil and let sit 5 minutes.

Rux Martin ◆ *Underhill Center, Vermont*

Seafood Paella

"A colorful dish that is elegant enough to serve for company, this paella adapts well to substitutions. The paprika imparts a hotter bite than the more expensive, traditional saffron."

◆

Yield: 6 servings
Preparation time: 2 hours

◆

6½ cups	chicken stock
1 bunch plus 5 Tbsp.	parsley
½ tsp.	thyme
1	onion, peeled
6	peppercorns
	salt to taste
¼-⅓ cup	olive oil
6	chicken thighs, skinned
½ lb.	ham, cut into 1" pieces
¾ lb.	firm-fleshed fish, such as halibut, shark or swordfish
1 lb.	shrimp
1	green pepper, chopped
1-2	small dried hot red peppers, crumbled
4 cloves	garlic, minced
1	medium tomato, sliced
3 cups	white rice, preferably short-grain
2 tsp.	paprika
2 cups	lima beans or peas
1 lb.	fresh small littleneck clams in shell, or mussels in shell
1 bunch	scallions, chopped

Variations: Italian sausage or pieces of pepperoni may be used in place of ham, along with whatever fish and shellfish are available.

Simmer stock with 1 bunch parsley, thyme, onion, peppercorns and salt. Preheat oven to 325 degrees F.

Heat olive oil in skillet and sauté chicken on high heat until golden. Set aside and keep warm. Sauté ham lightly and set aside. Cut fish into pieces, sauté briefly and set aside. Sauté shrimp just until they turn pink and add to the other meats and fish.

Sauté green and red peppers, garlic and tomato in the oil. Stir in rice, adding more oil if necessary, so it does not stick to the pan and burn. Sauté about 5 minutes, stirring, until it is translucent. Add strained stock, 5 Tbsp. parsley, paprika and lima beans. Cook, stirring occasionally, for about 10 minutes, until most of the liquid has been absorbed but some remains.

Spoon into a wide baking pan (an earthenware casserole dish is excellent for this). Bury the chicken, ham, fish and shrimp in the rice, and poke the clams or mussels in so their shells are pointing upward. Bake, uncovered, in the oven for 20 minutes, or until shells open. Remove from oven and cover with foil. Let sit 10 minutes before serving. Serve garnished with chopped scallions.

Rux Martin ◆ Underhill Center, Vermont

Preparation Hint: Scrub clams and mussels well and remove beards from mussels before adding them to paella.

Couscous with Chick-Peas & Summer Vegetables

Couscous, a staple in Morocco, Algeria, Tunisia and Egypt, is a fine grain made of semolina. It is nourishing, easily digested and found in most supermarkets near the rice.

◆

Yield: 4-6 servings
Preparation time: 1½ hours

◆

4 cups	vegetable or chicken stock
½ tsp.	cumin
1 Tbsp.	grated ginger, or 1 tsp. powdered ginger
½ tsp.	turmeric
¼ tsp.	saffron
2 cloves	garlic, chopped
2 lbs.	cubed chicken
1	leek, sliced
8	white onions
3 stalks	celery, chopped
1	large carrot, sliced
1	zucchini, sliced
1	summer squash, sliced
3	tomatoes, cubed
½ lb.	mushrooms, sliced
19-oz. can	chick-peas, drained
1 cup	couscous

HOT SAUCE
2 Tbsp. cayenne pepper
1 Tbsp. olive oil
1½ tsp. coriander powder

Boil cayenne and 3 Tbsp. water briefly, then stir in oil and coriander.

Place stock in a large pot, add spices, including garlic, and simmer ½ hour. Bring to boil, add chicken, leek, onions and celery, boil for 15 minutes. Add remaining ingredients except couscous, reduce heat, and simmer 30 to 45 minutes. Serve over couscous, with hot sauce on the side.

To make couscous: Boil 2 cups water; whisk in couscous, cover and set aside until water is absorbed, stirring once.

Melissa McClelland ◆ *Burlington, Vermont*

Meat & Fruit Pilaf, Indian-Style

This extraordinary dish of Indian origin is a type of biryani, or mixture of fruit, nuts, meat and rice. It can easily become the centerpiece of an elegant buffet.

◆

Yield: 6-8 servings
Preparation time: 1 hour

◆

¼ cup	butter
2	onions, chopped
1" piece	ginger, peeled and finely chopped
1 clove	garlic, finely chopped
1 tsp.	ground cumin
1 Tbsp.	coriander seeds, crushed
1 tsp.	cardamom seeds, crushed
1 tsp.	peppercorns, crushed
3"-long	cinnamon stick
1 lb.	boned leg of lamb, cut into ¾" cubes
4 oz.	dried apricots, cut in half
4 oz.	sultana raisins
2 oz.	cashew nuts, slit in half
2 oz.	slivered almonds
2	bay leaves
2 tsp.	salt, or to taste
2 cups	chicken stock
2 cups	basmati rice, washed, soaked in cold water for 30 minutes, and drained
3 Tbsp.	butter, melted
½ tsp.	saffron threads, soaked in 2 Tbsp. boiling water for 10 minutes
2 oz.	pistachio nuts

Melt butter in a large, heavy skillet. Add onions, ginger and garlic, and fry, stirring occasionally, for 5 minutes, or until the onions are soft and translucent but not brown. Add cumin, coriander, cardamom, peppercorns and cinnamon stick, and fry, stirring constantly, for about 2 minutes.

Dry lamb cubes with paper towels and add to the spice mixture, taking care not to splatter. Fry them for about 10 minutes, or until they are seared and brown. Add apricots, raisins, cashews, half the almonds, bay leaves and 1 tsp. salt. Pour in chicken stock, cover pan, and simmer until lamb is tender, about 35 to 40 minutes. Taste the mixture and add more salt if necessary. Remove pan from heat. Remove and discard cinnamon stick and bay leaves. Set aside and keep warm.

Preheat oven to 350 degrees F. In a large saucepan, bring 3 pts. water to boil over high heat. Add remaining salt and rice, and boil for 1 to 2 minutes. Remove pan from heat and drain rice in a colander.

Pour 1 Tbsp. melted butter into a large, ovenproof casserole dish. Put one-third of the rice in the bottom. Sprinkle with one-third of the saffron water. With a slotted spoon, transfer half the meat and fruit mixture to the casserole dish. Add another third of the rice and saffron water. Add the remaining meat and fruit mixture, reserving the pan juices. Finish with a last layer of the rice sprinkled with the remaining saffron water. Pour the reserved pan juices over all. Sprinkle with pistachios, remaining almonds and remaining melted butter.

Cover casserole dish and bake for 20 to 30 minutes, or until the rice has absorbed all the liquid. Remove from oven and serve immediately.

Ina Fitzhenry-Coor ◆ *Burlington, Vermont*

Suggested Accompaniments: Indian bread, chutney and Raita (page 222).

CASSEROLES & POTPIES

*"You better come on in my kitchen
'Cause it's going to be raining outdoors."*

Robert Johnson

In what has become an annual pilgrimage, we band together with friends and make a 75-minute trek through the mountains to the diminutive village of Groton, home of 667 people and one of Vermont's most generous harvest suppers. On this evening, the town streets are choked with cars and people streaming toward the Community Center. This is rural fundraising at its best, and all four sittings are typically sold out; reservations are essential.

Last year, we made the mistake of arriving near the end of the last sitting, which is immediately followed by a community dance. The room was full of unfamiliar faces, but we were instantly swept up by the friendly chaos of dining hall din. The room-long tables were decked in white church-supper paper, and a bevy of volunteers stood ready to keep the chicken potpie and all the trimmings coming.

No sooner had we tucked in our chairs than our food arrived. We ate, were immediately offered seconds and, within minutes, had been served our apple and pumpkin pies with coffee. It was clear that latecomers were not expected to linger over their meals, and we hurriedly cleaned our plates, hardly daring to take the time to look at each other. Suddenly, in a scene befitting an old slapstick movie, the townsfolk moved into action, clearing the dishes and snapping the folding chairs up to make room for the dance. We were still sitting at our places when they grabbed the soiled tablecloth and started rolling it hastily down the long table toward us. We took this to be a gentle signal that the dinner portion of the evening was over. To this day, we can't help laughing whenever the subject of potpie comes up—a dish that will forever be associated with rough-and-tumble service and the recollection of scrambling to avoid a white paper steamroller.

Potpies and casseroles fit squarely into the tradition of moveable feasts and appear at large, communal events: at church suppers, town meetings, square dances or school P.T.A. suppers. At home, casseroles and potpies give comfort in foul weather and variety to monotonous winter fare, providing rib-sticking, satisfying nourishment. Originating from a sturdy, basic formula, they may be infinitely varied—as economical as Betty Hay's Salmon Strata or as festive as Torta Milanese, a pastry with layers of spinach, red peppers, ham and cheese.

The casserole takes its name from its traditional serving vessel, a squat, earthenware pot with bulging sides, handles and a tight-fitting, slightly arched lid. This design allows uncooked foods like beans to be baked slowly, basted by their own juices, which condense on the lid and "rain" down on the contents. In modern times, the casserole dish is more often a shallow, rectangular oven dish used to bake layers of precooked foods. In either case, oven baking or "casseroling" produces an oven-to-table meal, requiring no fussy last-minute adjustments, which can be spooned directly from the dish in which it is served.

Making a good casserole lies in knowing how to make the best out of simple ingredients. Preserving the flavors and textures of the ingredients is essential. If these are to be precooked, the vegetables should be slightly undercooked and the pasta should be *al dente*. The sauce should be a bit on the wet side as the other ingredients can be expected to absorb moisture. If the dish is to be uncovered during the baking, a layer of bread crumbs is often added to protect the food underneath from drying out. Choosing a handsome serving dish of the correct size and shape is also important; its capacity can be measured simply by filling it with quarts or cups of water. Allowing the casserole to "rest" for five to ten minutes before serving will give the juices time to be fully absorbed and the sauce layer to firm up before setting it out for a hungry crowd.

—*JoAnne B. Cats-Baril*

Chicken Potpie

Preparation Hint: "This hearty dinner pie is best baked and served in an earthenware casserole dish."

Τhis easy variation on a traditional chicken potpie is enhanced by the abundance of herbs.

◆

Yield: 6-8 servings
Preparation time: 2 hours

◆

	Basic Pastry Crust for single 9-inch pie shell (*see page 201*)
¼ cup	butter
6 Tbsp.	flour
1 cup	milk
1 cup	dry white wine
1 cup	chicken stock
¼ tsp.	rosemary
¼ tsp.	savory
1 Tbsp.	parsley
1 tsp.	salt
¼ tsp.	pepper
¼ tsp.	marjoram
3 cups	diced raw chicken
1½ cups	thinly sliced carrots, cooked until slightly soft
1½ cups	peas
1 cup	sliced mushrooms, sautéed
	optional: broccoli, squash, asparagus or potatoes may be substituted for any of the other vegetables
1	egg yolk, mixed with 1 Tbsp. ice water

Make the pastry and chill. Melt butter in a large saucepan over medium heat; blend in flour until smooth. Add milk and blend. Add wine, stock and seasonings, and stir until thick. Add chicken. Cover, and simmer for 5 to 10 minutes, stirring occasionally. Cool to room temperature and blend in vegetables. Spoon into ungreased 2-qt. casserole dish.

Place pastry on a lightly floured surface and flatten into a circle about 1 inch thick. With a floured rolling pin and short quick strokes, roll out into a circle about 3 inches larger than casserole dish. Place 3 to 5 slits in the top, or use a pie vent, and dampen the edges of the dish. Place the pastry on the dish and crimp the edges to seal. Mix egg yolk with water to make a glaze, and brush onto the crust. Do not cover vent holes.

Bake at 425 degrees F for 30 to 40 minutes until brown and bubbly. (Check occasionally; if edges are browning too fast, cover them with aluminum foil.)

Ruth Hafer ◆ *Germantown, Maryland*

Basic Pastry Crust

This is an excellent potpie crust, easy to make and delicious. Many pastry cooks believe lard produces the most tender and flavorful crust, but vegetable shortening can be substituted with good results.

◆

Yield: double 9-inch pie shell
Preparation time: ¼ hour, plus chilling time

◆

2 cups	flour, sifted before measuring
¾ tsp.	salt
8 Tbsp.	butter
4 Tbsp.	lard

This pastry can be made by hand with a pastry cutter or in a food processor. Make the pastry by working butter and lard or shortening into the flour and salt until it has the texture of cornmeal. Add 3 Tbsp. ice water and stir in briefly. Wrap dough in plastic wrap and refrigerate, preferably overnight or for at least 4 hours.

JoAnne B. Cats-Baril ◆ Charlotte, Vermont

Tourtière

This recipe for pork pie is from Quebec; though there are endless variations, this one is a favorite.

◆

Yield: 4 servings
Preparation time: 1¼ hours

◆

Preparation Hint: This *tourtière* freezes well.

	Basic Pastry Crust for double 9-inch pie shell *(see above)*
2 lbs.	pork butt, trimmed and finely chopped
1	medium onion, peeled and finely chopped
1 clove	garlic, crushed
¼ cup	water
¼ cup	cognac or rye whiskey
¼ tsp.	celery salt
¼ tsp.	ground cloves
	salt and freshly ground pepper to taste
¼ cup	dry bread crumbs

Put all ingredients, except the bread crumbs and crust, in a saucepan and simmer until tender, about 20 minutes. Stir in bread crumbs and cool.

Roll out half the dough on a floured surface and place in the bottom of a 9-inch pie plate; trim the dough, leaving a ½-inch overhang. Fill the pan with the pork filling and smooth the top. Roll the remaining dough, cut a vent hole in the center, and drape the dough over the filling. Roll the edges under and crimp decoratively. Bake in a preheated 350-degree F oven for 35 minutes or until nicely browned. Let set for 5 minutes before serving.

JoAnne B. Cats-Baril ◆ *Charlotte, Vermont*

Vermont Cheddar-Crusted Scallop Pie

See photo page 72.

A flaky, buttery crust made with Cheddar cheese encases a savory filling of scallops, apples and bacon. Decorate the top crust with a scallop shell made from the leftover pastry dough.

◆

Yield: 4-6 servings
Preparation time: 1 hour

◆

CRUST

4 cups	all-purpose flour
1 tsp.	salt
1 cup	butter, cut into small bits
1½ cups	grated sharp Cheddar
1	egg, lightly beaten

FILLING

6-8 slices	bacon, cut into thirds
2 Tbsp.	butter
2 Tbsp.	olive oil
1½ lbs.	scallops
2½-3 Tbsp.	flour, plus extra for dredging scallops
2	Granny Smith apples or any crisp baking apples, cut into bite-sized pieces
¼ cup	dry white wine
2-3	shallots, finely chopped
1 cup	cream
2 cups	cider, reduced by boiling to ¼ cup
	salt & pepper
1	egg white, lightly beaten

To make the crust: Sift flour and salt together and cut in butter and grated cheese. Add egg and mix in ½ to ¾ cup water. Knead dough into a ball, wrap in plastic, and refrigerate for at least 30 minutes.

Roll out dough about ¼-inch thick and line a 10-inch, deep pie plate. Roll out top crust and refrigerate until needed. (You will have extra pastry, which may be used to decorate the top crust.)

To make the filling: Preheat oven to 425 degrees F. Blanch bacon in boiling water for 1 to 2 minutes; remove, drain and reserve. Heat a large sauté pan over high heat and melt butter and olive oil. Toss scallops in flour, and sauté on both sides until golden brown. (If your pan is hot enough, this should only take 1 to 1½ minutes per side.) Remove to large mixing bowl and set aside.

In the same pan, sauté bacon and apples until the apples are lightly browned. Add to reserved scallops. Deglaze the pan with white wine, scraping up browned bits, and add chopped shallots, cream and reduced cider. Heat but do not boil. Season with salt and pepper to taste.

Toss scallops, apples and bacon with 2½ to 3 Tbsp. flour. Brush bottom crust with egg white, and fill pie shell with scallop mixture. Pour cream mixture over scallops. Cover with top crust and decorate with extra dough. Brush with beaten egg white and bake for 20 minutes, or until golden.

R. Kent Cummings ◆ *North Ferrisburg, Vermont*

Torta Milanese

"**I** served this puff pastry filled with colorful layers of omelet, cheese, ham and red peppers to 40 diplomats' wives in Ottawa. They loved it." Puff pastry is found in the freezer section of the supermarket.

See photo page 77.

◆

Yield: 6-8 servings
Preparation time: 2 hours

◆

1 lb.	puff pastry
1 Tbsp.	oil
1 Tbsp.	butter
1 lb.	fresh spinach, blanched and well drained
2 cloves	garlic, minced
¼-½ tsp.	nutmeg
	salt & freshly ground pepper
2	large red peppers, cut into 1" pieces and blanched
8 oz.	Swiss cheese, thinly sliced
8 oz.	ham, thinly sliced
1	egg, beaten

5	eggs
2 tsp.	chopped chives
2 tsp.	chopped parsley
1 tsp.	chopped fresh tarragon, or ½ tsp. dried
	salt
4 Tbsp.	butter

Preparation Hint: Timing is everything in this layered dish: you must work quickly to assemble it. Our tester recommends measuring the ingredients for the omelet in advance and placing the first omelet on a plate for readiness. The top crust should be made in advance and refrigerated. Then, while the second omelet is cooking, begin layering the torta.

Lightly grease 8-inch springform pan. Roll out ¾ of the pastry ¼-inch thick and line bottom and sides of pan. Roll out remaining pastry; refrigerate.

Heat oil and butter in large skillet. Add spinach and garlic and sauté 2 to 3 minutes. Season to taste with nutmeg, salt and pepper. Remove from skillet and allow to drain. Add red pepper to skillet and sauté briefly. Remove from heat and set aside.

Make two omelets. Beat together eggs, chives, parsley, tarragon and salt. Melt 2 Tbsp. butter in a 7-to-8-inch skillet or omelet pan and add half of the egg mixture. Cook until set, turning pan so omelet cooks evenly; do not stir. Remove to plate. Melt remaining butter and cook second omelet.

Position rack in lower third of oven and preheat to 350 degrees F. Layer ingredients in prepared pan in following order: 1 omelet, half the spinach, half the cheese, half the ham and all the red pepper. Repeat layering in reverse order, using remaining ham, cheese, spinach and omelet.

From remaining pastry, cut out 8-inch circle. Place over omelet and seal well to pastry lining with egg and by pinching with fingers. Decorate with pastry scraps and brush with beaten egg. Place pan on baking sheet and bake until golden brown, about 70 to 75 minutes. Cool slightly. Release from pan and serve warm, slicing with a sharp, thin knife.

Pam Collacott ◆ North Gower, Ontario

Microwave Moussaka

Tis innovative and delicious moussaka persuaded HARROWSMITH editors to depart from tradition. No oil is used to cook the eggplant, which is traditionally fried before it is baked. The combination of seasonings here—cinnamon, garlic and oregano—is characteristically Greek.

◆

Yield: 6 servings
Preparation time: 2¼ hours

◆

2	medium eggplant, about 1 lb. each
	salt

2 Tbsp.	oil
⅔ cup	chopped onion
1⅓ lbs.	lean ground lamb or beef
2	medium tomatoes, chopped (about 1 cup)
5½-oz. can	tomato paste
1 clove	garlic, minced
1 tsp.	dried oregano leaves
½ tsp.	cinnamon
	salt and freshly ground pepper to taste
6 Tbsp.	Parmesan cheese
	paprika

BÉCHAMEL SAUCE

1⅓ cups	milk
2 tsp.	butter
2	eggs
3 Tbsp.	flour
¼ tsp.	salt

Regular oven: Bake at 325 degrees F for 30 minutes, then at 400 degrees for 10 minutes, or until brown and bubbly.

Peel eggplant and cut into slices ½-inch thick. Sprinkle the slices lightly with salt, set on paper towels, cover with a layer of paper towels and a heavy tray to weight, and let stand for ½ hour. Pat dry.

Arrange eggplant slices in a circle around the edge of a heatproof plate. Cover with plastic wrap and microwave on high for 4 to 6 minutes, or until cooked. Repeat until all eggplant slices are cooked. Place half of the eggplant slices in an overlapping layer in an 8x10x2-inch glass baking dish. Set the rest of the eggplant aside.

Place oil and onion in a large casserole dish. Microwave on high for 3 minutes, or until onion is soft. Stir in meat. Cover, and microwave on high for 5 to 6 minutes, or until no pink color is visible. Stir twice during cooking. Add tomatoes, tomato paste, garlic, oregano and cinnamon. Microwave on high, uncovered, for 7 minutes, or until the filling is thick and most of the moisture has evaporated. (Cooking the filling on the stove over medium heat will take about 20 minutes.) Stir 2 or 3 times during microwaving. Season to taste with salt and pepper.

Spread meat filling evenly over eggplant layer in the baking pan, and sprinkle with 2 Tbsp. Parmesan. Layer the rest of the eggplant slices over the filling and sprinkle with 2 more Tbsp. Parmesan.

Make béchamel sauce. In microwave, heat 1 cup milk and butter in a 4-cup glass measuring cup on medium for 2 minutes, or until scalded (150 degrees on probe). Whisk remaining milk, eggs, flour and salt in a medium bowl. Slowly whisk hot milk into egg mixture. Pour the mixture back into the measuring cup and microwave on medium for 3 minutes, or until thick. Whisk several times during cooking.

Pour béchamel sauce over the top eggplant layer in the baking pan, and sprinkle with remaining 2 Tbsp. Parmesan and a bit of paprika. Microwave on high for 20 to 25 minutes, or until moussaka is hot and bubbly. Let stand for 10 minutes before serving.

Pam Collacott ◆ *North Gower, Ontario*

Layered Polenta Casserole

Polenta, or coarse cornmeal, found in health food stores, is preferable to the finely ground type.

Polenta—cornmeal boiled until it acquires a creamy consistency—takes the place of noodles in this lasagnalike casserole, topped by layers of spinach, tomato sauce and cheese. Unlike traditional polentas that need at least 45 minutes of vigilant stirring, this one can be made in a scant 15 minutes.

◆

Yield: 4 servings
Preparation time: 1¼ hours

◆

1½ tsp.	salt
1½ cups	coarse cornmeal
19-oz. can	chick-peas, drained
1	bay leaf
1 tsp.	dried basil
2 cloves	garlic, chopped
1 Tbsp.	olive oil
28-oz. can	Italian tomatoes, crushed, with puree
20 oz. (2 packages)	frozen spinach, thawed and squeezed dry, or 16 oz. fresh, steamed and chopped
	salt & pepper
8 oz.	part-skim mozzarella

Boil 4½ cups water and salt, and whisk in cornmeal briskly to prevent lumps. Lower heat to gentle boil, add chick-peas, and stir with wooden spoon for 15 minutes. Pour into 9x11-inch oiled pan, and set aside in refrigerator while making tomato sauce. Preheat oven to 350 degrees F.

Sauté bay leaf, basil and garlic in olive oil, add tomatoes. Simmer ½ hour. Discard bay leaf, and season with salt and pepper. Cover polenta with layer of spinach, and cover with tomato sauce. Cover casserole with foil and bake 25 minutes. Slice mozzarella into 12 pieces (1x3x¼-inch). Remove casserole from oven, and top with two rows of 3 Xs made with cheese slices. Return to oven uncovered just until cheese melts, about 5 minutes.

Melissa McClelland ◆ *Burlington, Vermont*

This puffy popover shell with cheese can be filled with any meat, seafood or vegetable combination.

◆

Yield: 6 servings
Preparation time: 1¾ hours

◆

THE GOUGÈRE

1 cup	sifted all-purpose flour
½ tsp.	salt
½ tsp.	pepper
1 cup	milk
¼ cup	butter
4	eggs
¼ lb. (1 cup)	sharp Cheddar, diced
1 tsp.	Dijon-type mustard

THE FILLING

1 cup	chopped onion
4 Tbsp.	butter
½ lb.	mushrooms, sliced
2-3 Tbsp.	flour
1 tsp.	salt (optional)
¼ tsp.	pepper
1 cup	chicken stock
2	large tomatoes, peeled, quartered and seeded
6 oz.	ham, in thin strips
2 Tbsp.	shredded Cheddar or grated Parmesan
2 Tbsp.	chopped parsley

Gougère with Mushrooms & Ham

To Serve: Cut shell with a pie server and spoon over the filling.

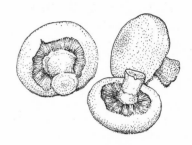

To make the gougère: Sift flour, salt and pepper. Heat milk and butter in large saucepan to boiling. Add flour and seasonings all at once and stir vigorously until mixture forms a ball. Cool slightly, then add eggs one at a time, beating well after each addition. Stir in diced cheese and mustard. In greased 10-inch pie plate, shape pastry into a ring around edge of pan, leaving center open.

To make the filling: Sauté onion in butter until soft. Add mushrooms. Cook 2 minutes. Sprinkle with flour, salt and pepper. Cook 2 minutes. Add chicken stock, and mix well. Heat to boiling, stirring constantly. Simmer 4 minutes, or until floury taste is gone. Remove from heat. Cut each tomato quarter into 4 strips and add to filling mixture. Add ham strips and mix gently. Fill center of pastry ring with filling. Sprinkle with cheese. Bake in 400-degree F oven for 40 to 45 minutes, until pastry is puffed and brown. Serve at once, garnished with parsley.

Pam Collacott ◆ North Gower, Ontario

Curried Vegetables with Cream Biscuits

This unusual potpie is spicy but not too hot, and is nicely balanced by the biscuits.

◆

Yield: 4 servings
Preparation time: 1 hour

◆

1 cup	carrots cut into rounds
2 cups	leeks cut into rounds
1 cup	sliced celery
2 cups	chopped red bell pepper
2 small cloves	garlic, crushed
1½ Tbsp.	peanut oil
½ tsp.	Chinese hot oil
2½ cups	bite-sized broccoli florets
3 tsp.	aromatic curry
½ cup	crushed tomato
¾ tsp.	salt
1½ Tbsp.	peanut butter
3 Tbsp.	yogurt

Sauté carrots, leeks, celery, red pepper and garlic in peanut and hot oils. Transfer to a bowl and add the broccoli, curry, tomatoes, ⅓ cup water, salt and peanut butter; stir and set aside until cool.

Stir in yogurt. Put into a soufflé dish, cover with aluminum foil, and bake in a preheated 450-degree F oven until the mixture starts to bubble, about 25 minutes.

Meanwhile, prepare the biscuits.

CREAM BISCUITS

2 cups	sifted flour
1 Tbsp.	baking powder
½ tsp.	salt
⅓ cup	butter
2	large eggs
½ cup	heavy cream

Sift flour, baking powder and salt. Cut in butter. Add eggs and cream, barely mixing. Turn dough onto floured surface and knead just enough to hold dough together so that it can be cut into biscuits.

Pat the dough into a ½-inch thickness and cut biscuits with a floured juice glass or biscuit cutter. Place the biscuits, touching, on top of the hot mixture, and bake for 12 to 15 minutes longer, or until the biscuits are golden brown. Any extras can be baked on a baking sheet.

JoAnne B. Cats-Baril ◆ *Charlotte, Vermont*

Zucchini Mushroom Potpie

Mushrooms, zucchini, Monterey Jack cheese, sour cream and walnuts are tucked into a biscuit dough crust sprinkled with Parmesan.

◆

Yield: 6 servings
Preparation time: 1¼ hours

◆

Preparation Hint: Make the dough first, since it is needed to cover the bottom of the pan.

BISCUITS

4 cups	flour
1½ Tbsp.	baking powder
1½ tsp.	salt
1⅓ cups	butter
1½-2 cups	milk
½ cup	Parmesan cheese

FILLING

3-4	medium zucchini, halved lengthwise and sliced ¼" thick (4 cups)
3 cups	sliced mushrooms
1	medium onion, chopped
16 oz.	sour cream
¼ cup	flour
¼ tsp.	salt
⅛ tsp.	pepper
⅓ cup	chopped walnuts
1 cup	shredded Monterey Jack cheese (4 oz.)

To make biscuits: Sift dry ingredients into a large bowl. Cut butter into dry mixture until well mixed. Add milk ½ cup at a time, mixing well. Dough should be moist, not sticky.

Divide dough in half. Set one half aside; roll the other half out to a ½-inch thickness, 13 inches wide. Spread into a lightly greased 9x13x2-inch pan. Sprinkle with ¼ cup Parmesan. Bake in a 350-degree F oven for 10 to 15 minutes, until golden.

To make filling: Place zucchini, mushrooms and onion in a steamer over boiling water. Cover and steam 8 to 10 minutes, until crisp-tender. Remove; set aside.

In a large bowl, stir together sour cream, flour, salt and pepper. Stir in zucchini mixture and walnuts. Turn into pan; spread evenly over crust. Sprinkle with Monterey Jack. Top with second piece of dough, rolled to ½-inch thickness. Sprinkle with remaining Parmesan. Bake at 350 degrees F for 30 to 40 minutes, until top is golden and filling heated through.

Judy Sheppard-Segal ◆ *Falmouth, Maine*

"You Can Serve It To Company" Shepherd's Pie

Julienned zucchini, summer squash and carrots present a colorful cross section when this splendid shepherd's pie is sliced. It can be made spicy or mild by varying the quantity of cayenne in the filling and sauce.

◆

Yield: 6 servings
Preparation time: 2½ hours

◆

1½ lbs.	ground beef
½ lb.	ground pork
2	eggs, lightly beaten
½ cup	very fine bread crumbs
3 Tbsp. plus 1 stick	unsalted butter
¾ cup	finely chopped onion
¾ cup	finely chopped celery
¾ cup	finely chopped bell pepper
3 cloves	garlic, minced
1 Tbsp.	Worcestershire sauce
½ tsp.	Tabasco sauce

MEAT SEASONINGS

2 tsp.	cayenne
1½ tsp.	salt
1½ tsp.	black pepper
¾ tsp.	ground cumin
¾ tsp.	dried thyme

¾ cup	evaporated milk
6	medium potatoes, peeled and quartered
1	egg
	salt, to taste
1 tsp.	white pepper
1½ cups	julienned carrots
1 cup	julienned onion
1½ cups	julienned zucchini
1½ cups	julienned yellow squash

VEGETABLE SEASONINGS

½ tsp.	salt
¼ tsp.	white pepper
¼ tsp.	chili pepper
¼ tsp.	garlic powder
¼ tsp.	cayenne

Preheat oven to 450 degrees F. Combine beef, pork, eggs and bread

crumbs in large bowl. In 1-qt. saucepan, melt 3 Tbsp. butter, and add onions, celery, bell peppers, garlic, Worcestershire, Tabasco and meat
seasonings. Sauté on high for 5 minutes, stirring often. Remove from heat.

Add sautéed vegetables and ¼ cup evaporated milk to meat and mix. Pat
into an 8x12-inch loaf in a baking pan. Bake at 450 degrees F for about 30
minutes, or until browned on top. Remove from oven, pour off drippings,
reserving 2½ Tbsp.

Boil potatoes until tender, drain, reserving 1 cup of liquid. Place in large
bowl with 1 stick butter, ½ cup evaporated milk, egg, salt and white pepper, and mash until very smooth. Use some of the reserved liquid if they
become too dry.

In a large skillet, with reserved drippings, sauté carrots and onions on
high for about 2 minutes. Add zucchini and squash, and continue to
sauté for 3 to 4 minutes, stirring often. Remove from heat. Stir in vegetable seasonings. Lay vegetables on top of meat, then the potatoes on top of
the vegetables, and bake at 525 degrees F until potatoes are brown, about
8 to 10 minutes. Serve with the following sauce.

SAUCE

½ cup	chopped onion
½ cup	chopped green pepper
¼ cup	chopped celery
¼ cup	chopped jalapeño peppers (use chili peppers for milder sauce)
¼ cup	olive oil
¼ cup	flour
¼ tsp.	cayenne
½ tsp.	black pepper
3 cups	beef stock, heated

Mix vegetables in bowl. Make a roux with olive oil and flour. Add vegetables to roux and sauté for 3 to 5 minutes. Season with cayenne and pepper, add beef stock, and continue to stir until smooth.

Liz Foster ◆ Hinesburg, Vermont

Greek Fish

"**I** created this dish one night when my mother
came to dinner. She was trying to lose weight, and I was deter-
mined to serve something more interesting than plain fish. Simple,
colorful and delicious, it fit the bill."

◆

Yield: 6 servings
Preparation time: 1¼ hours

◆

2½-3 lbs.	white fish fillets
1 Tbsp.	oil
1 lb.	fresh spinach
1½ cups	chopped onion
1 clove	garlic, minced
1½ cups	chopped tomatoes
	parsley
	salt & pepper to taste
1 cup	white wine

Preheat oven to 350 degrees F. Place fish in 9x13-inch baking dish, sprinkle with oil, if desired, and surround with spinach. Top with onion, garlic and tomatoes. Sprinkle with parsley, salt and pepper. Pour wine over all. Bake, covered with foil, for 30 minutes; remove foil and bake 5 more minutes.

Linda Messier ◆ North Ferrisburg, Vermont

Rice & Lentil Casserole with Spicy Shrimp

"**I** developed this Indian-style casserole for my family, who once though lentils were boring and tasteless. Not anymore!"

◆

Yield: 4 servings
Preparation time: 4 hours

◆

SHRIMP

1	onion, chopped
3 cloves	garlic
1 thin slice	ginger root, peeled and minced
2 Tbsp.	lemon juice
2 Tbsp.	peanut oil
½ tsp.	ground cumin
½ tsp.	ground turmeric
dash	cayenne peppper
1 tsp.	ground coriander
½ tsp.	salt
1½ lbs. (about 45)	large shrimp, peeled and deveined

RICE & LENTILS

1 Tbsp.	butter
1 Tbsp.	peanut oil
1	onion, finely chopped
1 tsp.	curry powder

2½ cups	chicken stock
4	whole cloves
½ cup	uncooked long-grain rice
⅔ cup	brown lentils
	salt to taste

Place onion, garlic, ginger, lemon juice and peanut oil in blender. Mix until smooth. Pour into bowl, stir in cumin, turmeric, cayenne, coriander and salt. Add shrimp. Cover and refrigerate for 2 hours, stirring from time to time.

Meanwhile, prepare rice and lentils. In saucepan, heat butter and oil, and sauté onion until golden. Stir in curry powder, chicken stock and cloves. Bring to a boil over high heat. Add rice and lentils. Season with salt, reduce heat, cover and simmer 25 minutes, or until liquid has been absorbed.

Thread shrimp on skewers and broil 4 minutes on each side, or until cooked through. Remove shrimp from skewers and place in center of serving dish; surround with rice and lentils (which have been kept warm). Bake in oven at 325 degrees F for 5 minutes.

Helene Gauvreau ◆ *Victoria, British Columbia*

Fettuccine Casserole with Shrimp

"**E**legant" is how our tester describes this baked one-pot of fettuccine, cheese, fresh asparagus and mushrooms. It is even better, of course, when made with homemade pasta.

◆

Yield: 4 servings
Preparation time: 1¾ hours

◆

6 Tbsp.	butter
1 clove	garlic, minced
6 Tbsp.	flour
1½ cups	milk
¾ lb.	Cheddar or Colby cheese, grated
¾ lb.	fresh asparagus tips or broccoli florets, cooked
½ lb.	fresh mushrooms, cooked
1 lb.	shrimp, peeled
	salt & pepper to taste
9 oz.	fresh or frozen fettuccine noodles

Melt butter and sauté garlic until translucent. Blend in flour to make a paste. Add milk and stir until thick. Add grated cheese and stir continuously over low heat until the cheese has melted into the sauce. Add vegetables, shrimp and salt and pepper.

Cook noodles in boiling, salted water for no more than 2 minutes (if they are cooked completely, they will dissolve in the sauce). Drain, and mix with the cream sauce. Bake in a greased casserole dish at 350 degrees F for 20 to 30 minutes.

Ruth Hafer ◆ Germantown, Maryland

Salmon Strata

Few will guess that the salmon in this rich casserole is canned. Caraway seeds are the lively seasoning, uniting the layers of fish, apple and potato.

◆

Yield: 4-6 servings
Preparation time: 1½ hours

◆

15½-oz. can	salmon, drained and flaked
½ cup	chopped onion
½ cup	chopped celery
4	eggs
2 cups	milk
1 tsp.	salt
1 tsp.	caraway seed
⅛ tsp.	black pepper
6 cups	thinly sliced potatoes
3	apples, peeled, cored and sliced
½ cup	dry bread crumbs
¼ cup	chopped fresh parsley

In large bowl, combine salmon, onion, celery, eggs, milk, ½ tsp. salt, caraway seed and pepper. Mix well. Place half the potato slices in a single layer in a greased 1½-qt. casserole dish. Sprinkle with remaining ½ tsp. salt. Place half the apple slices in a layer over potatoes, and spread half the salmon mixture over. Repeat with a layer of potato and of apple slices, topping with salmon mixture. Sprinkle with bread crumbs. Bake, uncovered, at 350 degrees F for 1 hour, or until potatoes are tender. Just before serving, sprinkle with parsley.

Betty Hay ◆ Lexington, Kentucky

Shrimp & Mushroom Feast

"**P**lumped full of shrimp and mushrooms, this casserole can be prepared in individual ovenproof dishes and frozen to serve as fancy lunches or as appetizers for unannounced guests."

◆

Yield: 6 servings
Preparation time: 2 hours

◆

2 lbs.	raw medium shrimp, peeled and deveined
1 lb.	small mushrooms, cleaned and towel-dried
2	medium onions, finely chopped
3 Tbsp.	butter
2	tomatoes, peeled and chopped
	salt to taste
½ tsp.	pepper
¼ cup	white wine or sherry
½ tsp.	Worcestershire sauce
2 Tbsp.	flour
½ cup	cream
3 cups	cooked rice
½ cup	fine bread crumbs
	sweet paprika
sprigs	fresh parsley

Sauté shrimp, mushrooms and onions in 2 Tbsp. butter until shrimp turn pink, about 3 to 4 minutes. Add tomatoes, salt and pepper. Cover, and simmer for 5 minutes on low heat. Add the wine and the Worcestershire.

Blend together flour and cream to form a smooth mixture. Stir into the shrimp pot and bring to a boil, mixing constantly and gently. Reduce heat and continue cooking for 1 minute. Mix with rice and place into 3-qt. casserole dish.

Melt remaining butter and toss with bread crumbs and paprika. Sprinkle over casserole and place under broiler until golden brown, or bake until bubbly and browned. Garnish each serving with a sprig of fresh parsley.

Linda M. Powidajko ◆ Kingston, Ontario

Tuna, Cannellini & Noodle Casserole

Shopping Tip: Look for cannellini beans in the Italian section of the supermarket.

Smooth, nutty-flavored cannellini beans replace the usual canned mushroom soup as a binder in this healthful rendition of tuna-noodle casserole.

◆

Yield: 2 servings
Preparation time: 1 hour 10 minutes

◆

½ lb.	egg noodles
2 Tbsp.	olive oil
2 cloves	garlic, chopped
1 can	albacore tuna in water, drained and flaked
19-oz. can	cannellini beans
½ cup	fresh or frozen lima beans
1	carrot, diced
½ cup	green beans cut small
½ cup	corn kernels
½ cup plus 2 Tbsp.	grated Romano cheese

Preheat oven to 350 degrees F. Boil water for noodles and cook them until still firm to the teeth. Drain and blend with 1 Tbsp. olive oil to prevent sticking.

Sauté garlic in remaining 1 Tbsp. olive oil. Place tuna in large mixing bowl and stir in garlic, cannellini beans, limas, carrot, green beans and corn. Mix well. Gradually add noodles and ½ cup Romano. Place mixture in oiled casserole dish and bake, covered, for ½ hour. Uncover, sprinkle remaining cheese on top, and return to oven for approximately 10 minutes, or until cheese melts.

Melissa McClelland ◆ Burlington, Vermont

Layered Tomato & Eggplant Casserole

This tasty vegetarian casserole is baked in a springform pan, and the sides of the pan are slipped off after baking so that the casserole stands free. It can, of course, be made in an ordinary baking dish.

◆

Yield: 4 servings
Preparation time: 1¼ hours

◆

6 oz. or 1 small	eggplant, sliced
	salt
6 Tbsp.	oil

1	large onion, chopped
3 cloves	garlic, crushed
1	green pepper, chopped
14-oz. can	tomatoes, drained
½ tsp.	cumin powder
½ tsp.	coriander powder
½ tsp.	pepper
2 Tbsp.	chopped parsley
	lemon juice
6 oz.	flat noodles, cooked and drained
4 Tbsp.	dry bread crumbs
2 oz.	Parmesan cheese
4 Tbsp.	butter

Sprinkle eggplant slices with salt and set aside for 20 minutes. Drain. Rinse and pat dry. Heat 4 Tbsp. oil in frying pan and fry eggplant for 2 to 3 minutes on each side. Drain on paper towels.

Heat 2 Tbsp. oil and fry onion and garlic in a saucepan. Add green pepper and tomatoes, cover, and simmer 10 to 15 minutes. Add seasonings, parsley and lemon juice to taste.

Grease a springform pan and arrange ⅓ of the noodles on the bottom. Layer with ½ the eggplant slices and cover with some of the tomato mixture. Repeat layers again and complete, covering the top with remaining noodles. Mix bread crumbs and cheese together. Sprinkle over the top. Dot with butter.

Cover with foil and bake in preheated 350-degree F oven for 30 minutes. Remove foil and bake for 5 to 10 additional minutes. Cool slightly before removing from springform pan. Serve immediately.

Marian da Costa ◆ *Etobicoke, Ontario*

Malaysian Chicken & Rice Casserole

The flavors of Southeast Asia make this casserole an exotic choice for company. Our tester was won over by the combination of fresh ginger and crunchy coconut, and reports that although the aroma is sweet, the result is nicely balanced.

◆

Yield: 8 servings
Preparation time: 65 minutes

◆

4 Tbsp.	vegetable oil
2	small onions, thinly sliced
2	cinnamon sticks, 2-3" long
2 cups	uncooked rice
¾ cup	plain yogurt
1 tsp.	salt, or to taste
3 lbs.	chicken pieces
2 Tbsp.	minced fresh ginger root
8	whole cloves
⅔ cup	finely grated fresh coconut
1½ cups	canned tomatoes
1½ tsp.	turmeric
¼ tsp.	hot cayenne pepper
½ tsp.	freshly ground black pepper

Heat 1 Tbsp. oil in a large heavy pot. Add 1 onion and the cinnamon sticks, and sauté until onion is tender. Stir in rice, yogurt, 3 cups water and salt. Bring to a boil, turn heat down, cover, and simmer on low heat until liquid is absorbed and rice is tender. Uncover and set aside while preparing the chicken.

Remove skin and fat from chicken and set aside. Heat remaining oil in a heavy frying pan. Add remaining onion, and sauté until tender. Add ginger and cloves, stir and cook 1 minute. Add chicken pieces, and cook a few minutes, turning and stirring to coat chicken. Add coconut, tomatoes, turmeric, cayenne and black pepper. Simmer, uncovered, for 20 minutes, turning chicken to cook evenly. Remove chicken pieces; set aside.

Add the cooking mixture to the rice and stir gently. In a large casserole dish, layer half the rice mixture, top with the chicken pieces and spoon the remainder of the rice on top. Cover with a tight-fitting lid, and bake 40 minutes at 350 degrees F.

Irene Louden ◆ *Port Coquitlam, British Columbia*

Fresh coconut is far superior to the stale, sweetened, packaged variety. Choose coconuts that make a sloshing sound when shaken. To open, punch a hole in one or two of the round eyes near the stem end with an ice pick or screwdriver. Drain the milk, which is delicious, and bake the coconut in a preheated 350-degree F oven for 20 minutes. Crack the shell with a hammer and pull it off. Pare off the brown skin with a knife and grate the white meat with a hand grater or in a food processor.

Lemon Chicken Casserole with Bulgur & Peppers

"A friend, who works long hours in a newsroom and has little time to cook, likes to serve this casserole to company. It features carefree preparation, healthy ingredients and the refreshing zing of lemon juice."

♦

Yield: 6- servings
Preparation time: 1 hour 35 minutes

♦

2 Tbsp.	olive oil
1 (about 3½-lb.)	broiler-fryer chicken, skinned and cut into small serving pieces
	salt
	freshly ground black pepper
3	medium onions, chopped
3 cloves	garlic, minced
1	large green pepper, cut into 2" chunks
1	large sweet red pepper, cut into 2" chunks
2 tsp.	minced fresh jalapeño pepper, or ½ tsp. cayenne
1½ cups	bulgur
½ tsp.	ground cardamom
½ tsp.	ground coriander
½ tsp.	ground cumin
	grated rind and juice of 1 lemon
3 cups	chicken stock

In a large skillet, heat olive oil, add chicken, and brown pieces on all sides. Place in large casserole dish and season with salt and pepper. Add onions and garlic to skillet, and sauté until onions are translucent. Add peppers and sauté briefly until they are coated with oil. Add bulgur to the skillet and sauté until it is slightly browned. Add spices and lemon rind and juice to the bulgur, mixing well. Spoon bulgur mixture over chicken. Bring stock to a boil and pour over the casserole. Cover with foil, and bake in a preheated 350-degree F oven for 1 hour, or until liquid is absorbed and chicken is done.

Rux Martin ♦ Underhill Center, Vermont

FINISHING
TOUCHES

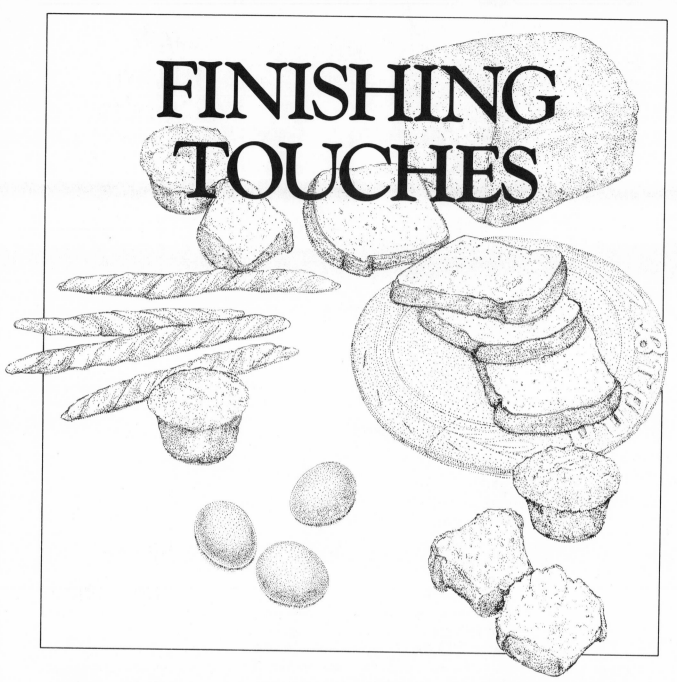

"Imagine, if you can, what the rest of the evening was like. How they crouched by the fire which blazed and leaped and made much of itself in the little grate. How they removed the covers of the dishes, and found rich, hot savory soup, which was a meal in itself, and sandwiches and toast and muffins enough for both of them."

Frances Hodgson Burnett

This is a great coleslaw. Made with no oil whatsoever, it emphasizes the natural tang of the cabbage. It can be tossed together in a few minutes' time and served with almost any one-pot dinner.

◆

Yield: 4-6 servings
Preparation time: ¼ hour

◆

4 cups	slivered cabbage
1	large green pepper, chopped
⅓ cup	chopped onion
¼-⅓ cup	sugar
⅓ cup	vinegar
1 tsp.	Dijon mustard
½-1 tsp.	celery seed
1 tsp.	salt
¼-½ tsp.	paprika
⅓ cup	parsley
	pepper to taste

Toss together cabbage, pepper and onions. Mix remaining ingredients in a food processor or blender, pour over vegetables and toss.

Meredith Gabriel ◆ Ferrisburg, Vermont

Fresh Winter Coleslaw

Preparation Hint: The flavor is at its best when this dish is made 1 to 2 hours ahead. Its color darkens if it is allowed to sit longer.

Flecked with fresh coriander, this refreshing slaw is a perfect match for Chinese dishes.

◆

Yield: 4 servings
Preparation time: ¼ hour

◆

4 Tbsp.	rice vinegar
2 Tbsp.	chopped fresh coriander
2 Tbsp.	sugar
½ tsp.	sesame oil
pinch	salt
3-4 cups	curly-leaf Nappa cabbage, cut into 3" julienne slices

Mix vinegar, coriander, sugar, sesame oil and salt in a bowl until sugar is dissolved. Add cabbage and toss to coat. Chill for a few hours, then serve.

Steve Bogart ◆ Worcester, Vermont

Chinese Nappa Salad

Preparation Hint: The coriander will darken if allowed to sit for too long.

Cabbage Apple Salad

This winter salad goes exceptionally well with baked beans or soup.

◆

Yield: 6-8 servings
Preparation time: ¼ hour

◆

1	medium cabbage, coarsely chopped
3-4	apples, McIntosh or Red Delicious, cored, unpeeled and cut into cubes
⅓ cup	raisins, or more to taste
1 cup	chopped walnuts
⅔-1 cup	mayonnaise and vanilla yogurt, in equal proportions
2 Tbsp.	maple syrup
1 tsp.	nutmeg

Mix cabbage, apples, raisins and walnuts together. Mix mayonnaise and yogurt together and stir in maple syrup and nutmeg. Add to cabbage mixture and stir until well blended. Sprinkle with a little nutmeg.

Nancy Davis ◆ *Underhill Center, Vermont*

Raita

"Cooling" is the word for this Indian dish of cucumber and yogurt, which is traditionally served as a condiment or liquid salad with spicy curries. The mixture of yogurt and sour cream used here approximates the consistency of Indian yogurt.

◆

Yield: 6-8 servings as a condiment
4-6 servings as a salad
Preparation time: ¼ hour

◆

Variation: 16 oz. of yogurt may be substituted for the mixture of yogurt and sour cream.

12 oz.	plain yogurt
4 oz.	sour cream
1	cucumber, peeled and finely chopped
1	large firm tomato, finely chopped
2	scallions, green tops included, finely chopped
1 tsp.	salt
⅛ tsp.	white pepper
½ tsp.	ground cumin

⅛ tsp.   cayenne pepper
⅛ tsp.   paprika

Beat yogurt and sour cream until smooth. Stir in cucumber, tomato, scallions and all the seasonings except paprika. Sprinkle paprika over top. Cover and refrigerate 4 to 6 hours, so that flavors meld.

Ina Fitzhenry-Coor ◆ *Burlington, Vermont*

Cheese-Herb Dumplings

These fluffy dumplings with crusty tops are excellent with chicken stew and may be adapted for beef stew by substituting rosemary and thyme for chervil and omitting the cheese.

◆

Yield: 2 dozen
Preparation time: ¼ hour

◆

2 cups	flour
1 tsp.	salt
4 tsp.	baking powder
1 tsp.	chervil
⅓ cup	grated Cheddar cheese
1	egg, beaten
3 Tbsp.	melted butter
⅔ cup	milk

Sift flour, salt, baking powder and chervil together. Stir in cheese. Mix egg, butter and milk together and stir into flour mixture to make a moist, stiff batter. Using 2 teaspoons, drop dumplings over bubbling stew. Cover, and cook for 15 minutes, keeping stew at a slow boil. Cook, uncovered, for 5 minutes longer.

Rux Martin ◆ *Underhill Center, Vermont*

My family dumplings are sleek and seductive, yet stout and masculine. They taste of meat, yet of flour. They are wet, yet they are dry. They have weight, but they are light. Airy, yet substantial. Earth, air, fire, water; velvet and elastic! Meat, wheat and magic! They are our family glory!
—Robert P. Tristram Coffin

Parsley Dumplings

These dumplings contain just the right amount of parsley to brighten chicken soups and fricassees.

◆

Yield: 16 dumplings
Preparation time: 20 minutes

◆

2 cups	cake flour, measured after sifting
½ tsp.	salt
¼ tsp.	freshly ground pepper
¼ cup	minced fresh parsley
2	eggs
¼ cup	melted butter or oil
¾ cup	milk

Sift dry ingredients into a bowl. Mix in parsley. Beat together eggs, butter or oil and milk, and add to dry ingredients. Stir only until moistened. Drop by teaspoonfuls on the top of simmering soup or stew. Cover and continue cooking for 12 minutes; do not lift the lid.

Emma Carlson ◆ Fonthill, Ontario

Drop Biscuits

With little or no fuss in the preparation, this recipe produces golden, crisp biscuits with a tender crumb.

◆

Yield: 1½ dozen
Preparation time: 25 minutes

◆

3 cups	flour
5 tsp.	baking powder
½ tsp.	salt
6 Tbsp.	butter
1½ cups	milk

Sift dry ingredients into a bowl. Cut in butter and then add milk. Stir only until dry ingredients are moistened. Drop from a large soup spoon onto an ungreased baking sheet. Bake at 450 degrees F until browned, about 18 minutes.

Kathryn MacDonald ◆ Yarker, Ontario

Fluffy Biscuits

The original, light, fluffy biscuits, a hit at HARROWSMITH lunches. "I can add anything to these—wheat germ, oat bran, oatmeal, whole wheat flour, browned onions, Cheddar and herbs, and so on—and they always turn out lofty. I always add honey to my whole wheat biscuits, but not to white."

◆

Yield: 1 dozen
Preparation time: 20 minutes

◆

3	eggs
¾ cup	milk or cream
¼ cup	honey (optional)
3 cups	flour
4½ tsp.	baking powder
1 tsp.	salt
12 Tbsp. (1½ sticks)	softened butter

Beat eggs and add milk or cream. Stir in honey if whole wheat flour is used. Sift dry ingredients together. Cut butter into dry ingredients so it is in pea-sized lumps. Add wet ingredients and mix until they are just blended; do not overmix. Dough will be wet and sticky.

Turn out onto a well-floured board, dusting top of dough with flour. Pat to 1-inch thickness. Cut into 2½-inch rounds. Place on an ungreased baking sheet, with the rounds barely touching, and bake 12 to 15 minutes at 425 degrees F, or until lightly browned and crisp.

Meredith Gabriel ◆ *Ferrisburg, Vermont*

Variations: Buttermilk may be used in place of milk, with ½ tsp. baking soda added to it to counteract its acidity, which can interfere with the action of the baking powder.
• Add ½ cup chopped onions, browned in butter and cooled; or
• ½ cup grated Cheddar cheese; or
• up to 2 tsp. dried herbs.

Substitutes for flour:
• 1 cup wheat germ **or** oat bran, plus 2½ cups white flour; or
• 1½ cups whole wheat plus 2 cups white flour and ¼-½ cup honey.

Oatmeal Biscuits

Oats give these dense, tender biscuits a deliciously toasty flavor.

◆

Yield: ½ dozen
Preparation time: 20 minutes

◆

1 cup	flour
3 tsp.	baking powder
½ tsp.	salt
1 cup	rolled oats, cut fine in a food processor
⅓ cup	butter, chilled
2	eggs
¼ cup	milk

Sift flour, baking powder and salt into a bowl. Add oats. Cut in butter. Beat eggs and milk together and add all at once. Moisten dry ingredients by stirring and lifting with a fork. Handle gently. Pat into a circle and cut with a biscuit cutter dipped in flour. Place on lightly greased baking sheet and bake at 450 degrees F for 10 to 15 minutes.

JoAnne B. Cats-Baril ◆ *Charlotte, Vermont*

Rosemary Biscuits

These biscuits are permeated with aromatic scent. Fresh rosemary is especially good in this recipe.

◆

Yield: 1 dozen
Preparation time: 20-25 minutes

◆

2 cups	all-purpose flour
1 Tbsp.	baking powder
½ tsp.	salt
2 Tbsp.	rosemary
¼ cup	butter
¾ cup	milk

Preparation Hint: To make crispy biscuits, place them far apart on baking sheet; for fluffy biscuits, place them close together.

Mix dry ingredients together in a food processor (if not using a processor, crush the rosemary before mixing). Knife in butter until blended into fine particles. Add milk, stirring just enough to make particles cling together.

Turn out onto a floured surface and knead for about 1 minute, then pat or roll out. The dough should be ½ to ¾ inch thick. Cut into rounds or squares. Bake on an ungreased baking sheet in 450-degree F oven for 12 to 15 minutes.

R. Kent Cummings ◆ *North Ferrisburg, Vermont*

Buttermilk- Cheddar Biscuits

The tang of buttermilk and Cheddar make these biscuits savory companions for soups and stews.

◆

Yield: 8-10 biscuits
Preparation time: 25 minutes

◆

2 cups	flour
2 tsp.	baking powder
½ tsp.	baking soda
½ tsp.	salt

½ tsp.	sugar
4 Tbsp.	grated Cheddar cheese
7 Tbsp.	butter, chilled
⅔ cup	buttermilk
1	egg yolk

Preparation Hint: Handle the dough quickly and gently for especially tender and flaky results.

Sift dry ingredients into a bowl. Sprinkle grated cheese on top and distribute with a fork. Cut in butter. Add buttermilk and egg yolk. Stir until just moistened.

Pat into a circle and cut into 2-inch rounds using a biscuit cutter. Place on lightly floured baking sheet; bake at 400 degrees F for 15 to 20 minutes.

JoAnne B. Cats-Baril ◆ *Charlotte, Vermont*

Bran Corn Bread

A moist, whole-grain corn bread that retains its freshness the next day.

◆

Yield: 6-8 servings
Preparation time: 50 minutes

◆

1 cup	milk
1½ cups	All-Bran cereal
½ cup	shortening
½ cup	sugar
2	eggs, beaten
1 cup	flour
½ cup	cornmeal
3 tsp.	baking powder
½ tsp.	salt

Pour milk over cereal and let stand 5 minutes. Cream together shortening and sugar. Mix in eggs. Mix dry ingredients together and add to shortening mixture, along with milk and cereal, mixing only until ingredients are moistened. Place in a greased 9x9-inch pan and bake at 400 degrees F for 30 to 35 minutes, or until done.

Nancy Hill ◆ *Greensboro, Vermont*

Mexican Corn Bread

Fresh corn and jalapeño peppers add crunch and fire to this south-of-the-border accompaniment to chili.

◆

Yield: 8x10-inch pan
Preparation time: ¾ hour

◆

1 cup	cornmeal
1 cup	flour
2 Tbsp.	baking powder
1 tsp.	salt
3 Tbsp.	sugar
2	eggs
4 Tbsp.	butter
1 cup	milk
1 cup	yellow corn, fresh or frozen
2 Tbsp.	chopped jalapeño peppers

Mix dry ingredients together. Stir in eggs, butter, milk, corn and peppers. Blend well and pour into a greased 8x10-inch baking pan. Bake for 25 to 30 minutes at 350 degrees F.

Nancy Davis ◆ Underhill Center, Vermont

Prune-Nut Muffins

With just a touch of sweetening, these prune muffins are made for pork and lamb dishes

◆

Yield: 1 dozen
Preparation time: ½ hour

◆

1¾ cups	all-purpose flour
¾ tsp.	salt
¼ cup	sugar
2 tsp.	baking powder
⅓ cup	chopped prunes
⅓ cup	chopped walnuts
2	eggs
3-4 Tbsp.	butter, melted
¾ cup	milk

Preheat oven to 400 degrees F. Sift dry ingredients together. Fold in prunes and nuts. In another bowl, lightly beat eggs, add butter and milk.

Combine dry ingredients in a large mixing bowl. Whisk together the rest of the ingredients and gently but thoroughly fold them into the dry ingredients. Fill greased muffin tins and bake in a preheated 400-degree F oven for 20 minutes, or until done.

JoAnne B. Cats-Baril ◆ *Charlotte, Vermont*

Honey-Mustard & Cheddar Dinner Muffins

"These savory muffins are among our favorites—tangy with mustard, sweet with honey and rich with Cheddar. They can accompany almost any soup."

◆

Yield: 1 dozen
Preparation time: 25 minutes

◆

2 cups	all-purpose flour
1 Tbsp.	baking powder
¼ tsp.	salt
	freshly ground pepper to taste
1 cup	grated sharp Cheddar cheese
1	egg
3 Tbsp.	Honeycup Prepared Mustard
2 Tbsp.	honey
1¼ cups	milk
¼ cup	butter, melted

Honeycup Prepared Mustard is a commercially prepared hot-sweet mustard that is difficult to duplicate at home. It is available in specialty stores and some supermarkets in the U.S. and Canada, or it may be ordered from Stone Country Specialties, Inc., P.O. Box 133, Postal Station S, Toronto, Ontario M5M 4L6.

Combine dry ingredients in a large mixing bowl. Whisk together the rest of the ingredients and gently but thoroughly fold them into the dry ingredients. Fill greased muffin tin and bake in a preheated 400-degree F oven for 20 minutes, or until done.

JoAnne B. Cats-Baril ◆ *Charlotte, Vermont*

Scones

Variation: To make these scones more hearty, use equal proportions of whole wheat and white flour.

Relatively low in fat, these scones are light-textured and simple to make.

◆

Yield: 8 scones
Preparation time: 20-25 minutes

◆

1	egg
1½ tsp.	sugar
¾ cup	milk
1 Tbsp.	melted butter
2 cups	flour
4 tsp.	baking powder
pinch	salt

Preheat oven to 500 degrees F. Cream egg and sugar, and add milk and butter. Combine dry ingredients. Make well in the center of them and add wet ingredients. Mix. Turn out onto floured board, turn dough once, pat to a ¾-inch-thick circle. Cut into 8 wedges, and bake 10 minutes on floured baking sheet.

Melissa McClelland ◆ Burlington, Vermont

Gougère

These rich, cheesy buns, formed into a cluster, are made with Gruyère or Cheddar cheese from a cream-puff-like dough. They are good served warm or cold.

◆

Yield: 17 buns
Preparation time: 55 minutes

◆

½ cup	butter
1 cup	flour
4	eggs
1½ cups	grated Gruyère or Cheddar cheese
1 tsp.	Dijon mustard
1 tsp.	salt
½ tsp.	dry mustard
dash	hot pepper sauce

Preheat oven to 450 degrees F, and lightly greased 10x11-inch baking sheet.

Combine butter and 1 cup water in a heavy saucepan and bring to a rolling boil over medium-high heat. Add flour all at once and beat with a wooden spoon until the mixture forms a ball and comes away from the sides of the pan. Remove from heat, and add eggs one at a time, beating vigorously after each addition, until the dough is smooth and shiny. Blend in remaining ingredients.

Make a ring 9 inches in diameter with tablespoons of dough, sides touching, on baking sheet. Make a second ring of dough just inside the first, again with sides touching.

Bake 10 minutes at 450 degrees F. Reduce heat to 350 degrees and bake 10 minutes longer. Reduce heat again, to 325 degrees, and bake 10 to 15 minutes more, until puffed and browned. Remove from oven, poke holes in buns with a fork to let steam escape. Pull apart and serve.

Cheryl Veitch ◆ *Bella Coola, British Columbia*

Sage Popovers

Serve these sage-scented popovers with poultry or pork dishes.

◆

Yield: 6-8 servings
Preparation time: ¾-1 hour

◆

2	eggs
1 cup	milk
1 cup	sifted flour
½ tsp.	salt
1 Tbsp.	salad oil
¼ cup	finely chopped fresh sage, or 2 Tbsp. dried

Mix all ingredients together. Beat only 1 to 2 minutes—do not overbeat. Grease custard cups, muffin tins or popover pan very well. Fill the cups ½ full with batter.

Bake in a preheated 475-degree F oven for 15 minutes. Lower oven temperature to 350 degrees and bake for 25 minutes more, or until popovers are browned and firm. Prick with fork to let steam escape, and serve immediately, or hold in a turned-off oven with door ajar for up to 30 minutes for dry, crisp popovers.

JoAnne B. Cats-Baril ◆ *Charlotte, Vermont*

Mom's Popovers

Preparation Hint: Begin popovers in a cold oven.

"**M**y mom makes these popovers whenever we come to her house." Worth making a pilgrimage for, they are temptingly crusty and puffy. Do not peek until the end of the baking time, or they may fail to "pop." They are delicious plain or with cottage cheese and preserves.

◆

Yield: 10 large popovers
Preparation time: 40 minutes

◆

5	large eggs, slightly beaten
1 scant tsp.	salt
1⅔ cups	milk
1⅔ cups	flour

Beat ingredients together until blended. Generously grease 10 custard cups or a popover pan and fill with batter. Place in cold oven and turn oven to 450 degrees F. Bake for 35 minutes. Do not open oven door until baking time is up. Turn off heat and let stand in oven 5 extra minutes.

Nancy Davis ◆ *Underhill Center, Vermont*

Focaccia

Variation: Focaccia can be covered with caramelized onions, coarse salt, ripe olives or Parmesan cheese after the initial baking. Bake an additional 10 minutes.

This puffy Italian flat-bread is simply pizza dough flavored with olive oil. Because it only rises once, it is relatively quick to make.

◆

Yield: 2 loaves
Preparation time: 1¾ hours

◆

1 Tbsp.	yeast
1 tsp.	salt
2 Tbsp.	olive oil
½ tsp.	sugar
2½ cups	flour, equal parts whole wheat pastry and white

Dissolve yeast in 1 cup warm water; add salt, oil and sugar. Gradually stir in flour until stiff enough to turn out onto a floured board. Knead for several minutes, adding flour as necessary, until dough is smooth. Oil bowl and place dough in it, turning once to coat. Cover with damp towel and let rise for 30 to 40 minutes.

Turn out onto board, cut in two, and roll into two circles. Make fan-shaped slashes in dough, and transfer to an oiled baking sheet or pizza stone. Pull dough apart slightly so that the slashes open. Brush loaves with olive oil. Let rest 20 minutes. Preheat oven to 450 degrees F.

Bake bread in top third of oven, for 20 minutes. Loaves may be sprayed with water during first 10 minutes for a good crust.

Melissa McClelland ◆ *Burlington, Vermont*

Easy Caraway Beer Bread

This densely textured, crusty loaf, flavored with cheese and caraway, can be baked free-form on a baking sheet, or in a loaf pan. It is particularly good with vegetable dishes.

◆

Yield: 1 large loaf
Preparation time: 1½ hours

◆

4 cups	flour
2 Tbsp.	baking powder
2 tsp.	salt
¼ cup	sugar
1 tsp.	caraway seeds
½ lb.	Cheddar, cut into ½" cubes
12 oz.	beer
1	egg, beaten

Sift together dry ingredients. Add caraway seeds and cheese. Make a well in the center, add beer and beaten egg. Mix together and shape into a loaf. Place on a greased baking sheet, and bake at 375 degrees F for 70 minutes. Allow to cool in the pan for 15 minutes, then run a knife around sides to release cheese, which sometimes sticks.

Linda M. Powidajko ◆ *Kingston, Ontario*

INDEX